MS-DOS AND PC-DOS

Editor-in-Chief/Executive Editor: David T. Culverwell
Production Editor/Text Designer: Michael J. Rogers
Art Director/Cover Design: Don Sellers
Assistant Art Director: Bernard Vervin

Typesetting: Creative Communications Corporation, Baltimore, MD
Printing: R. R. Donnelley & Sons, Harrisonburg, VA
Typefaces: Helvetica (display), Palatino (text), Typewriter (computer display)

MS-DOS AND PC-DOS

User's Guide

Peter Norton

Robert J. Brady Co.
*A Prentice-Hall Publishing
and Communications Company*

Bowie, MD 20715

MS-DOS and PC-DOS: User's Guide

Library of Congress Cataloging in Publication Data
Norton, Peter, 1943-
    MS-DOS and PC-DOS: a beginner's guide to the microsoft disk operating system.
    Includes index.
    1. MS-DOS (Computer operating system) I. Title. II. Title: MS-DOS and PC-DOS III. Title: MS-DOS and PC-DOS.
QA76.6.N68   1983   001.64'2   83-15498
ISBN 0-89303-645-5

Prentice-Hall International, Inc., London
Prentice-Hall Canada, Inc., Scarborough, Ontario
Prentice-Hall of Australia, Pty., Ltd., Sydney
Prentice-Hall of India Private Limited, New Delhi
Prentice-Hall of Japan, Inc., Tokyo
Prentice-Hall of Southeast Asia Pte. Ltd., Singapore
Whitehall Books, Limited, Petone, New Zealand
Editora Prentice-Hall Do Brasil LTDA., Rio de Janeiro

Printed in the United States of America

84 85 86 87 88 89 90 91 92 93 94   10 9 8 7 6 5 4 3

CONTENTS

1 Introduction and How to Use This Book   1

2 Basic Computer Concepts   5
  2.1 The Computer as Worker   5
  2.2 What a Computer Can and Can't Do   12
  2.3 The Importance of an Operating System   14
  2.4 Two Ways of Using a Computer—Interactive and Batch   15

3 Getting Started with DOS   17
  3.1 The Very Best Way to Start   17
  3.2 What You'll Have to Do Once You Know How to Do It   17
  3.3 What You Need to Know First   18
  3.4 The First Things to Do   22

4 Fundamentals of DOS Commands   27
  4.1 Keeping Track of Drives   27
  4.2 Where Commands Could Come From   29
  4.3 Common Command Notation   32
  4.4 Files, File Names, and Other Wild Stuff   33

5 Overview of Elementary Commands   35
  5.1 The Time Commands—DATE and TIME   35
  5.2 Checking Out Your Disks—DIR, CHKDSK, and *CAT*   37
  5.3 The Diskette Preparation Commands—FORMAT,
      SYS, and DISKCOPY   40
  5.4 Moving and Removing Files—COPY, DEL, ERASE,
      REN, and TYPE   44
  5.5 Elementary Commands for DOS-2—VER, VOL, and CLS   46
  5.6 Where to Find the Rest of the Commands   47

6 Overview of Advanced Commands   49
  6.1 Comparing Copies—COMP/FC/FILECOMP and DISKCOMP   49
  6.2 Editors, Word Processors, and EDLIN   52
  6.3 The Snooping Tool—DEBUG   54
  6.4 Assembling—MASM and CREF   56
  6.5 Building Programs—LINK and LIB   56
  6.6 Converting Program Formats—LOCATE/EXE2BIN,
      and EXEFIX   57

7 Getting the Most of DOS Editing Keys   59
  7.1 Setting the Stage for the Editing Keys   59
  7.2 How the Editing Keys Work   60
  7.3 Some More Special Keys   65

8 Special Things About DOS-2—Pumping the Pipeline   69
  8.1 Buzz Words—A Quick Outline of the Ideas and Terms   69
  8.2 Telling 'em Where to Go   72
  8.3 Filling Up the Pipeline—SORT, FIND, and MORE   75

8.4 *Telling DOS Where to Go* 78
8.5 *Planting a Tree—MKDIR and RMDIR* 79
8.6 *Finding Your Pathways—TREE, CHDIR, PWD, and PATH* 81
8.7 *Other Commands Special to DOS-2* 86

9 What You Need to Know About Disks and File Formats 89
9.1 What's Inside a Disk 89
9.2 All About File Names 92
9.3 The Importance of Filename Extensions 94
9.4 Wild Cards and Their Use 96
9.5 File Formats and What They Mean to You 97
9.6 Diskettes and Other Animals 103
9.7 *Special Things About Disks in DOS-2* 105

10 What You Need to Know About Programming Languages 107
10.1 What Are Programming Languages? 107
10.2 The Two Kinds of BASIC—Interpreted and Compiled 112
10.3 How Compiled Languages Work in DOS 114
10.4 Choosing a Programming Language 120

11 Batch File Secrets 127
11.1 Introducing Batch Processing—REM and PAUSE 127
11.2 Slightly More Advanced Batch Processing 132
11.3 *Even More Advanced Batch Commands—ECHO,*
    SHIFT, GOTO, IF, and FOR 133
11.4 Suggestions and Examples of Batch File Tricks 137

12 Odds and Ends You Need to Know 145
12.1 Finding Out What's at Your Command 145
12.2 Throwing Things Away and Other Information on Devices 148
12.3 The Importance of Where You Are 152
12.4 Programs You Ought to Have 154

13 Handy Tricks 157
13.1 Setting Up Your Disks and DOS 157
13.2 More On Setting Up Your Disks 160
13.3 Making Commands More Convenient 163
13.4 *Some Tricks For DOS-2* 164

14 Danger Areas 167
14.1 Mixing Your DOS's 167
14.2 Disastrous Interruptions 170
14.3 Ordinary Ways to Lose Your Data 171

15 Coping With Copy Protection 175
15.1 Tricks of the Trade 175
15.2 Something Worse than Copy Protection 179

16 Special Tricks For Hard Disks and Electronic Disks 183
16.1 A Little Background 183
16.2 The Special Uses of Electronic Disks 186

16.3 *The Special Uses of Hard Disks* **189**
16.4 Common Problems and Tricks **193**

17 Making Some Software Choices **197**
17.1 Choosing Any Program **197**
17.2 Choosing Word Processors **201**
17.3 Choosing Spreadsheets **203**
17.4 Choosing Accounting Programs **204**
17.5 Choosing Multi-function Packages **205**
17.6 Choosing Programming Languages **206**

18 Avoiding Shortsighted Mistakes **209**
18.1 Hardware Mistakes **209**
18.2 Software Mistakes **211**
18.3 Operational Mistakes **213**

19 The EDLIN Editor **215**
19.1 Introducing EDLIN **215**
19.2 Ordinary EDLIN Commands **218**
19.3 Advanced EDLIN Commands for DOS-2 **225**

20 The DEBUGer—A Technical Tool **227**
20.1 Some DEBUG Background **227**
20.2 The DEBUG Commands **230**
20.3 Using DEBUG to Patch **235**

21 Reference Summary of Commands **239**
21.1 Separate Commands **239**
21.2 EDLIN Commands **245**
21.3 DEBUG Commands **247**

22 Narrative Glossary **249**

Index **261**

Acknowledgments

Many people helped in the preparation of this book. Tracy Smith and Dave Culverwell of The Robert J. Brady Co. initiated the project. Alan Boyd of Microsoft kindled my initial enthusiasm for a book on Microsoft DOS, and Microsoft's Chris Larson helped enormously by providing essential technical information. My own introduction to DOS was with the IBM Personal Computer, but three people were extremely helpful in providing the perspective of other computer manufacturers: Victoria Lerner of Heath/Zenith, Margaret Spillane of Wang, and Paul Burkett of Compaq. Harry Gaines of Brady provided those essential kicks in the seat of the pants, while Eileen Harris provided aid and comfort.

Copyrights

In this book many copywritten items are mentioned. Here are their owners:

Microsoft, MS, MS-DOS, and Multiplan are trademarks of Microsoft Corporation.
CP/M and CP/M-86 are trademarks of Digital Research.
UCSD, and p-System are trademarks of the Regents of the University of California.
Wordstar is a trademark of Micro Pro, Inc.
VisiCalc is a trademark of VisiCorp.
JET is a trademark of Tall Tree Systems.
IBM and IBM Personal Computer are trademarks of International Business Machines Corporation.
Compaq is a trademark of Compaq Computer Corporation.
Wang is a trademark of Wang Laboratories, Inc.

Equipment

You might be interested in knowing the computer equipment that was used in the writing of this book. Two different DOS computers and four different versions of DOS were used.

The two computers were the IBM Personal Computer and the Compaq computer, an excellent portable computer system. The IBM PC has 512K of memory, two diskette drives, and a 10 megabyte IBM fixed disk system (which the text of this book calls home). The Compaq has 256K of memory, two diskette drives, and a nicely padded carrying handle. A third computer, the Wang Professional Computer, was also used in this book's research, though none of this book was written on the Wang PC, which is slightly ironic since writing tools, or word processing, is Wang's specialty.

Parts of this book were written under the supervision of DOS 2.00, and parts under 1.10 and 1.25, two equivalent versions of the 1-series of DOS releases.

An interesting, curious, and—so far as I know—bootleg variation on DOS, known as 1.85R, was used during part of the writing of this book.

No standard word processing program was used to write this book. Instead an excellent editor program (which is half of what a word processor is), Vedit by CompuView Systems, was used to compose the text of this book. Spelling checking was done by two programs—for fast, convenient, and occasionally faulty spelling, EasyProof from Norell Data Systems, was used. For a final, slow, and laborious—but rigorous—check, the ProofReader (also called the Random House Dictionary spelling checker), from Aspen Software, was used.

Printing of draft copies was done on two computer printers—one popular Epson MX-80 printer, which is the standard printer for the IBM PC—cheap, and reliable, if not pretty. The other, a letter quality printer, was a Daisywriter 2000.

Software and hardware, I love it all.

About the Author

Peter Norton was raised in Seattle, Washington, and educated at Reed College in Portland, Oregon. During the past 20 years, he has worked with a wide variety of computer equipment, from personal computers to the largest "mainframes," and he has worked on every kind of software, from the most intricate system programming to thoroughly mundane commercial applications. Although Mr. Norton continues to develop software for small computers, his work now concentrates on writing about the use of personal computing. Mr. Norton lives by the beach in Venice, California, and avoids wearing shoes that have laces.

Note to Authors

Do you have a manuscript or a software program related to personal computers? Do you have an idea for developing such a project? If so, we would like to hear from you. The Brady Co. produces a complete range of books and applications software for the personal computer market. We invite you to write to David Culverwell, Editor-in-Chief, Robert J. Brady Co., Bowie, Maryland 20715.

1

Introduction and How to Use This Book

This book is about getting started in computing for computers that use the Microsoft Disk Operating System, called MS-DOS. But it is also about much more.

There are two parts to this book, although you won't find them laid out in two separate sections. One part teaches you the most basic things that you need to know about getting started with MS-DOS, and then getting the most out of it. The other part tells you things that any user of a small personal computer needs to know in order to be wily, smart, and effective with your little machine. The first part will tell you things like how to make good use of the commands that are built into MS-DOS. The second part will tell you things like how to choose intelligently among the hundreds of programs offered for sale.

One of the things that sets this book apart from many others is that it is full of practical advice about how to do things, about what works and what doesn't, about what to buy, about what to use. This advice is based on a solid foundation of four things from the author's experience:

- over a decade of experience with all sorts of computers;
- fairly recent conversion to working with a small computer, so that the experience of being a beginner isn't lost in the swamps of time;
- heavy, full-time use of a personal computer for the last year; actually it isn't quite accurate to describe it as full-time use—it's been ten hours a day, six or seven days a week, so that I've compressed lots of personal computer experience into one short year;
- a healthy dose of common sense.

We won't go into all the technical details of using MS-DOS. Your computer's manual will do that nicely. What we will do for you is help you understand what those manuals are about and help you get started. And we'll do something that your computer's manuals cannot, or dare not, do—give you advice about what's good and bad in software that you are considering buying.

Perhaps you are the enthusiastic first-time owner of a personal computer. Perhaps your work is forcing you to use a computer that you aren't really sure you want to deal with. Perhaps you are considering getting a small computer,

1

and you want to first learn a little of what computers are all about (and how to spend your money wisely). If you fit into any of these three descriptions, then this book is for you.

This is a help book for beginning computer users, people who will be working with MS-DOS computers. How can you get the most help from it?

- Pay attention to the cartoons. Some of them are just for fun, but most of them have important messages to help you understand your computer.
- If you are completely new to computers and don't understand them at all, read Chapter 2, which explains the most fundamental ideas about how a computer and its operating system, MS-DOS, work. Also, make use of the narrative glossary in Chapter 24; it defines some of the most commonly used technical terms about computers, and ties the definitions together into a narrative form.
- Find out which of the two main versions of MS-DOS you will be working with. A complex computer program like MS-DOS grows and expands and evolves, so there are various versions of DOS, grouped into two series—the 1-series (1.00, 1.10, 1.25) and the 2-series (2.00, etc). For simplic-

ity, we'll refer to the two series of versions of MS-DOS as DOS-1 and DOS-2. Everything that applies to the 1-series also applies to the 2-series. Most of this book concerns the common material that applies to both DOS-1 and DOS-2. The 2-series is substantially richer but more complicated to understand and use. To avoid confusing people using DOS-1, **everything specific to DOS-2 has been put in this distinctive typeface.** If you don't already know which version of MS-DOS you are using, you can easily find out by looking at your DOS manual or by starting up your computer—it should show the DOS version number. *If you are in doubt,* pass over the material about DOS-2, since it is more advanced, and might, at first, just make it harder for you to understand things.

- Check out the chapter headings. They will guide you into the material you need. To get going with DOS, look to Chapter 3, "Getting Started," Chapter 4, "Fundamentals of DOS Commands, "Chapter 5, "Overview of Elementary Commands," and Chapter 6, "Overview of Advanced Commands." The use of disk storage is at the heart of using your computer, so when you need information to understand your disks and files, look to Chapter 9. For advice on choosing software, using programming languages, and avoiding expensive mistakes, look to Chapters 10, 17, and 18. For tricks and tips and danger areas, see Chapters 11 through 16.

Most of all, this book is here to help you through the small traumas of beginning to use your MS-DOS computer. Every new experience brings its pleasures and pains—and the pains tend to come first. And the problems of "computer phobia" are now legendary. Whether you are a reluctant beginner or a starting enthusiast, this book will help make your transition into the use of MS-DOS easier. Computers are now for everybody.

2

Basic Computer Concepts

If you are going to use your computer successfully, you need to have a working idea of what it is and how it functions. By this I don't mean the computer technician's understanding of what's going on under the cover of your machine. I mean a simple, practical, working idea of what's what—just the sort of understanding that you need to have of a car in order to be a safe driver; not what a car mechanic needs to know, but what a car driver needs to know. As the "driver" of a small computer, you have to have an elementary idea of what's going on in your machine. In this chapter we'll try to lay out for you that kind of understanding of basic computer concepts.

We'll set it out in four parts: First, the metaphor of the computer as an office worker. Then we'll consider what a computer can do and what it can't. Next we'll look at the importance of an operating system, like our DOS. Finally, we'll wrap up this chapter with a very practical matter—the two quite different ways that you can use your computer.

2.1 The Computer as Worker

The best way that I know of to comprehend how a computer works, to make sense of its various parts, and to understand how they work together, is to draw an analogy between the computer and a human office worker (and a not very bright one at that). In many ways, a computer is remarkably like someone doing simple clerical office work.

Let's suppose you are at work, and your boss brings someone up and introduces the newcomer as your new personal assistant—someone whose only task is to help you with your work. But, the boss tells you privately, your new assistant isn't very bright. Conscientious, yes; hard-working, yes; but bright, intelligent, imaginative? Absolutely not. A helper who will do whatever you ask to be done, but who has to be given instructions in laborious detail. A worker with lots of energy, but absolutely no initiative, no common sense, no independence.

5

You don't need us to tell you the identity of your new assistant—you know already it's your computer. Well now, let's consider what your computer assistant has to offer, what it needs to get any work done, and what you'll have to do to get any useful work out of it.

Your computer has, as they say, an "electronic brain." This brain (and as we'll see, it's a pea brain, for sure) is called various things in computer terminology. It is the central processing unit, or just the processor, for short. This is the most central and fundamental part of a computer; and sometimes people refer to this one part of a whole computer *system* as being *the computer itself*. That is pretty accurate, but naturally it can be confusing to call this one part the computer, so we'll mostly call it the processor.

Your computer's processor is quite analogous to the brain of a not-very-bright person. It is a fair analogy—the computer's processor, like a person's brain, is the part that has the ability to comprehend and carry out your instructions.

So far, we have the worker's brain: the computer processor. What comes next? If your assistant is going to get any work done, it needs a work place. For an office worker that would be a desk. What part of your computer is its work space, its desk? It might surprise you that it is the part that we call the computer's memory.

Now, we all know that a person has a memory, and most of us have heard about a computer also having something known as its memory—so it is natural to think that the computer's memory is analogous to our memory. Wrong. Our memory is—as stupid as this sounds—where we remember things; it is our brain's more or less permanent record of information. But the memory of a computer is not a permanent record of anything. Instead, the computer's memory is the part that it uses as a work space. The memory is where the computer places the information it is working on while it is doing the work. This is just like the desk of an office worker. When work is being performed, it is spread out on as much of the desk as is needed. When the work is finished, then it is cleared off the desk, ready for another task. So it is with the computer's memory. The computer uses its memory on a temporary basis. When the current job is done, the memory can be cleared for another task.

This analogy of the computer's memory and an office worker's desk goes even further. While in principle all of your desk is work space, part of it is probably taken up by a telephone or a pencil cup. It is the same way with a computer's memory. Certain parts of it are dedicated to one specialized use or another; but on the whole, most of the memory is available as working space for the computer.

Some things that you do at a desk take up very little space. To scribble a letter, you don't need much space. But if you are writing a report, you would need more space—space for your writing pad, for your notes, for a dictionary. Nearly any desk has room for that sort of work. But if you were doing a very complicated task—let's say some complex accounting job that required looking information up in all sorts of account books and journals—then you would need much more space. Maybe more space than there is on an ordinary desk.

Things are just the same way with a computer. First, the more complicated the task, the more memory the computer needs as a working space. Second, like desks, computer memory usually comes in some rather standard sizes. For a computer, the size of its memory is usually measured in "K," or thousands of characters of memory capacity. One K is exactly 1,024 characters (bytes, in computer terminology); but for convenience, we can think of each K as simply a thousand characters—the amount of space taken up by 150 words of English. That's about the size of this paragraph. A typical size for home hobby computers is around 48K of memory. Personal computers for professional use usually start at 64K, and often have 128K, or even more. These are the most common work space sizes for personal computers—64K or 128K. Larger sizes are available, and it is not unusual for a personal computer to have 256K or even 512K.

There is another way that a computer's memory is like a worker's desk. For common simple tasks, not much of the memory/desk is used. For more complex jobs, more will be used until, finally, some job will be too large to fit into the available space. This is why it is good to have plenty of memory in your computer; since memory is relatively cheap, having plenty is inexpensive insurance against having a problem that is too large to fit. As with an office worker, having more work space generally doesn't affect how fast the work gets done—that relates to the worker's brainpower. The size of the work space mostly affects how large and complicated a job can be done.

Naturally you wouldn't get your assistant a desk the size of a football field, and you don't need to get your computer more memory than can be put to good use. For some guidance on what might be enough for your computer, see Chapter 18.

So far in understanding the parts of our computer, we've covered the processor (brain) and the memory (desk/work space). What about the rest of the computer parts? Let's consider what disk storage represents to your computer.

Disk storage is the computer's equivalent of the office worker's filing cabinet. Disk storage comes in several forms: as flexible "floppy" diskettes, as rigid disk cartridges, or in the form of permanently mounted, non-removable fixed "hard" disk systems. They may be called disks, diskettes, fixed disks, hard disks, Winchester disks, cartridges, or mini-disks. Functionally, they all do the same job for our computers—they act as a place to store information, which could be either data or programs, when the computer is not actually working on it. When the computer *is* working on the data, the data is in memory (on the desk top, so to speak), and not in the disk storage.

Disk storage acts like a filing cabinet for the computer, and it even borrows some of the terminology of filing cabinets: inside disk storage, our information is organized into "files." Each file contains whatever kind of data is appropriate to its purpose. This might be written text, accounting numbers, or sets of instructions (programs) for the computer. When the computer needs information from a file, it "opens" it, reads or writes it, and then "closes" the file. Here the computer terminology closely matches what human workers do with files. There is only one major difference in the way a computer uses a file and the way a person does. If you or I were to work with a file from our filing cabinet, we would place the whole file folder on our desk to work with it. But the computer's way of using a file is a little different—it works with small parts of a file at a time, similar to what we would do if we took only a page at a time from a file folder. Part of the reason why a computer works this way is to reduce the amount of memory that is needed to get its work done.

Like people, computers can, in a sense, read and write, and also talk on the telephone. Computers do this through what are called input/output devices, or I/O devices, or peripheral devices. A personal computer usually has a display screen to write information onto, and often a printer as well. A printer is the computer's equivalent of having a typewriter at hand. The computer does most of its reading (other than reading from its disk filing cabinet) from its keyboard—it "reads" what we type on the keyboard. The computer also can use the telephone to talk to other computers or to distant peripheral devices— such as writing through a telephone line to a printer that is located somewhere else. To use a telephone, a computer needs special parts to connect it to the phone lines. These special parts are called a communications adapter and a modem; they perform the translation necessary to change computer talk into telephone talk. These parts, the adapter and the modem, may be built into your computer, or they may be separately attached parts.

There are many possible kinds of I/O devices, or peripheral devices, that can be connected to your computer—many of them designed for very special purposes. There are special printers designed to draw pictures, called graphics printers or plotters. There are special input devices which the computer can read—such as a light pen (which can read a position on the display screen), a joy stick (mostly used for games), or a mouse (which is a joy stick for people who are too serious to play games). And naturally there is much, much more. The disk storage on a computer is also an I/O device—we just discussed it separately, since it has its own special importance.

So that is basically the full set of a computer's parts—the processor (brain), the memory (work desk), the disk storage (filing cabinet), telephone (adapter and modem), typewriter (printer), and so on. That is the hardware, the physical computer as worker. What about the computer software we hear so much about?

Our analogy of the computer as a faithful but not-very-bright office worker helps to explain software—computer programs—as well. A person normally has a general education, general mental skills, and knowledge that we call job skills. A computer, like an imbecile, has few job skills of its own. But the computer, like a loyal and dim-witted assistant, can do anything that we can explain how to do in meticulous detail.

The computer doesn't know how to do anything by itself; it needs programs to tell it what to do—as if our office assistant could do nothing but follow an elaborate manual of office procedures. So to accomplish any work, the computer must first turn to its disk file for the program instructions that will tell it exactly what to do.

When we use the computer, the first step to getting it to work is to tell it which program, which book of instructions, to follow. The program could be anything that people have taught computers to do—from accounting calculations to game playing. Some of the programs we run on our computers are aids to make it easier for us to write further programs.

One of the programs that a computer can run is a master program—a program which makes it easier to run other programs. This master program is called an operating system, and it is the computer's analogy to a human worker's general education, or an office worker's general office skills. If you or I were working as clerks in an office, we would be expected to have training in specific jobs—like a computer has programs for specific work—but we would also be expected to know how to do common ordinary things, like how to sharpen a pencil, or even how to find things in a filing cabinet. This kind of very basic skill is given to a computer by its operating system. The operating system takes care of the most ordinary tasks which all programs need to carry out, including the very important task of taking care of the filing cabinet, the computer's disk storage. The main subject of this book is an operating system, one particular one: the Disk Operating System, called DOS, from Microsoft.

So now, I think, we are ready to see how a personal computer works as a whole, keeping our analogy to the dumb-but-faithful office assistant in mind.

When we first need our computer, we turn it on—it reports to work. The first task we give it is to start up its operating system. Our office assistant has forgotten everything overnight, so its first task in the morning is to take its general instruction manual (operating system) out of the filing cabinet (disk storage), and place it ready on its desk (computer memory).

Once the computer is running—the office worker ready for work—then we can tell it what to do first. We give it the name of a program, which might be a word processing program, like WordStar, for us to write with; or a spreadsheet program, like VisiCalc, for us to do financial planning with. With the name of the job to be done, our worker takes the specific instructions (program) out of the filing cabinet (disk) and gets it ready on its desk (memory). For a while, we have our computer do that kind of work; when we're done, it puts the program away. When we want to do something else, we give our computer assistant the name of another program—and so it goes. As the computer works for us, it uses its disk storage to fetch and save our information. It uses the display screen to speak to us; it uses its printer to give us a written record; it uses the keyboard to take our commands. It may use the telephone to pass information to and from another computer. But whatever it does, it is just a simple helper for us.

Like my example of a dim-witted assistant, there are times when the computer can be very helpful, and times when it is more of a nuisance than an assistant. We have to teach it how to do things (which is laborious), and we have to learn the limitations of its ways (which can be equally time consuming). For some things it helps; for others it doesn't. But on the whole, it can be very useful.

2.2 What a Computer Can and Can't Do

There are some things that a computer can do, and many, many things that it can't. Even more important, there are many things that you might try to do with a computer, which are better done by hand.

First, let's consider what the computer can do, and do well. It's a real whiz at arithmetic—fast, and unfailingly accurate. Arithmetic is what computers do best; in fact, when you are using a computer for something else, like writing a letter with a word-processing program, *most of what the computer is doing*, behind the scenes, is arithmetic. So when we need arithmetic done, the computer is just dandy at it. The computer's most famous and best success with arithmetic has been with "electronic spreadsheets," the sort of program pioneered by VisiCalc.

VisiCalc is a fine example of computing at its best—it is quick and handy, and it makes it possible for many people to do all sorts of financial planning and numeric calculations, which they wouldn't have even tried before there were programs like this. Doing the kind of work that VisiCalc does by hand was so difficult that we might as well say it was impossible.

So computers can make impossibly lengthy calculations as easy as scratching your tummy.

The next thing that computers are very good at is record keeping—but only certain kinds of record keeping. With their large disk storage, computers can save large amounts of data. And, under the right circumstances, computers can be efficient about searching out just the information that we need. But it is also true that many kinds of simple record keeping are more work to keep on a computer than to keep by hand. This is something really worth knowing. Once you fall even a little in love with what a computer can do, it is easy to become infatuated and try to get it to do everything for you. Beware. You wouldn't turn to your computer to add 2 + 3, but you would use your computer to add up the square roots of a hundred numbers—that's more in its line of work. So it goes with record keeping. If you have any information that is reasonably easy to keep organized by hand, then it would probably be more work to use your computer to keep track of it. On the other hand, when your manual records get out of hand, it's time to call in the computer.

We people are still learning how to master the talents of computers, so we are expanding the range of things that it is practical to have computers do for us. Some things which don't fit into a computer's natural skills of arithmetic and record keeping have turned out to be very good things to have a computer do anyway. The best example of this is word processing, which means computer work related to the written word—accepting written text, changing (editing) it, keeping track of it, checking its spelling and grammar, and formatting it into tidy printed pages. This is the kind of work that the computer learned (through our programming) how to do fairly recently. And yet it has become one of the computer's greatest successes. So there are now, and will be in the future, many jobs a computer can do well, even though they don't involve much computation.

There are some things, though, that computers can't do now, and may never be able to do, and that is anything that involves intelligence and judgment. Computers do very well by rote, but when a task calls for imagination, intuition, and the like, it is, at least for now, a job for people—perhaps a job at which a computer can assist, but still a job for humans.

So, you can expect your computer to be able to do anything that is mechanically straightforward, but you can't expect it to do anything that involves judgment. And you can expect to have *success* with your computer in any work that is in the right scale—neither too big for your computer to handle, nor too small for it to be worth putting on your computer.

2.3 The Importance of an Operating System

So far we've seen roughly what a computer is and the sort of things that it can do, and we've had a little bit of an explanation of the role of the computer's operating system—DOS—but that is all. So far it seems that the operating system is no big deal. Actually, the operating system is a very big deal, for several reasons.

The first reason why an operating system is very important is because it sets the environment in which you interact with the computer and the environment in which your programs work. So the operating system establishes the character of how your computer works, just as much or more than the particular kind of computer you have does. Likewise, the operating system sets many of the practical limits of your computer's usefulness, just as the specific hardware does.

The operating system, in effect, completes your computer. Without it, your computer is a useless hunk, like a car with no fuel. With it, your computer takes on both life and a particular character. Your friends who grew up in big cities have a different character and style, on the whole, than your friends who grew up in the countryside. With one operating system, your computer will have one style, and with another system another style. Because this style will permeate much of your interaction with your computer, the character of your operating system affects how you use the computer.

There are other reasons why your operating system is important. Computer programs will not work with any operating system, willy-nilly. Programs generally have to be matched to their operating system, and this means that the list of programs available for your computer is heavily influenced by the popularity of the operating system that it uses. Thanks partly to the enormous success of the IBM Personal Computer—which pioneered the Microsoft DOS operating system—and partly to the strong reputation of Microsoft, DOS has become the dominant operating system for the current 16-bit generation of computers. In many ways it does not matter to us if our operating system is better or worse than some other system; what does matter deeply is how popular it is—that is, how many programs are available for it, and how many different computers use it. The popularity of our operating system mostly determines how good a choice of program tools we have available to us. Thank heavens that we have, in DOS, a runaway popularity winner.

There is yet another reason why our operating system is important to us—the future. It is possible for an operating system to have itself open to the expected future of computing, and it is possible for an operating system to cut itself off from the expected future. Again, fortunately for us, DOS has a well-planned and orchestrated future ahead of it, based upon a compatible family of operating systems. Our DOS, particularly DOS-2, is part of Microsoft's planned family of systems.

When—not if, but when—you change from one personal computer to a newer one, you do not want to have to discard all of the computer skills and experience that you have acquired. Here again, DOS is a plus for us because by being the dominant operating system in its part of the computer world, we are ensured that it is very likely that our next computers will use either DOS or a big brother to DOS; thus, salvaging the usefulness of our skills and probably our programs as well.

2.4 Two Ways of Using a Computer— Interactive and Batch

Before we finish this chapter on computer fundamentals, you should learn about a subject that will become increasingly important to you as your use of a personal computer widens—the two basic ways of using a computer.

When you first start using your computer, you will probably be giving it your full attention. You will be working with the computer interactively, which means that you do something (type something at the keyboard), and then the computer does something (shows a result on the screen), and you type something else, and so on and so on. This is interactive computing, one of the two fundamental modes that computers can operate in. This interactive mode may seem so natural to you, that you may wonder why you might ever want the computer to work in any other way.

But, the simple fact is that when you are working with the computer interactively, the computer is keeping you busy just as much as you are keeping it busy. This isn't always ideal.

Now, when you need some computer help with your work, it is natural to have an interactive computer. But there are some things that we want the computer to do that do not require our attention. This is when the computer does its work more or less on its own, unattended by us, and, thankfully not needing our attention. This style of computer operation is called—for no particularly good reason—batch mode.

So your computer can be working either in interactive mode or batch mode. There isn't a strict division between the two—it's just a matter of degree of how much attention your computer requires when it is doing some work.

Now there is a very good reason why we are pointing out to you that computers can, under the right circumstances, work on their own unattended.

You may begin using your computer only occasionally, but it is inevitable that as time goes by, you will want your computer to do more and more work for you. Does this have to take up more and more of your own time? Not if you are aware of the possibilities of the computer's unattended batch processing capability.

As an example, consider an accounting program that I use. One of its operations is quite lengthy. Unfortunately for me, when this program is doing its lengthy operation, it repeatedly asks me if I want it to continue (I always do). The darned thing won't carry on without me. This wastes my time just sitting around telling it to get on with its business. Ugh. If this nasty program had been written with a batch mode in mind, it would be enormously more useful to me.

The moral of this story is twofold. First, you should be aware of the possibilities of unattended batch operation, and second you should be careful in buying, or writing, programs to see that they do not unnecessarily require attention from people. People have better things to do than pay attention to fussy programs.

The secret of successful batch operation lies in two things—programs which don't require unnecessary interaction, and the good use of DOS's batch processing files, which you will find discussed in Chapter 11.

This, then, has been a quick course in the fundamentals of computers, with emphasis on the parts that are most likely to end up being useful to you. Next we'll move on to how you get started with DOS.

3

Getting Started with DOS

Things are often topsy-turvy when you are just getting started at some new endeavor. The way it usually works is that you need to know everything at once. What do you learn first? What do you do first? It usually seems that before you can learn one thing, you need to know everything else. We'll grapple with this problem as we learn how to get started with DOS.

3.1 The Very Best Way to Start

The very best way to start using DOS and your DOS computer is not to do it alone. If you can get someone who knows the ropes and isn't impatient, get your friend to lead you by the hand through these basic steps. With the help of someone experienced, you can skip over the rest of this chapter.

The next best way to start is to read on.

3.2 What You'll Have to do Once You Know How to do It

There are some fairly urgent things that you need to do "before you get started." *Not* really before you get started, but still quite early in the game. But you can't—or shouldn't try to—do these early steps, which have to do with safeguarding your DOS system, before you are at least slightly comfortable with your computer.

So that you don't feel lost, here is what we are working towards: first, we're going to get just a little working knowledge of what DOS does when we work with it. Second, we're going to learn to do the most preliminary steps that are needed to get going—getting diskettes ready for use (called formatting), and making copies of our data, so that we don't have to worry about damaging our only copy.

So, once we have an idea of what we are doing, we are going to do the most basic diskette operations: formatting, copying, testing, and, of course, using the diskettes.

But, before we are ready to get down to work, we need to understand some things.

3.3 What You Need to Know First

The very first things you need to know are these, which we'll talk about in this section:

- how DOS settles in at its desk when it begins its working day
- how you tell DOS to do some work
- what are the dangers of starting out
- how the safeguards to these dangers work
- what setting up diskettes is all about.

Let's begin with what DOS does when it starts its working day. When your computer "wakes up" it doesn't know very much, since it doesn't have an ordinary program loaded into it. But your computer does have two special programs built into it, so it does know how to do two things—one is how to do a little self-testing, to see that things are in working order, and the other is a program that knows how to start up DOS. This start-up program is usually called a bootstrap loader, since it "pulls DOS up by the bootstraps." This simple start-up program reads the very first part of a diskette, where DOS has left a program that knows how to get DOS all set up.

This bootstrap operation works in three interesting stages. First there is the tiny program built into your computer. It doesn't know anything about DOS— it just knows how to read the beginning of a diskette and run it as a program. This tiny program built into the computer doesn't know, or care, if it is starting DOS or some other operating system. It just reads the beginning of a diskette, where DOS's own starting routine is.

The second part of this start-up routine, which is part of DOS, is just smart enough to get the rest of DOS going; so it reads the rest of DOS from the disk, and, voila, DOS is running.

All this, however, goes on behind the scenes. We don't see the details, we just watch the computer working away until DOS is started up. When DOS is ready to start, it first asks us to tell it the current date and time so that it can keep track of it. It is a very good idea to faithfully put in the right date and time, because that lets DOS keep track of when our data is created (which can become very important later).

The exact form that DOS asks for the date and time may vary slightly from computer to computer, but this is typical. DOS displays this on your screen and waits for you to key in the date:

```
Current date is Tue 1-01-1980
Enter new date:
```

You key in the date, using the hyphen (-) or the slash (/) to separate the year, month, and date. After this is done, DOS does the same thing for the time:

```
Current time is 0:00:12.34
Enter new time:
```

Again, you key in the time, using a colon (:) to separate hours, minutes, and seconds. DOS uses a 24-hour clock, which means that if the time is past noon,

DOS UP AND READY TO GO!

you would enter an hour of 12 or more. For example, 2 PM is 14, and so forth.

After these preliminaries, DOS announces that it is ready for work, with a few messages which usually give the brand of your computer and the version of DOS. This is a typical example:

```
The Wonderful Computer DOS
Version 2.00
(C) Copyright The Wonderful Computer Corporation
(C) Copyright Microsoft, Inc
```

(By the way, this is what we call DOS's starting message, and in Chapter 20 we'll show you how you can change it, if you want to.)

There is one thing you should pay attention to, right away, and that is the version number. If you don't already know which version of DOS you are using, look at the version displayed. (Our example shows version 2.00; yours might be 1.10, 1.25, or something else.) For this book, you need to know if you have a 1-series DOS, or a 2-series DOS, since there is a significant difference in the features between them. There is much less difference in the minor version numbers after the decimal point.

This is, in simple terms, how DOS begins its working day. Next let's see how we tell DOS to do some work for us. The process works as a simple, and very terse, dialogue between DOS and us. DOS tells us that it is ready for a command, and then we tell DOS what to do. DOS tells us that it is ready for a command by displaying the DOS "prompt," prompting us to put in a command. The typical prompt is like this:

A:

or like this:

A>

A capital A followed by a colon, or by a "greater than" symbol. Whether the colon or the greater than symbol is used depends upon your computer and version of DOS; there is no significance to which is used. The A part of the prompt indicates which disk DOS is currently using. It might be another letter of the alphabet than A, but the effect is the same. (We'll go into what this letter means in the next chapter on elementary commands.)

If we see the DOS prompt, "A:" or "A>" or "B:", and so on, then we are talking to DOS, and DOS wants us to tell it what to do—DOS wants a "command," an instruction of what to do next. On the other hand, if we see something else on the display screen, then it isn't DOS waiting for a command, it's some program, one of the DOS commands, asking us for instructions.

To get DOS to do some work, we must give it a command. What are the commands and what can they do? A command, in simplest terms, is the name of a program that you want the computer to carry out. That program command might be the name of one of your own programs. Or it might be the name of a program which you have bought—like VisiCalc or WordStar. Or it might be a program that is a part of DOS itself—like the command TIME which changes the setting on DOS's clock, Finally, it might be the name of a special kind of DOS program called a batch execution file, which we'll cover in Chapter 11. So, you might say that there are four kinds of commands—our own programs, store bought programs, DOS's own programs, and DOS batch programs. But this is just dividing commands up into four logical categories for us to think about. There is very little basic difference between these four. At heart, they are all just programs which we can get DOS to carry out for us.

In Chapter 4 we'll start looking more closely at what commands are, and we'll find out which commands can be used at any given moment.

How do we get commands to work? A very simple way. We key in the name of the command and press our computer's *enter* key. DOS takes it from there—figuring out what sort of command it is, finding the program, and making the program work. DOS does all this for us. All we have to do is type in the command name.

So far, we've seen how DOS gets started, and how it takes commands from us. Now, what are the dangers? And how do we protect ourselves from the dangers?

The dangers are few, and they are mostly about losing our data. It's pretty hard to break the computer itself, short of dropping it out the window, or pouring coffee inside it. If you were driving a car, rolling along at a good speed, and then suddenly shifted into reverse, you'd break your car quickly. Driving into a tree would do a lot of damage, too. But with a computer, you can't break it by "bad driving." You can damage your computer by physical abuse, but not by typing the wrong thing at the keyboard.

No, the major danger we face as users of a computer is of losing our only copy of some information. We can lose data in two ways. One is by physically damaging a diskette that stores the data—the equivalent of taking a phonograph record and breaking it. The other is by telling the computer to throw data away—the equivalent of taking a cassette recording of some music and erasing it. There are ways you can reduce the chance that you'll do the computer equivalent of breaking a record or erasing a tape, but the most important safeguard against losing data is simply to have copies around.

And that is the simple reason why the first thing to do is to make copies of your DOS diskette, so that you can start working with it or with the copy— with the safe feeling that if you do anything wrong, the original is safe.

DOS IS SAFE WHILE A COPY DRAWS THE FIRE...

There is one more thing to learn before we can begin—we need to know the basics of setting up diskettes. We make copies of our diskette data, including the DOS diskette, onto blank diskettes. But a blank diskette can't be used just like that—it has to be "formatted." What is formatting? It is something like taking a blank piece of paper and ruling lines on it, so that we have guidelines to make our handwriting even. A blank diskette is just that—blank—but our computers need the equivalent of guidelines written onto the diskette to create a framework for our data. Formatting a diskette creates this framework, the guidelines for writing on our diskettes. With a formatted diskette, we can copy our data onto the diskette.

When a disk is formatted, it can include a copy of DOS or not. This may seem odd, but that is the way it is. (We'll get a clearer idea of why in Chapter 9 when we learn more about diskettes.) Why would we want a copy of DOS on our diskettes, or why would we not want it on our diskettes? If we format our diskettes with DOS, then we can start our computer system using these diskettes. That can be very handy. Any diskette that you have put DOS onto can be used to start your system, so you don't have to look for a special start-up diskette; any one with DOS on it will do. On the other hand, having a copy of DOS on a diskette takes up some space on the diskette, so that there is less room for our own data.

When we get deeper into the subject, we'll learn how to decide when it's a good idea to put DOS onto a diskette, and when it's better not to. We'll see more about that in Chapter 5, on elementary commands, and in Chapter 9, on diskettes, including the advantages and disadvantages of a shortcut called DISKCOPY.

For now, we'll follow the simplest and safest rule—we'll put DOS on all of our diskettes.

With that background out of the way, let's proceed to safeguard and play with our DOS.

3.4 The First Things to Do

Now we're ready to start up DOS for the first time, make safe-keeping copies of your DOS, and start playing around.

To begin, you'll need four things. The first, naturally, is your computer. The second is the computer's introductory instruction manual, to check to see how each operation is done for your particular computer. The third is the DOS diskette which came with your computer's DOS manual. And the fourth is a few blank diskettes.

With these parts ready, place the DOS diskette in your computer's first disk drive opening, close the hatch, and then turn your computer on. For most computers, it will take a short while for the computer to warm up and then to test itself. When that is done, the computer will begin reading the DOS diskette; and DOS will start, as we described in the last section, by asking you for the date and the time, like this:

```
Current date is Tue 1-01-1980
Enter new date: XX/XX/XXXX      (we type in where the X's are)
Current time is 0:00:12.34
Enter new time: XX:XX           (here, too, we type where the X's are)
Your Computer DOS
Version X.XX
(C) Copyright Your Computer Company
(C) Copyright Microsoft, Inc.
```

When that is done, DOS is ready for us to start work, and DOS will give us the command prompt, which might be

```
A: or A>
```

The next thing we want to do is to format some diskettes, to get them ready for use. Formatting diskettes is a very basic and everyday operation, so we might as well get some practice at it.

If you have read any of your computer's beginner's manual, you've probably seen the discussion of what you do if you have one or two diskette drives. DOS and your computer need to have two diskette drives to work with, so that we can do things like copy data from the diskette in one drive to another diskette in the other drive. Your computer probably has two diskette drives. But what if it has only one? DOS solves this problem by pretending that the computer has two anyway. It pretends that there are two drives by first treating the one disk drive as the first drive (known as the "A" drive), and then treating the same drive as if it were the second drive (known as the "B" drive). If you actually have two disk drives, then the two just merrily work away. If not, every time that DOS switches from treating the one real drive as A or B to treating it as the other, DOS stops and tells you to change the diskette from the one that is supposed to be in the A drive to the diskette that is supposed to be in the B drive (or vice versa). So, with only one disk drive, DOS switches the use of it back and forth between the two drives that it needs, A and B.

From now on, we'll always just refer to your computer's A drive (the first one) and B drive (the second one). If you only have one real drive, DOS will take care of maintaining a pretense that there are two drives, as long as you will co-operate by switching the diskettes in and out of the one drive. (When this happens, you'll quickly learn why you should have two drives.)

So now we are ready to format some diskettes. First, we have to give DOS the command to format them. The command looks like this (we'll explain the parts of it in a moment):

```
FORMAT   B:  -S
```

There are three parts to this command. First, there is the command itself, "FORMAT". Then there are two parameters, which tell FORMAT just how to operate. The first parameter, "B:", tells the FORMAT command that the diskette to be formatted is in the B drive. The second parameter, "-S", tells the FORMAT command that we want it to place a copy of DOS onto the formatted diskette. (As we mentioned before, a diskette can have a copy of DOS on it, or not, which means that the disk can or can't be used to start up DOS; we'll see more about this in Chapters 4 and 8.) By the way, some computers require a slash (/) before the S rather than a hyphen (-). If your computer manual shows things this way, or if the FORMAT command complains about the hyphen, substitute a slash.

With this done, we press the *enter* key and the FORMAT command begins working. When FORMAT is ready to start formatting our diskette, it will stop and ask us to put our diskette into the B drive, and then press any key. After we do that, the FORMAT command program will work away, formatting the diskette. When it is done, it will give a little report on its work. The exact nature of the report will depend upon your computer and the kind of diskettes that it uses, but this is typical:

```
Formatting...Format complete
System transferred
362496 bytes total disk space
 40960 bytes used by system
321536 bytes available on disk
Format another (Y/N)?
```

We should take this opportunity to format several diskettes, so answer "Y" to the question about formatting another. After that, FORMAT will remind you to put a new diskette into the B drive.

Keep doing this formatting until you have a small working supply of diskettes. They will come in very handy shortly. After you have enough, maybe four or five, answer "N" so that the FORMAT command will come to an end.

At this point we now have several diskettes, each formatted, and each with a copy of DOS. Having a copy of DOS means that the system can be started from that diskette; but it does not mean that all the parts and tools of DOS are copied onto the diskette—just the most fundamental parts. Our next step is to copy everything from our original DOS diskette onto one of these new diskettes. This will become our main working copy of DOS, so that we can put the original copy of DOS away for safekeeping.

So far we have experimented with one single DOS command: FORMAT. Now, we'll get a chance to try another one, the COPY command. COPY is a command which will do several different interesting things for us, as we'll see later in Chapter 5. In fact, many of the commands that make up DOS have more than one use. But for now, the feature of the COPY command that we will use is its most simple and straightforward: copying data from one diskette to another.

The copy command, as we use it to copy everything that is on the diskette in drive A to the diskette in drive B, is done like this:

```
COPY   A:*.*   B:
```

While we'll put off understanding the details until the next chapter, we can easily see the main parts of what is going on; and it's not much different from what we saw with the FORMAT command. There are three parts here: the command name (COPY) and two parameters. In this case, the first parameter indicates what to copy from. It says, with the "A:" part, copy from drive A, while the "*.*" part is a way of saying copy everything. The second parameter, "B:", says to copy to drive B. While the first parameter had a "*.*" part to indicate that everything was being copied, the second parameter doesn't have any such specification. Why? Because it's implied that whatever is found on drive A should be copied as it is to drive B. We'll dig deeper into how these things work in the next chapter.

So, if we type this command in and press the *enter* key, then DOS's COPY command will dutifully copy everything it finds on the diskette in drive A to the diskette in drive B.

Do exactly this, and then you will have in drive B a diskette with a copy of everything that was on the diskette in drive A. This new diskette we can use as our working copy of DOS. We can now put the original copy of DOS away in safekeeping without having to worry about doing it any harm.

And that finishes a short lesson on how to get started in DOS. It has done several things for us. For one thing, it "got our feet wet." Without having to understand too much about DOS, we've been able to put it to work a little and get a useful result out of it—namely we've got some formatted diskettes to work with, and we have a copy of the DOS diskette to use. What we're ready for now is to understand the principles behind what we've done and more about the commands of DOS, ordinary and advanced. This will occupy us for the next three chapters.

Fundamentals
of DOS Commands

Before we can move on to start really looking at the DOS commands, we have to learn the fundamentals of how they are laid out and used. In this chapter we'll pause to master the basics of DOS commands.

4.1 Keeping Track of Drives

Our real goal in this entire book is to get you comfortable with DOS—to speed you, as quickly as possible, toward thinking of DOS as an old friend, an old tool, which you use with ease and hardly a second thought. One of the things that will help you most in getting comfortable with DOS is to understand how important disk drives are to DOS.

DOS is, after all, a *Disk* Operating System; and disks are very much at the core of the way DOS operates and the way it organizes itself. So if we want to understand DOS, we need to understand the way that DOS thinks about disks.

One of the first things we need to realize about how DOS works, is to realize that DOS is focused more on the disk *drive* than on the *diskette* that is in the drive. Your computer probably has one or two diskette drives in it and maybe a high-capacity hard disk system. DOS needs a consistent and uniform way of keeping track of this disk gear, and it does this by giving a letter code to each of the drives. The first drive is referred to as A, the second as B, and so forth. Your computer probably has at least two drives; but if it doesn't, as we mentioned in the last chapter, DOS will turn your one drive into a "let's pretend" pair of drives, A and B. Many DOS command operations need two disk drives, and, when there is only one drive, it is easier and more consistent for DOS to fake having a second drive, a B drive, than to try to do everything with only an A drive.

Now if we have a diskette that we want to work with, and we put that diskette in our A diskette drive, then we'd tell DOS to look to the A drive to find what is on that diskette. We'd get the same result if we put the same diskette in the B drive and told DOS to look there. The idea is simple—DOS doesn't know what we're doing with diskettes, which we might be switching around behind its back. But DOS does know what's what with the disk drives, so that is where DOS's focus is.

This means that whenever we do anything with data or programs on a disk, we have to let DOS know which drive we want it to look to. This is done by giving the drive letter, followed by a colon, like this:

    A: or B: or C: (or A> or B> or C>)

(By the way, DOS will happily take either an upper or lower-case letter and treat them the same. In our examples, we'll always show things in upper-case, but you can type them in either way at your convenience.)

When *any* of your computer manuals refer to the *drive specification*, what you see above is what they are referring to: the drive letter, followed by a colon. So "A:" or "B:" is a drive specification.

Since much of what we do with the computer involves disk data, it could be a real nuisance to have to keep typing in the drive specification, A: or B: or whatever, all the time. DOS simplifies the process by having a *default* drive. DOS keeps track of the current default drive; and any time we refer to a disk, or one of our programs refers to a disk, without giving a drive specification, then DOS assumes we intend to use the default drive. By the way, DOS-2 adds a considerable enrichment to the idea of a default drive; we'll cover that topic in the last section of Chapter 8.

We've already mentioned that DOS prompts us for commands with something like this:

A: or, on some computers   A>

You're probably ready to guess that the "A" in this prompt tells us that A is the current default drive. If the default drive were changed to B, then DOS's prompt would be

B: or   B>

This is really quite clever, when you think about it. If the default drive can be changed, it would be very helpful for DOS to give us reminders of where the default is now. But it would be a nuisance to have DOS repeatedly putting a message on the screen like "The default drive is now X." So the DOS command prompt is a compact, handy, and unobtrusive way for DOS to remind us of the default drive.

What if you want to change the default drive? (We'll postpone talking about *why* you would want to change it; that makes sense only after you have a feel for how you use DOS.) There is a very simple way to change the default drive: you just type in a drive specification *as a command by itself.* DOS takes that to be a command to change the default drive, and away we go. Here is a dummy example:

A>   (DOS prompts us, saying the default drive is A)
  B: (we enter a B drive spec, with no command)
B>   (DOS has now changed the default drive)

Whenever we are working with disks, we have a free choice of using the default drive or specifying the drive. We can specify the drive even if it is already the default drive—there is no harm in that. So if for any reason we want to be very specific about things, we can indicate the drive we want to use, and it will work just fine, default or not.

Most of the time, though, having a default drive is a real convenience, because it cuts down on the keystrokes we have to type in.

4.2 Where Commands Could Come From

The next thing that we need to know about commands in general is where they come from. All commands that we ask DOS to carry are, in one way or another, programs. The question is, then, what kind of programs are they, and where are the programs located.

This brings us to a topic that DOS calls internal and external commands.

There is a problem inherent in DOS having a nice, large number of services, or commands, available for us to use. On the one hand, we would like to have these command services on tap, instantly, at all times. But to do this, the programs that provide these services would have to be resident in memory, which means that they would be taking up some of our working memory space all the time, both when we were using them and when we were not. So, on the other hand, we would like to have as little as possible of our memory, our working desk top, taken up by these command programs.

This is an obvious conflict, and to resolve it DOS has worked out a compromise. A handful of the command programs which are smallest and most useful are made a resident part of DOS, which means that they are in memory all the time once DOS has been read off the disk and started up. These are called the *internal* commands, since they are internal to DOS. All of the other command programs are called *external,* and they are kept in the disk "filing cabinet" until the time comes when they are needed.

The internal commands are built right into DOS, so there is no question that they are a part of DOS. The external commands are also provided with DOS, and they are rightly considered to be a part of DOS as well. But, actually, any program which can be used from the disk can work just like all of the DOS commands. So there is only a fuzzy distinction between the external commands which are DOS commands, and all other programs, which are also a form of commands. Shortly we'll see a list of the commands that are internal, and those that are external.

So, depending upon which kind of command we happen to select to use, DOS will either be able to carry it out immediately, or else it will have to look into its disk filing cabinet for the command program. The practical significance of this is that the command's program *must be on the disk* when DOS goes looking for it. At first this may seem a silly point, since you expect to have your DOS diskette in a disk drive. But soon you'll learn that it isn't that simple. Unless you have a high-capacity hard disk system, you'll soon be using more command programs than will fit onto a single diskette. In fact, all of the parts of your DOS probably take up more than one diskette as it is. What do you do when you have more programs than you can keep on one diskette?

The answer is very simple: you organize your diskettes functionally, combining all the parts that you need to carry out one kind of work, leaving other programs off each diskette. In Chapter 13 we'll give you some advice about doing just that. Right now, the important point is that DOS can only carry out those commands that it has access to the programs for. The internal commands are always on tap, and you can ask for any external command whose program disk is currently loaded.

Of course, all it takes to get access to other commands is a change of diskettes. You take out one diskette, put in another, and you can have a whole new set of commands at your service. *But DOS can't do that for you.* So, if you ask for a command that isn't internal, and isn't on your current diskettes, then DOS can't perform the command. Instead, DOS will tell you something is wrong by displaying the message

```
Bad command or filename
```

THE SEARCH FOR A COMMAND PROGRAM.

At first you might be confused by this message, which is part of the reason why we're discussing it. As you learn more about how external commands are stored on disk, you'll see that a command's name is the same as the name of a file on a disk, which explains the "or filename" part of the above message. The important thing for you to know is that when you see the above message, DOS is telling you that it couldn't find a command program which matched the command name that you entered.

There are two reasons why DOS might not be able to find a command you have entered. One reason, which we've been discussing, is that the command program is on another diskette. The other reason, which you have to be prepared for, is a simpler one: you keyed in the command name wrong. So, the first thing that you should do when you get the "Bad command" message, is to check what you typed as a command name—it may not be what you intended.

4.3 Common Command Notation

There is a standard format for asking DOS to carry out commands, a notation or syntax to the way we are supposed to enter commands. This section will explain the normal way that DOS commands are requested. Unfortunately there is a little too much variety in the way that you can enter commands, which can lead to some confusion about the best way to express commands. We'll try to clear all that up here.

First, all commands start out in this basic format:

```
COMMAND-NAME   PARAMETERS-IF-ANY
```

For example, in the last chapter on setting up our DOS diskettes we used this copy command:

```
COPY   A:*.*   B:
```

The command name was "COPY" and two parameters were needed, the first indicating what to copy from ("A:*.*") and what to copy to ("B:").

So far, we have the most basic part: that a command begins with the name of the command, followed by whatever parameters are needed.

Some kind of punctuation must be used to separate the command name and the parameters. In our examples, we've always used spaces, but DOS allows other things to be used for punctuation—commas, semicolons, and some other symbols. (The exact list of punctuation symbols may vary from computer to computer, but usually the equal sign (=), and the *Tab* key can also be used.)

It is best, for various reasons, to use the space character, the comma, and the semicolon. You'll probably get the best results and have the fewest problems if you always use the blank space character to separate commands and parameters, except for one special circumstance, which we'll discuss next.

While most commands need only one or two parameters, some special command programs, such as compilers for programming languages, need a longer list of parameters, some of which may be left off. For this kind of command, there is a very useful convention: each of the parameters is separated by a comma. If a parameter is being left off, then two commas appear in a row. When no more parameters follow (even if there might be more), a semicolon indicates the end of the list. Here is an example showing how this is done:

```
COMMAND  1st,2nd,,4th,,6th;
```

You'll notice that the third and fifth parameters don't appear, but the commas serve to hold their places, so that it is clear that the 4th parameter *is* the 4th parameter.

When you need to specify command parameters this special way, feel free to do so—but otherwise, for simplicity, I recommend you always use spaces to separate a command name from its parameters, and the parameters from each other.

There is one more thing you need to know about how commands and their parameters are written. Some commands divide their parameters into two categories, regular parameters and what are called switches. As a simple way to understand what switches are, we could give this short guiding rule:

- COMMANDS indicate what is to be done (such as copying data)
- PARAMETERS indicate what the command is to be performed on (e.g., what to copy)
- SWITCHES indicate how it is to be done (e.g., should the copy be checked for correctness?)

To make it easier to separate parameters (what to act on) from switches (how to carry out the action), there is a special notation that is used. The switch is preceded by a special character. On some computers the switch identifier is a slash (/); on others it is a hyphen (-). You'll have to check your computer's manuals to see which is used. (In this book, for consistency, we show the hyphen format, which is the normal DOS form.) You've already seen one example of a switch in the last chapter—we used one, "-S", when we used the FORMAT command.

Usually switches are very short and simple, typically just a single letter. The idea of a switch is that it is an instruction to do or not do some variation on the basic operation. For example, the "-S" switch in the FORMAT command tells it to include a copy of the operating system on the formatted diskette. Another example: the COPY command has a "-V" switch, which tells it to Verify the copy, checking to see that it is right. Remember to check to see if your computer uses "/" or "-" to mark its switches. The quickest way to check that is to look up the FORMAT command, and see if it shows the "S" switch with a slash (/) or a hyphen (-).

4.4 Files, File Names, and Other Wild Stuff

Most DOS commands are doing some operation either on an entire disk or on files that are stored on a disk. You will see that most parameters are either just a disk specification (telling the command which disk to do its operation on) or the name of some files.

We'll put off going over all the details of file names until we cover disks in more detail in Chapter 9. But for now, we still need to know a little about them, because we're going to be seeing them a lot as we go over the DOS commands in the next two chapters. So here is a quick summary, that will do for now, and that will also give us a head start when we come to Chapter 9.

Data on a disk is organized into *files*. To identify the files, each one has a file name. Among all the files on one disk, the file name must be unique so that files don't get confused. The name of a file actually has two parts called the *filename* proper and the filename *extension*, or the extension to the filename.

The *filename* is at least one character, and it can be as long as eight characters but no longer. Filenames can be made up of letters of the alphabet, digits, and some punctuation characters (wait until Chapter 9 for details). You can't have a space character as part of a filename or any of the other punctuation characters that are used to punctuate a command and its parameters. We can use upper or lower-case letters in filenames, but DOS treats them as if they were all upper-case. Here are some sample filenames:

```
FILENAME
12
A
ABC123
```

The *extension* to the filename is a short appendage added on after the filename. The two are separated by a period so that a filename and extension look like this:

```
FILENAME.EXT
```

The extension is three characters at most, and it's an optional part—a file must have a filename part, but it doesn't have to have an extension part. If there is no extension part, then we drop the period that is used to separate the two parts.

Here are some more examples of file names, with and without extensions, to give you more of an idea of what they can look like:

FILENAME.EXT	(this is as big as they can get)
A	(this is the minimum file name)
12345678	(numbers are OK)
NEW-DATA	(hyphens can be OK)
ADDRESS.LST	(an example of how a file name can indicate contents)
JULY.83	(another informative file name)

The *intended purpose* of an extension is to indicate the category that the filename falls into. It is an informal—*not* a mandatory—way of indicating what type of file a file is. In Chapter 9 we'll look at some of the more common categories.

It is a little confusing to have a files's complete name be called a file name, and part of that name be called a filename, (with no space), but that is the terminology that is used with DOS, so we have to live with it. Whenever you run across either term, slow down and be careful to see what is being referred to.

There is a way to refer to more than one file at a time—through a mechanism known as wild cards. Wild cards are a way of partly specifying a file name so that several files may match the specification. For example, in the last chapter we did a COPY command with a file specification of "*.*" —which meant any filename and any filename extension. If we had written it as "*.COM" that would mean any filename, but only the extension "COM".

There is a rich way that wild cards can be used in a file specification, using two wild card symbols: the asterisk (*), which we've seen, and the question mark (?), which we haven't yet. More will be revealed in Chapter 9. For now, understand that we can use "*.*" as a way of saying any filename with any extension—or, in other words, all the files on a disk.

With this accomplished, we are ready to move on to look at some of the commands that DOS provides for us.

Overview of Elementary Commands

In this chapter we'll begin going over the commands that DOS gives us to work with and control our computers. Here we'll look at the commands that are easiest to understand and the ones that are the most commonly used, while we'll reserve the more complicated ones for the next chapter.

To make it easier to understand, we'll cover them grouped by topic rather than in alphabetical order. What we *won't* do here is to cover the precise details of how the commands work—that's a subject that belongs to your computer's manuals, particularly since some of these commands vary a little from computer to computer. What we *will* do here is to make sense of these commands for you, and give you tips and handy hints about how to get the most from these commands (and how to avoid problems with them, as well).

One small word of warning to help keep you from getting confused: some computer makers use slightly different names for the commands that are available in DOS. Where we can, we'll point this out. But be prepared for some minor differences between what you see here and what your computer manuals describe; for example, for the DISKCOPY command some computers drop the "I" and call it DSKCOPY. But whatever the name, the result is the same.

5.1 The Time Commands—DATE and TIME

DOS keeps track of the date and the time of day, which is a very handy thing. It is handy for all sorts of reasons, and one of the best reasons is that every time you create or change some information on a disk, the disk data is marked with the current date and time. This can be extremely valuable to you for answering questions like "which of these files did I work on last week?" or "which of these diskettes has the *latest* changes to my report?"

I have occasionally found it a lifesaver to know that all of my files have an accurate date and time stamp on them, and there is hardly a day when I don't find it at least useful to see time stamps on my files. (Later in this chapter we'll learn how you see these time stamps when we cover the DIR command.)

To make it possible for us to enter or change the date and time, DOS has two special commands called, naturally, DATE and TIME. These commands work independently so that you can enter or change either one without affecting the other. By the way, when DOS starts up, it automatically invokes both DATE and TIME as part of its start-up procedures. We saw this in action back in Chapter 3 when we described how DOS begins operation.

Both DATE and TIME work the same way, and both can be used two ways. The first way, which we might call interactive, happens when we just enter the command name, like this:

```
DATE
```

DOS then responds by telling us what its current record of the date (or time) is, and asks us for a new date (or time), like this:

```
Current date is Tue 01-01-1980
Enter new date:
```

At that point, we can either enter a new date (time), or just press enter to leave the date (time) unchanged.

The other way to use the DATE and TIME commands is more direct. If we key in the command name, followed by the date or time, and press *enter*, then DOS will just change the date or time without displaying or requesting anything else. Here is an example of how we would use DATE and TIME this way:

```
DATE  7-4-1984
TIME  14:15
```

Here are some tips and notes on the DATE and TIME commands:

- When we enter the date, it's punctuated with either hyphens (-) or slashes (/), at our choice. The time is punctuated with colons (:).
- You can leave leading zeros off the figures, so January can be entered as "1", rather than "01".
- When entering the date, we can leave off the century, the "19" in "1984".
- When entering the time, we can leave off the seconds, or both minutes and seconds, if we want.
- There isn't any way to get DOS to display the current date or time without having it wait for us to enter a new value (except for a tricky way that can be done with DOS-2).
- As long as it is running, DOS keeps track of when midnight passes and, under normal circumstances, automatically changes the date.
- DOS is smart enough to keep track of leap years.

The DATE and TIME commands are internal (except in the long obsolete 1.00 version of DOS), so that you can use them at any time, regardless of what you have on your disks.

Some computer systems have special hardware functions to keep track of the date and time even when the computer is turned off. This hardware, combined with the right supporting programs, can save you the trouble of entering

DOS SETS ITS WATCH AND CHECKS ITS CALENDAR.

the date and time when you start up DOS. However, you still have the option of using the DATE and TIME commands to change DOS's record of the date and time.

5.2 Checking Out Your Disks—DIR, CHKDSK, and *CAT*

There are two commands designed to let you find out what's on your disks, called DIR and CHKDSK, and a third which applies to some versions of DOS-2, CAT.

DIR is the *directory listing* command, designed to tell you the list of commands on a disk. There are several ways that DIR can be used. The most common way is to just put in the command DIR with a drive specification (or, implied, the default drive) like this:

```
DIR A:
```

This will ask DIR to list all of the files on a disk. The list will include the filename, the filename extension, the size of the file in characters or bytes, and the date and time the file was created, or last changed. You will recall that we mentioned in the preceding section, in discussing the DATE and TIME commands, that files were marked with time stamps like this. The DIR command is our way to see what the time stamp is as well as each file's size.

If you don't want to see a list of all of the files, but only the information on one, you can enter that file's name, and DIR will report on it only:

```
DIR THISFILE.EXT
```

Similarly, if you use the wild cards mentioned in the last chapter (and covered more in Chapter 9), then you can get information on just some files.

For example, this command would get directory information on all files which have an extension of "BAT":

```
DIR *.BAT
```

One of the incidental things that DIR reports is the amount of space left free on a disk. So you may want to use the DIR command not to see a directory listing but simply to find out how much space is available for use on a disk.

A disk can have "hidden" files on it; usually if it does, they are just secret parts of the DOS operating system (we'll see more about that in the next section and in Chapter 9). The DIR command acts as though hidden files were not there at all (but CHKDSK, which we're coming to, tells us about them).

There is one peculiarity of the DIR command that you need to know about. Most DOS commands work with wild card file specifications, like "*.*", which means "all files with any names." DIR works with wild cards as well, but it has one difference—DIR will assume a wild card where you didn't put one. So, if you enter the command

```
DIR
```

it will be treated just as if you had entered

```
DIR *.*
```

and if you put in a filename, with no extension, such as

```
DIR FILENAME
```

it will be treated as if you put in a wild card for the extension, such as

```
DIR FILENAME.*
```

The DIR command is the only one which acts this way. This special feature of DIR is rather handy, but it has one real drawback—it is inconsistent with the rest of DOS. Consistency is important in anything as complex as DOS, because it reduces the number of rules that you have to learn, and it increases your confidence that DOS will do what you think you are asking it to do. In this case, don't be worried if you find that DIR is acting a little different than all the other DOS commands. It isn't you misunderstanding things, it's just DIR doing things its own way.

DIR LISTS THE FILES ON A DISKETTE.

Your version of DOS may include switches in the DIR command to pause after the screen fills ("-P" or "/P"), or to eliminate the size and time stamp information ("-W" or "/W"). Both switches are intended to help you see the list of files better.

Some versions of DOS-2 also include a CAT command, which works like the DIR command but gives slightly different information, formatted in a different way. In many ways, though, CAT is just a variation on the DIR command.

While the DIR command shows us a list of files on a disk, the CHKDSK, or check disk, command is intended to give us a status report on our disks. CHKDSK does two main things—first it checks the disk over to see how much space there is, how much is in use, and if there is any discrepancy in the space usage. (It is rare for there to be any discrepancy, so you may never encounter one. How and why things can go wrong with the space allocation is a very interesting subject, but one that is too technical for this book.) Then it reports to us the total space, the space in use, the number of files, and incidentally if there are any hidden files.

CHKDSK is also prepared to repair any logical damage in the use of space. If any space has been "lost"—which is one of the possible discrepancies in the space usage—CHKDSK can recover it and also report or repair other kinds of mixups in the space (which is rare). DOS-1 and DOS-2 treat this repair work differently—DOS-1 does it automatically, while DOS-2 is more cautious and asks for our permission.

This check, report, and repair operation is a very valuable one, and so it is a very good idea to routinely do a CHKDSK on all of your disks occasionally. When you set up batch files, which we'll cover in Chapter 11, it would be good to include CHKDSK in many of your batch file operations.

Like DIR, CHKDSK reports on the amount of space available on your disks, and does something else nice that is completely unrelated to its check-your-disk function: it reports on the amount of memory available in your system. Just as you might use DIR just to find out about available space on disk, you might also use CHKDSK just to see how much memory you have.

DIR is an internal command, so you can use it at any time. CHKDSK, and CAT, are external commands and must be available on your disks to be used.

5.3 The Diskette Preparation Commands— FORMAT, SYS, and DISKCOPY

Since DOS relies so heavily on the use of diskettes, naturally there are commands to prepare diskettes for use. We took a short look at one of them, FORMAT, in Chapter 3. Now we'll look closer at all three setup commands, FORMAT, SYS, and DISKCOPY.

Each of these three commands is *external*, which means that we can only use them when we have a disk ready which contains the command programs for these commands.

The FORMAT command is used to to do the most basic preparation of a disk for use. It is the equivalent of drawing writing guidelines on a blank sheet of paper, to make it possible to later write evenly on the paper.

FORMAT actually does two important things with a diskette—it draws the electronic "guidelines" that make it possible for DOS to work with the diskette, and it also checks for any defects in the diskette. Because diskettes are so vulnerable, they may have damaged patches on them. But a diskette with a bad patch can still be used—the FORMAT command knows how to recognize these bad patches and put up a safety fence around them. When FORMAT finds bad patches, it reports them to you, indicating their size as well as the size of the usable part of the diskette. With this done, the rest of the diskette is ready to use.

Whether or not you want to use a diskette with a bad patch is up to you. Obviously a bad patch takes up part of the space on a diskette, and makes you wonder about the quality of the rest of the diskette. But usually bad patches are small and nothing goes wrong with the rest of the diskette. If you need every bit of space that a diskette has to offer, or if you are unusually worried about risks to your data, then put aside any diskette that has bad patches when it is formatted. Normally, though, I would say that there is no problem with using a diskette with bad patches that are a small proportion of the diskette.

FORMAT MARKS OFF THE DAMAGED SECTION.

Usually, diskettes format without any bad patches. If you encounter them a lot, it is a sign of one of two things—either you have a bad batch of diskettes, or the recording heads on your disk drives are dirty and should be cleaned. If you suspect that the problem is dirty heads, see your computer's manuals for cleaning instructions.

When you format a diskette, you have the option of putting the DOS operating system on the diskette. The advantage of including DOS on many of your diskettes is that you can then start your system using any of those diskettes—you don't have to use just one special start-up diskette. This can be a real convenience. The disadvantage is that having DOS on a diskette takes up some of the diskette's usable space. I would recommend, for starters, that you include DOS on every diskette until you learn from your own experience which ones you do and don't want DOS stored on. At first, it is better to have DOS on all of your disks. Later you can be more discriminating—for example putting DOS on all of your *program* diskettes but leaving it off your *data* diskettes. If you have formatted a diskette *without* a copy of DOS, then you *cannot* later add DOS to the diskette except by reformatting it (which would wipe out any data you had placed on the diskette). So, in general, it is better to include DOS in your formatting.

The system switch, "-S" or "/S", is used to tell FORMAT to include a copy of DOS on the diskette. (Remember that switches are marked with "-" or "/", depending upon your computer.)

When the FORMAT command sets up a diskette as a system diskette, it places three files on the diskette. Two of these files are hidden, which means that you can't ordinarily see them except through a CHKDSK command (discussed above) which reports on the number of hidden files on a diskette. The third file is not hidden—it can be seen like any other file, and it is named COMMAND.COM. We'll see more about the two hidden files and the COMMAND.COM file in a moment.

If you are using DOS-2, you can put a logical volume label on your diskettes when you format them. This label allows DOS to report to you what the name of the disk is whenever DOS refers to it. The label can be up to 11 characters long. Putting a label on each disk is a very good idea, and I highly recommend it. Choose your labels carefully—DOS doesn't give you any way to change them later. The "-V" or "/ V" switch is used to tell FORMAT that you want a volume label on the disk.

Your computer may work with more than one diskette format—for example, single or double-sided diskettes. If so, there will be switches in your version of the FORMAT command to control which format you want. Normally you should let DOS decide which format to use, unless you know that you need a special format which is used by another computer.

FORMAT is one of the most dangerous of all the commands in DOS because it can wipe out an entire diskette's worth of data at one go. If you format a diskette that has some valuable data on it, it is thoroughly gone, and nothing will bring it back. So be very careful when you format diskettes—check to be sure that the diskette doesn't have something important on it before you wipe it off the face of the disk with FORMAT. On the other hand, if you have to destroy some confidential data and need to be sure that it can't be reconstructed, FORMAT is the right tool to use.

There are times when you may want to transfer a copy of the DOS operating system to a diskette that is already formatted to hold it. The SYS command is intended to solve this problem. There are two reasons why you might need the SYS command. One is if you buy a program diskette which needs to have a copy of DOS on it. This is commonly done with copy protected programs (which we'll talk more about in Chapters 15, 17, and 18). Disks like that usually have space provided for DOS, but *don't actually have DOS on the disk.* So you have to transfer DOS to them. The second reason why you might need to transfer DOS is when you get a new version of DOS. Like all other good programs, DOS is occasionally updated and upgraded. And when you have a new version of DOS, you need to transfer the new DOS to your old DOS diskettes.

The SYS command is designed to transfer the two hidden files that are part of DOS from one diskette to another. SYS, however, *does not* transfer the third file that is part of DOS, the non-hidden file COMMAND.COM. So a complete transfer of the DOS operating system onto a diskette requires that you do two things—a SYS command to transfer the two hidden files, and a COPY command to copy the COMMAND.COM file. Whenever you read instructions about transferring DOS to a diskette, the instructions should mention both— SYS and COPY COMMAND.COM. (See more about the COPY command below.)

There is another way to set up a diskette for use besides the FORMAT command, and that is the DISKCOPY command.

DISKCOPY is a command that reads all the formatting and data from one diskette and copies it to another diskette. DISKCOPY is a quick and efficient way to make copies of diskettes. It is so quick and efficient in fact that you will find its use recommended to you over and over again. But there are some important problems with DISKCOPY, so I recommend that you be very careful about using it. *The preferred way to copy disk data* is with the COPY command, which we'll come to later.

One of the minor problems with DISKCOPY is that it is not included in all versions of DOS. So before you set out to use it (or even read any further about it), check your computer's manuals to see if your DOS includes DISKCOPY. Another minor problem with DISKCOPY is that some versions *do not transfer the formatting;* this means that you have to format a diskette first, and then DISKCOPY onto it. That eliminates most of the speed and efficiency advantages of DISKCOPY.

But the major disadvantage of using DISKCOPY is that it does not allow for bad areas on your diskettes. If either the diskette you are copying from or the one you are copying to have unusable bad areas on them, the sort of bad areas which we mentioned that FORMAT detects, then the DISKCOPY will not work properly. On the other hand, the COPY command, the preferred way to copy data, works nicely with bad patches on the diskettes.

Another advantage to COPY over DISKCOPY, is that COPY can improve the use of space on a diskette, while DISKCOPY can't. (Again, we'll discuss this improvement of storage space when we go to cover COPY.) Finally, DISKCOPY will wipe out anything that is on the target diskette, while COPY will merge new files with old to put more information on a diskette.

So there are many reasons not to use DISKCOPY, but there are still some good reasons to use it. For one thing, DISKCOPY is faster than COPY if the diskette is full of data. On the other hand, if there is only a little data on a diskette, COPY could be faster because it would copy only the data, while DISKCOPY would also faithfully copy all the unused diskette space.

Another reason for using DISKCOPY is to check a diskette for physical damage or for copy-protection. If you can DISKCOPY a diskette without any error messages, then the diskette is probably not damaged, and not copy-protected. This makes DISKCOPY a quick and easy way to check for these problems.

5.4 Moving and Removing Files—COPY, DEL, ERASE, REN, and TYPE

In this section we'll learn about changing files around—copying them, removing them, displaying them, changing their names. All of these commands are internal, which means that you can use them at any time. Let's begin with copying.

The COPY command starts out as something very simple—a tool to make copies of disk files—and then adds enough variations on the theme of copying that it ends up serving three distinct purposes.

The most straightforward kind of copying just duplicates files from one disk to another. For example,

```
COPY A:THISFILE  B:
```

would take a file named "THISFILE" from the disk in drive A and make a copy of it on the disk in drive B. The same thing could be done with wild card file names, so that the copy would copy several files. For example,

```
COPY A:*.*   B:
```

would copy all the files ("*.*") from drive A to drive B. Or we could copy all the files that begin with the letters "XYZ" like this:

```
COPY A:XYZ*.*  B:
```

You can see that we could work many variations on this idea, all of them duplicating files under the same name, but onto a different disk.

In the examples so far, we've specified the names of the source or *from* files, but we've only given the drive specification for the target or *to* files. In that case, COPY used the same file names. But we can, if we want, specify the names of the target files so that they could have different names than the original copies. For example,

```
COPY  THISFILE  THATFILE
```

would make a copy of a file named "THISFILE", and the copy would be named "THATFILE". Since we didn't specify any drives (like "A:" or "B:"), DOS uses its current default drive for both the source and the target. This means that both copies, "THISFILE" and "THATFILE", would be on the same disk—but that's just fine since the names are different.

If the copy is being made without any change of name, COPY requires that the source and target be in different places. But if the name is being changed on the copy, then the target file can be anywhere—where the source is or somewhere else.

So far we've seen two of the three different uses of COPY—to make duplicates on other disks, and to make duplicates under a different name. There is yet another use of copying—combining the contents of several files into one. This combining operation is advanced and tricky—which means you shouldn't try it until you have become more experienced in using DOS. So we won't go into all the details here, but leave that for a more advanced treatment of DOS commands. But you should know about this feature of COPY so that when you need it, you can study up on it. Here is an example of how it works: suppose we have two files, XX and YY, and we want to combine their contents into another file, ZZ. This copy command could do the trick:

```
COPY  XX+YY  ZZ
```

You should know there are dangers and pitfalls in doing this kind of copying as well as some special rules. So, when you need it, be careful.

No matter what kind of copying you are doing, the COPY command will proceed whether or not there is already a file with the target name. If there isn't a file with the target name, then a new file will be created. If there is one, it will be over-written—which might destroy some valuable data. There is no warning that an existing file is about to be destroyed, so *be careful* with all copies—this is one of the ways that you can clobber your valuable data.

On the other hand, COPY does require that the source files be there, naturally enough. How can you make a copy of something that isn't there? COPY will let you know if it can't find the source file you claim you want copied.

If you can duplicate files with COPY, creating new copies, you'd expect that you can destroy files as well. For that there is the DEL/ERASE command. This is one command, but with two different names: DEL for delete, and ERASE for erase. Under either name, it will throw a file away. We can ERASE files one at a time or en mass using "wild card" file names. DEL/ERASE gives us one small protection against erasing all our files with a slip of the hand: if we give it a wild card name, that means all files such as "*.*", then DEL/ERASE will pause to ask us if we are sure. But all other file deletion commands proceed without warning. So, this command will proceed automatically:

```
DEL  *.BAK
```

while this command will pause for confirmation:

```
DEL  *.*
```

DOS does not give us any way to recover files that have been erased; in fact the data from erased files is still on the disk, and can be recovered by a clever "un-erase" program. If this kind of program is available for your computer, buying it could be one of the best investments you can make; it acts like an insurance policy for your data. When I got my first personal computer, I saw that there wasn't an "un-erase" program available for it, so one of the first things that I did was to write one. That program saved the day for me many times, and I have a stack of testimonial letters from other people who thanked me deeply for creating a tool to rescue their data, too. So, if you possibly can, get yourself an "un-erase" program.

While erased data can, with luck, be recovered, data that you have lost by formatting cannot be recovered. For more information on the dangers of erasing and formatting, and some tricks to safeguard yourself against these dangers, see Chapters 11 and 14.

Related to both copying and erasing files is a DOS command to change the name of a file. REN, short for rename, will change a file's name as long as the name isn't also in use by another file on the same disk. Renaming is done like this:

```
REN  NAME.OLD   NAME.NEW
```

Like other commands, REN can be given wild card names to rename several files. For example, you could change every file with an extension of XXX to YYY, like this:

```
REN *.XXX  *.YYY
```

or any variation on this idea.

Finally, to finish this section, let's look at the TYPE command. TYPE is a handy way to get a quick look at the contents of a file. TYPE simply writes a copy of a file onto the display screen of your computer. (In fact TYPE is really just a COPY command, with the target of the copy being your display screen instead of another file.) The file you want to see must be something reasonable to look at—it had better consist of display characters, what is called a text file, or else what appears on your screen will be nonsensical. TYPE is done like this:

```
TYPE  SOMEFILE.TXT
```

5.5 Elementary Commands for DOS-2—VER, VOL, and CLS

There are some simple and ordinary commands which belong in this chapter that apply only to DOS-2. All of them are internal commands, available at any time.

When we covered the FORMAT command, we mentioned that with DOS-2 you can place a volume label on a disk. The VOL command will report a volume's label to you. You use the command like this:

```
VOL  B:
```

It is nice to have this command, but the same volume label information is also given by the DIR command, so VOL doesn't add anything new, it just gives a cleaner way to get only the volume label.

If you want to know the exact version of DOS that you are using, the VER command will display it. But it only works with DOS-2, so it can't be used to show which version of DOS-1 you might have. If you are whimsically inclined, you might say that there is a VER command in DOS-1, but the version it reports is this:

```
Bad command or filename
```

There is one more nice, simple command in DOS-2 which isn't in DOS-1, and that is CLS, or clear-screen. This command clears the display screen, which can be very useful.

5.6 Where to Find the Rest of the Commands

This brings to an end our discussion of the simple, necessary, and easy to understand commands. The next chapter gets into most of the more difficult ones—which you might want to read now, or skip over and come back to later when you are ready for them. But not all DOS commands are covered in this chapter and the next. There are several groups of commands which need a special discussion together with related information—so you will find more commands being discussed in Chapter 8 on special features of DOS-2, in the last section of Chapter 9 on paths, and in Chapter 11 on batch file processing. Chapter 21 brings them all back together with a reference summary of commands.

Overview of Advanced Commands

In this chapter we'll go over some of the more advanced commands. This chapter is really just a continuation of the last, but we've put a chapter boundary between them as a sort of warning that the material here could be a little harder to follow. If you find information on computers easy to understand, then plunge right ahead; if you think you might just get more confused, skip over this chapter and come back when you are ready.

We won't be covering all the advanced commands here: three groups of commands which need special discussion of related ideas will be covered later in Chapters 8, 9, and 11. This chapter takes care of the advanced commands that can be described pretty much on their own.

As we mentioned at the beginning of the last chapter, some computer makers choose their own names for commands, so be prepared for some differences between what you see here and what your computer's manuals show. The results should be the same.

6.1 Comparing Copies—COMP/FC/FILECOMP and DISKCOMP

When you make copies of files or disks, you may need to confirm that the copy is exact. To be honest, there is little reason to check a copy that you have just made—the copying process is extremely reliable, and it is very unlikely that there will be any errors in copying, unless the copying procedure itself tells you that there were problems.

The main reason for comparing copies of files or disks is to find out if there have been any changes made, although you can also use it to double check a copy that you have made just to confirm that there are no defects in the copy.

There are two comparison commands: one to compare files individually and one to compare an entire diskette. The file comparison program checks the contents of files to make sure that they match. On the other hand, the diskette comparison program compares two diskettes, and checks to see if they match *exactly*; if two diskettes contain the same data so that they are functionally

YOU CAN COMPARE TWO FILES OR TWO DISKS.

equivalent but differ in some minor way, such as the order the data is stored in, then the diskette comparison program will report them as different.

There is probably more difference in this area of comparison commands between different computers that use DOS than in any other aspect of DOS. Most other parts of DOS are quite consistent from one computer to another, but with these comparison programs there are lots of differences.

How do they differ? In three ways. First, not all DOS computers include the disk comparison program—some only have the file comparison command. Second, the names are quite inconsistent—the file comparison program is variously called COMP, FILECOMP, FILECOM, and just FC. The diskette comparison command is usually called DISKCOMP or DSKCOMP, but you might find it under another name. (This bewildering variety of names does us a real disservice in trying to find the common ground among all DOS computers.) And third, just to make things more interesting, there are two very different versions of the file comparison programs.

When should you use either of these comparison programs, and which one should you use (if you have both)? Whenever you are in doubt about whether one copy matches another, you can use these programs. Remember, though, that each file's directory entry holds a time stamp showing when the file was created or last changed; checking the time stamps is one of the most practical ways of checking how up to date files are. If you have the slightest worry about whether two copies are identical, then by all means use these comparison programs. Normally the comparison you will want to do is with the *file* comparison program. A file comparison checks for logical equivalence of two files and doesn't worry about extraneous matters, like where the files are stored on a disk.

The disk comparison is only for use when you want two disks to be identical in every detail, including such things as where the files are stored on the disk, and if there were any files that have been erased. The disk comparison primarily makes sense as a way of checking the disk copy operation, DISKCOPY.

The DISKCOMP command is easy to understand and use. To use it, you enter the command name, followed by the drive specifications where the two diskettes are. Both diskettes are read from front to back and compared; any differences are reported. Here is a typical example of using disk comparison:

```
DISKCOMP  A:  B:
```

The file comparison command, which might be called COMP, FILECOMP, FC, or something else, is usually the better one for you to use. There are two versions of this program, one which does only "dumb" comparisons, and one which can do both "smart" and "dumb" comparisons. The dumb version checks two files to see that they match exactly. This kind of uncompromising comparison gives us a check that files match exactly, but doesn't give us any help if they differ at all. To help distinguish minor differences between files, the "smart" version works better.

The smart file comparison has special features which make sense when we are comparing text files, files which contain written material like what you are reading here. The smart version is designed to help us two ways—first, it can ignore differences that may not matter much, such as whether letters are in upper or lower-case letters, and second, once it finds a difference between files it can search around to find a point where the files match again. This searching around, or "synchronizing," can be extremely useful when text files differ, and you want to know about the differences. The smart version of file comparison can be extremely useful when you need to know how two copies of a text file differ. Bear in mind that these smart features apply only to text files, not to any other kind of disk data files. (For more about text files and other kinds of files, see Chapter 9.)

How do you tell if you have the smart or dumb version of the file comparison command? You can check your computer manual—after you figure out what name the command is listed under (COMP, FILECOMP, FC, or whatever), and see if your version of the command has switches. Recall that switches are controlling parameters which describe how an operation is to be done; switches are always preceded by a hyphen (-) or a slash (/). If there are switches for your command, you have the smart version.

Smart or dumb, here is how file comparison is done. You provide the names of two files to be compared. If the two copies have the same name, on different disks, then you needn't specify the name of the second file, but just where it is located with a drive specification. Here are two examples of how you would start a file comparison if the name of the command is FC:

```
FC    COPY.ONE    COPY.TWO
FC  A:FILENAME  B:
```

With the dumb version of file comparison, the files are checked for an exact match, character for character, byte for byte.

With the smart version of file comparison, we can control the smartness of the comparison. If we want the comparison to be dumb, then the B-switch "-B" or "/B", will tell the file comparison program to make the comparison Blind, Binary, and dumB. If the B-switch isn't specified, then the comparison will be smart, and will try to resynchronize after any mismatch is found.

Two other switches add more smartness to the comparison. The C-switch, "-C" or "/C", makes the comparison ignore differences in the Case of letters. With the C-switch set, an upper-case A would match a lower-case a, and so forth. The W-switch makes the comparison ignore differences in white space meaning that differences in blank spaces, or tab characters, which are the equivalent of spaces, are ignored. With the W-switch set, any white space will match any other. This means that "A   B" would match "A B", but if there were no space at all, as in "AB", they would not match. By the rules that the file comparison follows, the end of a line is considered important, and the W-switch does not ignore line breaks.

When the file comparison finds a difference between the files, and it is allowed to be "smart," it will search several lines in each file for a synchronizing match. This search can't go on forever—a limit is set. The limit is normally 3 lines, but another switch, the #-switch, lets us set the number of lines from 1 to 9. Here is an example of how this switch is set:

```
FILECOMP  FILE.ONE    FILE.TWO   -#5
```

When we want to compare files, we usually have one of two things in mind: either we want to check that the files exactly match, or else we want to figure out what the differences are. When it matters what the differences are, the "smart" features of file comparison come in very handy. One of the greatest needs for this smart comparison is in maintaining computer programs, because it can be easy to lose track of the exact nature of changes that were made in a program. You can make good use of smart text file comparison whenever you need to know the differences between two versions of a written document.

6.2 Editors, Word Processors, and EDLIN

One of the commands that comes with DOS is a program called EDLIN. EDLIN is a simple example of a type of program called an editor. We'll look at EDLIN in more detail in Chapter 19, but this is a good opportunity to learn about editors, word processors, and EDLIN.

Editors are computer programs that are designed to help us enter and revise written text. This book, naturally enough, was written with an editor program.

Any program that you use to enter or revise written text is an editor.

You have almost certainly heard of a kind of program known as a word processor. Word processors are designed to provide the tools needed to work with written text—entering it, changing it, and printing it. As you can see, editors and word processors are closely related. In fact, a word processor is really nothing more than an editor program with—hopefully—rich and useful features. The main thing that sets word processors apart from editors is that word processors include tools to help control the printed format of written material. In short, a word processor is nothing but a fancy editor.

What do editors do for us? They give us the means to enter written text and to make changes in it. Changes might involve adding more text, removing old text, moving parts around, or shifting text from one file to another—in short, all the kinds of things that you might do when you revise a report on a written page.

We need editors for many purposes. We need them when we write letters and reports on our computers, and we need them for writing programs if we do programming. We also need an editor to get the best use of our DOS computers, because an editor is required to create batch processing files, which are one of the best tools for enhancing our use of the computer. (We'll look at batch files and what we can do with them in Chapter 11.) An editor is an essential part of our use of the computer.

Because of this, DOS comes complete with an editor, but a rather rudimentary one. Editors are very complex programs, and there are many opinions about what an editor should be like to work with. Editor programs are considered to be a specialty area, so DOS doesn't include a high-powered editor for the same reason that it doesn't include programs for other specialty areas, such as financial accounting, or VisiCalc-type spreadsheet calculation. The idea is that we will choose our own word processor or editor program, and there is no need for DOS to try to compete with the word processors.

Some kind of editor is all but essential to using DOS, so a simple one is included in DOS—the EDLIN editor.

To help you understand the limitations of EDLIN, and to understand why you will probably want to get a strong editor or word processor program, we need to explain the difference between *command* editing and *full-screen* editing. EDLIN is a command type of editor, but the best and easiest way to edit written text is with a full-screen editor. In full screen editing, the written text fills the display screen. The screen acts like a window which can be moved around to show different parts of a document. When changes need to be made they can be typed directly into the window, a fast and easy task. Command editing is much more laborious. To see parts of the document being edited, or to move around within the document, commands have to be typed in and executed. With a full-screen editor, browsing around within a file is very easy, while with a command editor it can be very tedious.

As an example, let's suppose that we are looking at part of a document, and we want to see the part just a bit earlier in the file. With a full-screen editor this would usually take only a single keystroke, requesting that the editor move the screen's display window back one page or screen. With a command editor like

EDLIN, the same operation would require typing in one command to move from the current location in the document to another, and another command to display some of the text; each of the two commands would require several keystrokes—a clumsy and laborious process. Changing the text with a command editor can be even more of a nuisance.

So, if you have a good word processor or editor, use it instead of EDLIN. If you don't have one, I highly recommend that you get one as soon as possible. And only if necessary, use DOS's line editor, EDLIN.

If you are reduced to using EDLIN, see Chapter 19 for some guidance on how to use it.

There is one more thing to mention before we finish the subject of editors. The BASIC programming language is part of your computer's DOS operating system, and BASIC contains within it a special purpose editor designed to make it easier to enter and change programs in the BASIC language. You will occasionally find that some large complex programs, like BASIC itself, incorporate special purpose editors. If you will be writing BASIC programs, you can either write them within BASIC, making use of BASIC's built-in editor, or you can use your main editor, and then pass your programs from the editor to BASIC. Each technique has its advantages and disadvantages, and you can choose which suits you best.

6.3 The Snooping Tool—DEBUG

DOS includes a command tool called DEBUG which can be used for all sorts of snooping around in your system. DEBUG is not an easy tool to use; in fact it was designed with the needs of advanced programmers in mind, and ordinary folks should steer clear of DEBUG. But it is good if you have an idea of what DEBUG can do, so that if you need to do any of the tasks that DEBUG was designed for, you will know where to turn.

Here we'll give you just an overview of DEBUG's features. For more details about how to use them, look to Chapter 20 which is devoted to DEBUG.

DEBUG is designed to provide the tools that are needed by some of the most advanced program developers. DEBUG allows you to display any part of your computer's memory so that you can see what is stored there. You can also type in changes to modify the contents of memory. You can also search through memory looking for the location of some particular information. Also, the contents of two parts of memory can be compared for differences or copied from one area to another.

Beyond the features that we have already mentioned, DEBUG can read a file from disk to memory, and then use its ability to search, display, change, compare, and copy parts of memory to do the same with the copy of the file. If changes are made, they can be written back to the disk, making a permanent change to the file.

Two special parts of the computer's equipment, the registers and the ports, can be read from or written into by DEBUG.

YOU CAN SNOOP AROUND WITH DEBUG.

When you display part of a computer program, it will appear in *hexadecimal* format, which is thoroughly unintelligible. To help make sense out of programs, DEBUG can "unassemble" programs, which means that it translates the hexadecimal into the format of *assembly language* (which is also called assembler language, or assembly code).

Provided that you can make sense of assembly language programs, you can use DEBUG's unassembly feature to help you see what programs are doing. DEBUG in DOS-2 also contains an "assemble" feature, which lets you enter assembly code instructions and have them translated into memory data.

It is also possible to use DEBUG to step through and trace the action of a program. DEBUG has the ability to load a program from a disk, and then execute the program, stopping it periodically as needed.

If you have a use for any of these features DEBUG is the command-tool for you. If not, it is at least interesting to know that they are there.

There are six more advanced DOS commands which are used in connection with program development. We'll take a look at them in the next three sections.

6.4 Assembling—MASM and CREF

Computer programs are written in some *programming language*, such as BASIC or assembly language. Your DOS computer will have available to it various *language translators*, which convert our programs into the form which the computer requires. Among these translators is Microsoft's assembler, called MASM, which is short for Macro ASseMbler.

For some computers the macroassembler is a separately purchased item. For others the macro assembler is included with the DOS operating system.

Assembly language is a rich and complicated subject, which fully deserves an entire book in itself—we won't try to teach assembly language programming here. But since your DOS may include the MASM assembler with it, you deserve to know a little about it.

Assembly language programming is done in a form that is close to what the computer itself actually uses, but assembly programs are written in a way that people can comprehend. The job of the MASM assembler is to translate our form of assembly language into the computer's machine language. For a better understanding of what programming languages look like, including assembly language and machine language, turn to Chapter 10, which covers what you need to know about programming languages. One of the features of MASM is that it allows programmers to use macros, which are small parts of programs that can be used and reused easily.

As an aid to assembly language programming, the MASM assembler comes with a companion program called CREF. CREF, working together with MASM, can provide a cross-reference of the symbolic names that are used in an assembly language program. This can make it much easier to work with a large program. CREF's cross-referencing abilities can be used for things other than just assembly programs, and CREF includes a description of how it can be made to work with other tools.

6.5 Building Programs—LINK and LIB

When large computer programs are prepared, they are usually built in smaller pieces and then put together into one working whole. It is similar to the manufacturing idea of combining parts into subassemblies, which are combined into finished products.

One of the DOS commands, the LINK program, is designed to do the programming task of combining parts into a whole. LINK combines, or "links together" or "link edits" program parts, and it takes care of the job of making sure that all the right connections are made. So if you do programming in any computer language—except for *interpretive* BASIC, which we'll learn about in Chapter 10—you will be using the LINK program.

Most programming languages make use of a library of handy and standard subprograms, which take care of routine work. A program library is a collection of these useful subprograms, kept in a form that is ready to be used by the LINK program. Most programming languages come with subroutine libraries, and their use is automatic—when we write programs in COBOL or Pascal or FORTRAN, we aren't aware of the use that we make of the accompanying subroutine library; but nevertheless, behind the scenes we are using it. When our programs are link edited, LINK finds the parts that are needed from our program libraries, and automatically incorporates them into our programs.

Some versions of DOS come with a program called LIB which allows us to change our programming libraries. With LIB we can build libraries from scratch or make changes to existing libraries—adding, replacing, or removing subroutines from the library.

Fortunately for those of us whose systems do not include LIB, we can use LINK to effectively create our own libraries of subprograms, though not as conveniently as it could be with the help of LIB.

If your version of DOS includes the LIB program, you can use it for program library work. You should understand, though, that library maintenance is a sophisticated chore, and few programmers have much of a need for it. So it is unlikely that you, or anyone working with you, will have much need for LIB. But again, it is interesting to know about.

6.6 Converting Program Formats— LOCATE/EXE2BIN, and EXEFIX

When computer programs are stored on disk in a ready-to-use form, they can be—and must be—in one of two formats that have been specially defined for storing programs. These two formats are known as COM and EXE, after the filename extensions that are used for them.

There are two formats for the simple reason that some programs require more help from DOS in being executed and others less. The EXE format is used for those programs that need the full range of DOS services in loading them for execution. For programs that do not need as much help, the COM format provides a more compact and efficient way to store them on disk.

Incidentally, since all programs must be stored in files which have filename extensions of either COM or EXE, you can see a complete list of all the programs on a disk by using the DIR command to list the two types of files. For example, these two DIR commands will list the programs on drive B:

```
DIR  B:*.COM
DIR  B:*.EXE
```

This list will not include interpreter BASIC programs for reasons we'll see in Chapters 9 and 10.

Any program could be kept in the richer but less efficient EXE format. But any program which meets the necessary technical rules can be kept in COM format. There are two programs provided with DOS to convert programs from one format to the other. One converts from EXE to COM format—this command is called LOCATE on some computers, and EXE2BIN on others. By either name, it does the same job of converting, when possible, from EXE to COM.

To reverse the process, EXEFIX will convert COM format to EXE format. EXEFIX is not included in some computer system's versions of DOS. Also it's not obvious to the uninitiated, including me, why anyone would want to convert from COM format to EXE format. But there is a program to do the job, if it needs doing.

Incidentally, the LINK program always produces programs in the EXE format. Eligible programs can then be converted to COM using LOCATE/EXE2BIN.

For your interest, you can see all of the stages that a program might have to go through to be prepared for use:

- first the program is written, using an editor;
- then it is compiled or assembled, using a language translator (which we'll discuss in Chapter 10);
- at this point it might be placed in a library, using LIB;
- then it is link edited using LINK and possibly incorporating parts of a library;
- finally, it can be converted to COM format, using LOCATE/EXE2BIN.

This brings us to the end of the advanced DOS commands, except for those which we've held for special discussion in Chapters 8, 9, and 11. Next we'll take a look at some special handy features that DOS provides us with, the editing keys.

7

Getting the Most of DOS Editing Keys

In this chapter we're going to take a look at an interesting feature of DOS which can—maybe—make your use of the computer quicker and easier: the DOS editing keys.

We can't promise you anything in this chapter. Some people find this part of DOS exasperating, annoying, and useless. Others find it very handy. You'll have to judge for yourself if this is something worth learning.

7.1 Setting the Stage for the Editing Keys

When we're using our computer, we're usually giving it instructions by typing away at the keyboard. Sometimes we're entering single keystrokes; for example, when we respond to a program's menu by typing the key that indicates our choice. At other times we're pounding away on the keyboard at length; for example, typing in a document to a word processing or editor program.

But surprisingly often, what we key into the computer is something in the middle between those two extremes. An awful lot of the time we key in a short line of information and press the *enter* key. A remarkably large proportion of our interaction with the computer involves typing single lines and then pressing *enter*. For example, whenever we give DOS a command, like COPY or FORMAT, we are entering a single line of information—a line made up of the command name and whatever parameters it needs.

Since this is done so often, there ought to be ways to make it easier, and that is what the DOS editing keys are about.

The DOS editing keys are a set of operations and functions, all based on the use of some special keys on the keyboard that help us enter or change a line of instructions. For example, one editing key lets you copy the last line you typed in, so that you can repeat something without having to type it in again. Other keys help you make changes to what you have already typed.

All this sounds rather handy—a fast and convenient way to speed your work to reduce the amount of key-pounding that you have to do. But it isn't that simple, and before you spend much time learning how to use them, you ought to know about the drawbacks to the editing keys.

The first problem with the editing keys is that they don't always work, at least that's the way we experience them. They *do* always work when they are available, but they aren't always made available to us. It goes like this: DOS provides a line editing service which any program, including all parts of DOS, can use to control what is keyed in. This line editing service is where the DOS editing keys take effect. As we key in a line *to DOS*, the DOS editing keys can be used to help enter and change the line. But only some programs take their input from this DOS service. Many programs do not, including lots of programs which are also used with operating systems other than DOS.

All the commands that are built into DOS naturally make use of the DOS editing keys, but we use plenty of other programs as well. With the other programs, we can sometimes use the DOS editing keys and sometimes not. Even worse, it isn't well advertised when we can and when we can't use them. This makes it more difficult to set our working style to incorporate the DOS editing keys. If you can't count on being able to use them, then they become an unreliable tool, an untrustworthy friend.

The second problem with the editing keys is simply that you have to learn them. That's the biggest problem in working with a personal computer—there is much too much to learn. To master your computer, you have to learn how the machine works, how diskettes work, how DOS works, how each of your main programs—say a word processor, a VisiCalc-like spreadsheet, perhaps an accounting program—works. It is too much to learn. No one can reasonably learn everything that we all ought to know in order to master our computers.

So one of the major tasks that faces us in dealing with our computers is to *reduce* the number of things that must be learned, and to decide what parts, of the thousands of things to learn, are the most important to us.

This brings us back to the DOS editing keys. They are yet another thing to learn about using your computer. They are something handy and productive, but mastering them is hardly essential to using your computer effectively. So you might decide that the DOS editing keys aren't important enough to be worth spending your time on. But, on the other hand, they can be useful, particularly the simplest ones (only an enthusiast could benefit from some of the fancier ones). And if you learn the most basic of the DOS editing keys right at the very beginning of your use of the computer, then they will become part of your general computer skills that you can use all the time with your DOS computer; learning the editing keys later means that you probably won't be able to integrate them into your comfortable style of computer use.

So, make a quick decision to press on in this chapter, and read about the DOS editing keys or skip over it. But don't skip the entire chapter—the last section, section 7.3, explains some special keys that you need to know about, even if you are not going to use the DOS editing keys.

7.2 How the Editing Keys Work

The DOS editing keys work on two simple ideas. The first idea is that you ought to be able to make simple revisions to what you have just typed before you press the *enter* key, which tells DOS to act on what you have keyed in.

The second idea is that DOS has kept track of the last line that you have entered, and you can use all or part of that previous line to make it easier to enter a new line.

In this section we'll explain how each of the different editing key functions works. Unfortunately we can't tell you exactly which keys to use on your computer to use these functions. Why? For the most ordinary parts of a computer keyboard, such as the letters of the alphabet, computers are very standard. But when it comes to function keys and keys for special operations, there is little common ground—each computer seems to go its own separate way. Some computers have plenty of function keys available, so that all of the DOS editing key operations can be done with the function keys. Other computers have few, so some of the DOS key operations have to be done with a combination of the *Control* shift and one of the alphabetic keys. Because of this, we'll have to describe the DOS editing keys in terms of what they do, and you'll have to check your computer's manuals to see just how they are keyed in.

Remember as we go over these DOS editing keys that they only apply in some circumstances. They work whenever we are entering DOS commands, and they work when we are entering information into DOS command programs, and they work with *some* other programs—but by no means all. Usually they will not work with many of the major programs that you use, such as a word processing program. But where they do work, they can be quite handy.

Let's start out by making simple corrections to a line that we have typed, but haven't yet told the computer to act on: so we have something typed in, but we haven't yet pressed the *enter* or *return* key. If there is something wrong with what we've typed in, how can we correct it? There are two ways.

The first way to make a correction is to cancel, or throw away, the entire line that we've typed in. There is a DOS editing key specially intended to *cancel* the entire typed line. On many computers the Escape key is used for the *cancel* operation; on your computer, it might be something different.

There is also another, completely separate key combination that *sometimes* has the same effect as the *cancel* editing key—this is the Control-C, or "break" operation, which we'll take a look at in Section 7.3 at the end of this chapter. Sometimes Control-C works just like the *cancel* editing key, but it can also terminate or cancel any program that you are running. So *don't* make a habit of using the Control-C break to simply cancel or discard a line that you have typed in. If you make a habit of this, at some time you will make one of your programs come to an abrupt end when you didn't mean to.

So, again, to cancel or throw away a line of information that you have typed, use the DOS editing key for *cancel*. This might be the "escape" key, or it might be another one—check your computer manual to be sure.

If we've typed in something really garbled, then we probably want to use *cancel* to get rid of it all. But more often, all we want to do is correct some simple typing mistake. Perhaps we typed one letter wrong—say our finger slipped and we typed "FORMA5" instead of "FORMAT"—or we left a letter out—"FOMAT" instead of "FORMAT"—and we want to correct that, without retyping the entire line. The way we do this is with the DOS editing keys for *backup*. When we use the DOS *backup* editing key, we move one space back in the line we've typed in, and the last character is erased, just as if we had never typed it in. With *backup*, we can erase what we have typed in, character by character, until we have erased the part we need to correct.

As with other DOS editing keys, your computer will have its own rules for what keys do the *backup* operation. The common, universal DOS code for this operation is Control-H. But it is likely that your computer will have two familiar keys that do the *backup* operation: the key that moves the cursor to the left (which is probably marked with an arrow, pointing to the left), and the backspace key. The backspace key is a standard item on typewriters, and your computer's keyboard probably has it as well; it might be marked "B.S.", or it might have an arrow pointing to the left, just like the left cursor key. Whichever keys your computer uses, they will backspace and erase one character of what you have typed in, which is what *backup* is supposed to do.

After we have gotten rid of what we have typed wrong, with the cancel or the *backup* editing keys, then we can type in the right information, and press *enter*, so that our computer will act on what we have typed in.

The *cancel* and *backup* keys let us make corrections to something that we are typing, but the rest of the DOS editing keys help us reduce the amount of typing that we have to do, by letting us reuse what we've entered before.

Now this reuse only does us any good when we are doing some repetitive typing—when we are entering the same information again and again, with minor changes. Unless we are doing that, repeating ourselves, these other DOS editing key operations don't do a thing for us. So that you have an idea of when this might be useful to us, let's consider an example.

Suppose that we need to copy a number of files from one diskette to another. This is a common operation. We might have a working disk that has two kinds of files on it—ones that we're changing, and ones that stay the same. For the files that change, we ought to make backup copies onto another diskette so that we don't lose our latest data. So we have a situation where we want to copy some of the files from a disk, but not all of them. It would be nice to be able to type in once:

```
COPY some-file
```

copy the one file, and then just change the file name for the others, without having to retype "COPY". This is the sort of thing that the other DOS editing keys let us do.

To do this, DOS keeps track of the last line that we have entered, and uses it as a template which we can copy from. The DOS template combines two ideas. First, DOS keeps track of the last command that we keyed in; this makes it easier to repeat a command. Second, DOS lets us make all kinds of changes to this last command; this is the template idea, which allows us to use an old command line as a model that is copied, adapted, and changed.

The first of the editing keys that works with the template is the *copy-all* function. This takes the entire template and copies it onto the screen, just as if we had typed in the entire line. If we want to duplicate exactly what we've typed before, *copy-all* does the job. If we need to make minor changes, particu-

DOS CAN COPY FROM A TEMPLATE.

larly at the end of the line, we can use the *backup* key to erase the part we want to change. Using the example above, we could press the copy-all key to duplicate the command "COPY some-file", then use *backup* to erase the "some-file" part.

Suppose it isn't convenient to copy all of the template. There are several ways that we can copy just part of it. One is the *copy-one* operation. Every time we press the *copy-one* key, one more character from the template is copied onto the display screen. In the example above, if we pressed *copy-one* five times, it would duplicate "COPY " (including the space), and we could then type in our new file name to be copied.

A quicker way to do the same operation is to use the *copy-up-to* editing key. To do this operation, we press the *copy-up-to* key, and then key in one of the characters in our template. The *copy-up-to* operation would duplicate the template up to, but not including, the key we pressed. For the above example, we could get "COPY " all in two key strokes, by pressing *copy-up-to* followed by "s", which is the first character that we *don't* want to copy.

So far, what you have seen of the DOS editing keys may seem somewhat handy, but perhaps trickier, and more elaborate than they are worth. From here, though, it gets even more elaborate—which reinforces my argument that learning the DOS editing keys may be more trouble than it is worth.

If you want to skip over part of the template, and then pick up copying it from some point, you can use the *skip-one* and *skip-up-to* keys. They work just like the *copy-one* and *copy-up-to* keys, but they skip over the template rather than duplicating it. From the above example, if we wanted to drop "COPY" but use "some-file", we would press *skip-up-to*, then press "s", then press *copy-all* to duplicate the remainder of the template. If you are good at this, it's a quick, efficient operation. Otherwise, it's confusing.

If you want to add something into the middle of a template, the *insert* key lets you type in new information, while keeping your place in the template. Without using insert, each character you type would also move you along in the template, so that any copying from the template would proceed from the point that is equivalent to how much you have typed. Using *insert* holds your place in the template, while you type in new information. The way it works is very simple: say you have copied part of a command from the template, and then you stop and press *insert*. At this point, the template is put on hold, so to speak, and anything that you type is added to your new command line, without passing over any of the template. After you have finished inserting new material, you could then copy from the remainder of the old template. Naturally, there is an *insert-exit* editing key to reverse the insert operation. If your computer has an "insert" key, as most do, this key will be used for both *insert* and *insert-exit*.

The final DOS editing key lets you set up a new template to work with without actually entering a line for DOS to act on. If you are using the copy-from-a-template idea, you ought to be able to set up a template from scratch and not just use the last line that you entered into DOS. This is what the *new-template* command is for.

As you can see, these DOS editing keys are rather elaborate, and yet they are only good when two circumstances are combined:

- the DOS editing keys are active (not true for many programs); and
- you want to repeat the same or similar lines several times.

If you don't meet both these conditions, then the DOS editing keys do nothing for you.

The reason why I suggest that you don't bother learning these editing keys is simple: why learn the tricky rules for an operation that you can only use sometimes? And when you can use the editing keys, they only save you a little work. But if they appeal to you, use them for all they are worth.

Here is a quick summary of the editing keys again:

Name	Operation	Common key used
cancel	throw the line away	Escape
backup	erase the last character	Backspace, left
copy-all	copy the template, in full	F3
copy-one	copy the next template character	F1, right
copy-up-to	copy up to the typed character	F2
skip-one	skip over one template character	Delete key
skip-up-to	skip up to the typed character	F4
insert	enter new stuff, keep place in template	Insert key
new-template	replace template with this line	F5

7.3 Some More Special Keys

There are some other special keys DOS uses that can be very handy for you, and we'll go over them in this section. They are only loosely related to the DOS editing keys, and you can get good use from them even if you never try the editing keys. There's even one here that some computer makers don't tell their customers they can use.

There are five of these special codes, each of them entered as a control shift of one of the letters of the alphabet. Like all of the control key combinations, they work by holding down the *Control* shift key and pressing the other key. Fortunately, when we're doing a control-letter combination, we don't have to worry about whether we're shifted into upper- or lower-case letters; either works just as well.

The most important of these five special control keys, is Control-C, which is also called *break*. Break, or Control-C, is a special instruction to the operating system to stop or break out of what it is doing. This break operation is very important, because it is our best way of stopping the computer from what it is doing, short of turning the power off. If your computer is going wild, or if you just want to interrupt what the computer is doing, *break* is the best way to do it. The break operation is so important that some computers, such as the IBM Personal Computer, mark a special key just for this operation. But whether your computer has a special break key or not, the Control-C combination will work just the same. In fact, Control-C is a universal code for small computers to mean Stop. To make it easier to remember this code, you can think of the "C" as standing for Cancel.

When we're working on our computers, the record of what we're doing—what we type in, and what the computer replies—rolls by on the display screen, and soon disappears. Sometimes we would like a permanent written record of what's happening. DOS provides us a way of doing this, with the *echo* feature. When *echo* is turned on, everything that is written on the display screen is also sent, or echoed, to the computer's printer. This works in a very straightforward way, so that we can automatically get a printed copy of what has been appearing on the display screen.

Usually we don't want a printed copy of everything that's happening, so echo can be turned on and off, and it is normally off. Two control keys are used to tell DOS if we want echoing. Control-P turns echoing on, and Control-N turns it off. To make it easier to remember, you can think of the "P" as standing for Print; you can make up your own mnemonic device for remembering the Control-N. As with the *break* operation, some computers will also have special keys to control echoing, and turning it on and off may be done with the same key, rather then with two separate keys. For example, the IBM PC uses Control-PrtSc for echoing. But whatever other keys are used, the standard universal DOS way to control echoing is Control-P to turn it on, and Control-N to turn it off.

You should know that echoing doesn't work with every program. Programs can produce display output in many different ways. Only if the output goes through official DOS channels can it be echoed. Usually it is easy to tell if the output of a program can be echoed, even without experimenting to try it. If a program writes its information to the display screen just as if the screen were a typewriter—which means writing everything at the bottom of the screen, and not jumping around to display some information here, and some there—then it should be echoable. But if a program works in full-screen mode, using the screen's ability to display information in controlled locations, rather than using the screen like a printer, then the output probably can't be echoed.

You probably won't be able to use echo with your word processing programs, or with most accounting programs, or VisiCalc-type spreadsheets. On the other hand, it will work with the commands which are a part of DOS.

The next interesting and handy special key is Control-S, to suspend output written to the display screen. Some computer operations write enough information to the screen so that some of it quickly disappears off the top of the screen. The *suspend*, or Control-S, key combination will temporarily halt DOS from writing anything more on the screen. Then we can look at the display information for as long as we want. When we're ready to have more information displayed, any ordinary key stroke will let DOS carry on. This Control-S suspend operation *does not* stop the computer, it just stops the display of information. So any program which isn't writing information onto the screen will continue to run. Don't make the mistake of thinking that you can stop a program just by typing Control-S—that just stops the display. Your computer may also have a special key for suspending computing, but that would be distinct from Control-S.

The last of the five special control codes is Control-Z. As you'll see in more detail in Chapter 9, disk files with written text material include special codes to indicate such things as where one line of text ends and another begins. Among these special formatting codes is a code which marks the end of the file. This end-file marker is quite important, and careful attention is paid to it by all programs which work with files of written text. Normally we never have to deliberately enter this Control-Z code at the end of a file—text processing programs take care of that for us. But there are some special circumstances where it must be keyed in, and the Control-Z key combination is used to enter it from the keyboard.

I doubt that you will ever need to use the Control-Z code. It is more likely, though, that you will see it mentioned in a book or article on personal computers, and so you should know what Control-Z is used for.

Here is a summary:

Control key	Function
Control-C	Cancel operation or end program
Control-S	Suspend screen output
Control-P	Start echoing screen output to the printer
Control-N	Stop echoing
Control-Z	Enter an "end-file" marker

This ends our discussion of the special key codes used with DOS. The next chapter contains special material which applies only to computers using DOS-2. If your computer is using one of the DOS-1 versions, you can skip over it, and pick up again with Chapter 9, where we will look at the inner workings of disks.

Special Things About DOS-2—Pumping the Pipeline

The larger, more complex versions of DOS numbered 2.00 and higher—which we're referring to as DOS-2—include some very powerful ways of controlling data that are not available in DOS-1. In this chapter we are going to look at the core of the special features of DOS-2.

8.1 Buzz Words—A Quick Outline of the Ideas and Terms

The subjects we have at hand are a bit technical so we'll be using some technical terms, what some people like to call buzz words. A buzz word means a technical expression—something that is useful for the knowledgeable to use, but which can leave beginners confused. What we have to cover here uses plenty of buzz words, many of them colorful, but most of them confusing. To help get you ready, let's run them by for a quick, early look, before we go into the details.

We'll be talking about trees and paths through the trees. We'll run a pipeline, and we'll put some filters in the pipeline. We'll work with standard input and standard output, and we'll be redirecting our input and output.

What Does All That Mean?

When we work with our computer, we "talk" to it, and it talks to us. We talk to the computer by typing on the keyboard, while the computer talks to us by writing information on the display screen. So the dialogue with the computer takes place over the keyboard and display. That is, it normally does.

There are times when it would be better to have some or all of this conversation take place elsewhere (we'll see why in the sections below). So one of the advances in DOS-2, over DOS-1, is to allow this conversation to be *re-directed.* In DOS-1, when a program writes out some display information it is written specifically onto the display screen. But in DOS-2, programs write out their information to a sort of switchboard called *standard output.* Normally *standard output* passes straight onto the screen—but the "switchboard" can *re-direct* the information, so that it goes elsewhere. Likewise, where a DOS-1 program reads from the keyboard, a DOS-2 program reads its information from *standard input,* which normally comes from the keyboard—but it can be redirected to come from somewhere else.

Normally we use programs one at a time and we can work with them directly, or we can re-direct the input or output for these programs. But there is another way we can use the idea of re-direction: we can hook programs together so that the output of one program becomes the input of the next program. This is done with a *pipeline.* A *pipeline* is a series of programs which are connected together so that each one takes its input from the one before and passes its output to the next program.

The idea of a pipeline only works with programs where that kind of operation makes sense. A program that generates data, a *generator,* could be

DOS-2's SWITCHBOARD CAN REDIRECT OUR INFORMATION.

used as the first part of a pipeline. Along the pipeline should be programs which read and write data while doing something useful with it—for example, sorting the data into the order we want it to be in. This kind of program is called a *filter.* We'll learn more about how *pipelines, generators,* and *filters* work in the following sections.

When we store our data into files on disks, we need to organize the files into separate groups, especially if we have lots of files on a high-capacity hard disk system. To help us do that, DOS-2 lets us create separate directories of files, where the files in each directory are kept quite distinct from the files in other directories. This helps us organize the files. But then we need to organize the directories—which brings us to trees and paths.

A disk has by itself a main, or *root,* directory. We can add to that root directory new sub-directories where files can be kept in distinct groups. Each directory, whether a root directory or a sub-directory, can have sub-directories branching off from it. With directories branching off of directories, they form a *tree-structure.*

With more than one directory on a disk, we need a way to find our way through them, and indicate which we want to use. *Paths,* or *pathnames,* are used to thread our way through the branches of the trees.

DOS-2 FINDS ITS PATH THROUGH THE TREES...

That, in a capsule summary, is the subject of this chapter. Now, let's move on to discover the details.

8.2 Telling 'em Where to Go

As we saw in the last section, the *standard input* and the *standard output* can be re-directed to somewhere other than their normal location, which is the keyboard for *standard input* and the display screen for the *standard output*. There are three different ways that this can be done, which we'll cover in three sections, this one and the next two.

One thing that you have to bear in mind is that this re-direction only works with *standard input* and *standard output*. That means two things. First, it only works with those two items—not with any other information that a program may read or write. If a program is designed to use a data file on a disk, then the re-direction of input or output will have nothing to do with that. Re-direction only works with what programs think of as their keyboard input and display-screen output.

The second thing to remember about re-direction working only with *standard input* and *output* is that not all programs use them when they talk with the keyboard and display screen. Many programs use methods other than DOS's standard methods for the keyboard and screen. This is particularly true of programs that work in full-screen mode, where information is displayed all over the screen. Most editor and word processor programs, and VisiCalc-type spreadsheet programs will not use *standard output* for their screen displays. There is no sure way to tell which programs do and don't use the standard input and output methods, but there are some simple rules that you can use to guess: if a program is a part of DOS itself, or if a program is very simple and straightforward, then it probably uses standard input and output which can be redirected. But if a program creates full-screen displays, or in general is complex and interactive, then it probably does not use standard input and output. When you are in doubt, you can check easily enough by just experimenting with re-direction of input and output.

As we mentioned before, there are three different ways to specify the re-direction of input and output. In this section we'll look at the simplest way to tell DOS what we want to do with input and output.

Let's take the directory listing command DIR as an example. If we enter the command

```
DIR
```

then we'll get a directory listing on the display screen. What if we would like to save that directory listing information in a data file? Then we can redirect the output into a file like this:

```
DIR   >FILENAME
```

After the command, we can specify where its output is to go to, or its input is to come from. The greater than symbol (>), is used to re-direct the standard output. We can think of this > symbol as an arrow which means "send it to." After the > we indicate where we want it to go to. Usually this will be the name of a file, and the standard output will be written into this file. If the file didn't exist, it is created; if there was a file with that name, then the old information in the file is replaced with the output data.

For commands and programs which need input, the same thing can be done to re-direct standard input. For input, the less than symbol (<), is used as an arrow which means "take it from." You'll recall that the FORMAT command expects to get some keyboard input: it needs keyboard input to tell it when a disk is ready to be used, and if more disks are to be formatted. The responses to these questions could be in a file; if the responses were in a file named ANSWERS, then FORMAT could be used like this:

```
FORMAT   <ANSWERS
```

In that example, FORMAT would read its responses from ANSWERS but still write its output information onto the display screen. To redirect both input and output, we would do this:

```
FORMAT   <ANSWERS   >QUESTION
```

Before we take a look at when and why we would want to re-direct input and output, there are two more details to cover.

When we re-direct output to a file, it wipes out any information that was in the file. But this doesn't have to happen. We can tell DOS to add the standard output to the end of the file, following anything that is already stored in the file. This is done with two > symbols, which means "append it to." As an example, here are two DIR commands whose output would be combined into one file:

```
DIR A: >INFO
DIR B: >>INFO
```

After these commands, the file INFO would contain the directory listings of the disks in drives A and B.

The one other thing about re-directed input and output is that it doesn't have to be done with a file. It can also re-direct to the name of one of your computer's devices, such as the printer. LPT1 is a standard device name for your computer's printer, so you can re-direct output straight to it like this:

```
DIR   >LPT1       or PRN ?
```

When and how can we make use of this re-direction of input and output?

The examples that we have used so far give a pretty clear idea of how we can use the re-direction of output. The main reason for re-directing output is to keep a record of it—either by sending it to a printer or saving it in a file so that we can work with the information later. Saving the data in a file gives us an opportunity to do all sorts of things with the information—like incorporating it into our word processing files, or using it with a batch file (see Chapter

REDIRECTION LETS DOS READ AND WRITE FROM FILES.

11 for more on this). Sending output to be saved in a file is extremely useful, and it clearly is the most important use you are likely to have for re-direction.

While re-directing output to the printer is very handy, you'll recall from the last chapter that the *echo* feature can be used to have screen output copied to the printer. Either way can work just fine for you, and so it is just a question of which one suits you best. Echoing will give you both a screen and a printed copy, while re-direction to the printer will keep your screen clear. If you have other devices besides a printer, re-direction can be used to send output to them, while echoing only goes to the standard printer.

There is one potential problem with re-directing output—if a program needs keyboard responses which you don't anticipate, you won't be able to see its messages telling you what it needs. This can happen when you don't expect it—a program may normally run just fine without needing any keyboard responses time after time, and then at some point run into an unusual situation and, to your surprise, call for a response. So be careful in your use of output re-direction.

Re-directed input is a trickier matter, and one that we generally have less use for. If you are using a program that needs information in a very standard and predictable form, then you might save yourself some repetitive work by putting these responses into a file that you can use by re-directing input. The uses for re-directed input, though, are much fewer than those for output. This is partly because often we can't reliably predict the exact input needed, and partly because we usually don't save much work by having an input response file for the program to read from.

Still, there are times when using input re-directed to a file can make your use of the computer easier, or faster, or more automatic; and for those occasions, it is nice to know that the facility is there when we want to take advantage of it.

I would warn you again, though, that there are dangers in using input re-direction, much greater than the dangers of re-directing output. One person I know managed to lock up his computer, thanks to an error in an input response file that was being read by the FORMAT command; his only way out of the problem was to shut his computer off and start over from scratch. So be cautious if you try to use re-directed input.

8.3 Filling Up the Pipeline—SORT, FIND, and MORE

Programs use data, so it is natural that the output of one program might be needed as the input to another program. DOS-2 provides a handy way of making this automatic. Before we see how DOS does this for us, let's consider how we could accomplish this with what we already have. If we have a program named ONE, which creates data that is needed by another program named TWO, we could use > and < and a working file name to pass the data like this:

```
ONE   > WORK
TWO   < WORK
```

The first program would write its data into WORK and the second would read back from it.

This is the basic idea that DOS-2 accomplishes with pipelines. A pipeline is just an automatic way of doing what we did with ONE, TWO, and the file WORK. In a pipeline, DOS takes care of creating the work file to pass data through. To create a pipeline, we just write the program names on the *same* command line, separated by a vertical bar, (|), which is the signal for a pipeline. Here is how we would pipeline the programs ONE and TWO:

```
ONE   |   TWO
```

If you want to, you can informally think of the data as passing directly between the two programs, but actually it is stored temporarily in a file that DOS creates especially for this purpose. The first program writes out all of its data and ends operation before the second program begins working and reads the first part of the data. When the whole operation is done, DOS removes the temporary files used to pass pipeline data so that they do not clutter up our disks. The whole process goes on quietly, behind the scenes, without needing any attention from us.

A pipeline can have as many programs in it as you want it to. For example:

```
ONE  |  TWO  |  THREE | FOUR  |  FIVE
```

There is an obvious difference between the programs at the beginning, middle, and end of a pipeline. Unless there is something unusual going on, the first program in a pipeline would be generating data. The ones in the middle would do something with the data, but still pass it on; this kind of program is called a *filter*. The last program in a pipeline could be a consumer of data, to balance the generator on the other end—but usually the last program of a pipeline is a filter, just like any of the ones in the middle. If the last program *is* a filter then it passes the finished result to *standard output*, and it will appear on our display screens.

DOS-2 PUMPS DATA THROUGH THE PIPELINE.

This leaves the subject of filters still a little mysterious. To understand them better, lets take a look at the filters that DOS provides us with. There are three main ones called SORT, FIND, and MORE.

Each of these three programs is a classic example of a filter—they read from *standard input,* do something with the data, and pass it on to *standard output.* SORT is quite obvious—it sorts the data that it is passed. SORT treats each line of data as a separate entity, so it is the order of the lines of data that SORT re-arranges. Normally SORT arranges the lines in first to last order, but a switch, "/R" or "-R", will make the sort work in reverse order. Another switch, "/+n" or "-+n" (where "n" is a number such as "/+12"), will make the sort start on the n-th column of each line. A common example of the use of SORT, and of the + switch, is with the DIR directory command.

DIR will list files in more or less arbitrary order. But if we combine it with SORT, we can get the directory listing in order by filename, or by the file-name extension, or by the size of the file. This pipeline will sort the files into order by name:

```
DIR | SORT
```

By using the + switch to shift the sorting over to the column where the file size is displayed, we can get the list in order by size:

```
DIR | SORT /+14
```

When we have information displayed on the screen, there is often more than can fit onto the screen at one time, so some of it may roll off the top of the screen before we get a chance to study it. The MORE filter is designed to display only as many lines of information as will fit onto your computer's screen, and then wait for a key stroke to indicate that you are ready to see more. Naturally MORE is only used at the end of a pipeline—it wouldn't make much sense to use it anywhere else.

The FIND filter is used to identify the lines of data which have, or don't have, some particular data on them. To use FIND, you must specify what you are looking for, enclosed in double-quotes. FIND filters out the lines which don't contain what we are looking for, and only passes on the lines that do. Here is an example of where we use FIND to look for error messages:

```
TEST | FIND "error" | MORE
```

As you might expect, FIND has some switches: the V-switch reverses the search so that lines with the specified information are filtered out and the others are passed through. The N-switch will add in the relative line numbers (which can help you know where the data was found), and the C-switch will give a count of the lines found only, without passing any other data on. On some computers, the FIND filter command is called FGREP.

While these three filter commands, SORT, MORE, and FIND, are intended to be used inside pipelines they can each be used by themselves. For example, we can use SORT together with ordinary > < redirection to sort the contents of one file and place it in another:

WE CAN PUT FILTERS IN THE PIPELINE.

```
SORT   < FILE.OLD  > FILE.NEW
```

Similarly, MORE can be used like the TYPE command, but with automatic pauses when the screen fills.

While DOS provides us with three handy filters (SORT, MORE, and FIND), these aren't the only filters we can have. Remember that any reasonable program that reads from *standard input* and writes to *standard output* can be used as a filter. If you have any ideas for useful filters, you can write programs that carry out your ideas and then make use of them in your pipelines.

8.4 Telling DOS Where to Go

So far we have seen two ways to redirect input and output, with < and > and with pipelines. Each of these two ways causes specific commands to have their input and output re-directed. When that is done, DOS carries on using the keyboard and screen for input and output.

But there is a way to get DOS to completely change its operation from the keyboard and screen to somewhere else. This is with the change console command CTTY.

In order to work, CTTY must be given the name of a device which can act as both the keyboard and the display screen—that means that it must be a character-type device (which the disks *aren't*), and it must be a device that can both read and write. Your computer could have something special on it which meets this requirement, but normally the only thing that it will have is a remote communications device, which is usually known to DOS as AUX or COM1. If we enter the command

```
CTTY AUX
```

then DOS will look to the communications line for all of its input and output. In effect, DOS will have turned over control of your computer to whatever is on the other end of the communication line. In fact, this is exactly what CTTY is intended for—to allow remote control of a computer. Using the CTTY command, a computer can be told to work with a remote terminal. This opens up all sorts of interesting possibilities—from your home base, you could use and control any number of computers located at remote sites. Or, reversing the situation, you could travel with a portable terminal, and still use your computer by calling it through the communications line from a telephone.

8.5 Planting a Tree —MKDIR and RMDIR

As we've mentioned, each of your disks has a main or root directory and other directories can be added to it. Each new directory branches out from its parent directory, and each one, in turn, can have any number of other sub-directories under it.

To create a new directory, the make directory command, MKDIR or MD, is used. When a directory is created, it is empty except for two reference entries known as "." and "..", which we'll discuss in the next section.

After a directory has been created, files (or other directories) can then be placed in it. All of the names in one directory—names of files or names of sub-directories—must be unique within that directory, but the same names can be used in other directories.

If we can make directories we should be able to remove them as well, and this is what the RMDIR, or RD, command is for. To avoid leaving any files or sub-directories without a home, RMDIR will not work unless the directory is empty.

It is possible to have directories branching out from directories without limits creating a complex "tree structure." You may be tempted to make use of this capability to create a thorough logical structure to your files. The idea is appealing—we create master directories for a major subject area, and sub-directories under it for more details. For example, you might create a directory for all accounting data, with sub-directories for each accounting year, or a master directory for each person who uses the computer with subject matter directories under them. There are all sorts of possibilities.

In practice, though, rich tree structures are a terrible idea. The main reason for this is that your computer has to do much more disk work to trace its way through complex directories, and disk access is usually the slowest part of your computer's operation. A secondary reason why complex trees are a bad idea is that the more complicated they are, the harder it is to keep track of them, find necessary data, and, especially important, discard unneeded data. There are nearly a thousand files on the hard disk of the computer system this book is being written with, and I'm often finding some neglected file that is cluttering up my disk space; if I had a complex tree structure, the problem would be much worse.

Sub-directories are really intended for use with only the fast speed and huge capacity of a hard disk system. Unless you have a lot of files on a disk, there is little need for organizing them into isolated groups by putting them in sub-directories. More important, the extra overhead of work that sub-directories require can cripple the operation of slower, diskette-type storage.

Sub-directories are practical only with the fast speed of a hard disk system—which works about five or ten times faster than an ordinary diskette system.

So, as a general rule, you only need sub-directories if you have a multi-million byte capacity hard disk system, and you can only afford the extra overhead of sub-directories if you have a hard disk. Otherwise, you should not use them.

From my own practical experience, I would recommend that you create as many sub-directories as you find a need for, but make your tree structure the simplest possible: place all your sub-directories onto the disk's root directory. Unless you have a really good reason to do so, don't create branches off of any other directory than the root.

Judging when you should create a directory at all is another question. There are advantages and disadvantages to creating lots of small directories. With many directories containing only a few files each, it is easier to keep track of the files that belong in one particular category. But it is more difficult to use files in different directories at the same time, so it can become inconvenient if you have your files split into lots of directories. The more sub-directories you have, the harder it becomes to manage the totality of your files.

The way you create and use your sub-directories will depend upon your needs and also your own taste. But let me recommend what I have found works very well for me. First, as I mentioned, I have only one level of tree. All of my sub-directories branch off my disk's root directory—there are no further sub-directories. When I created my tree I asked myself what sub-directories would do for me. The answer was to help keep track of my data, but not to keep track of my programs. So I placed all of my programs, including all of the DOS programs and other programs that I have written or bought, in the root directory. There they serve each of the sub-directories and don't clutter up the directories where I keep data. In the next section we'll learn more about the practical details relating to this.

8.6 Finding Your Pathways—TREE, CHDIR, PWD, and PATH

Since a disk can have numerous sub-directories, organized in a tree structure branching out from the root directory, we ought to have a way of finding out what all the branches of the tree are. The TREE command does this for us. TREE will display a list of all the branches of our directory tree for any disk.

With the potential complexity of a branching tree-structured directory, we need a way to find our way around it. We need ways to find and control where we are, and we need a way to indicate what part of the tree we are interested in: we need a notation, a way of writing down a location in the tree.

How we find our way to a particular sub-directory on a disk is referred to as a *path*. A path is the route we must follow to trace our way from a disk's main or root directory out to some point in the branching directory tree. The description of the path is called the *pathname*.

Let's suppose that we have a disk, which of course has a root directory. Then let's suppose that the root directory has a sub-directory named A, and it in turn has a sub-directory named AA, and finally in that sub-directory is the file we want to refer to, which we'll call just FILE. Then, to find our pathway out to the FILE, we need to describe the path something like this:

- Starting with the ROOT, find its sub-directory named A;
- then find its sub-directory named AA;
- then find its file named FILE.

Pathnames are written like that, but all the lengthy words are replaced with a short and simple slash (/). So our verbose path description shortens down to this:

```
/A/AA/FILE
```

You'll notice that we didn't say we were starting from the root—the first slash indicates that. If a pathname begins with a slash, that means "start the path from the root."

(Some computers' versions of DOS use a reverse slash, " \ ", for pathnames, instead of a slash. You'll recall that the switches that commands use
are marked off with a hyphen (-) or a slash (/). As you might guess, if a
computer uses the slash for the switch, then it needs to use something else,
the reverse slash, for writing out pathnames. The effect is the same, and the
difference isn't important—but it is important that you use the right one with
your computer.)

So with this way of writing a pathname, we can tell DOS where in any
disk's directory tree we want to work, and vice versa DOS can tell us where
things are. But if we are going to be working with various files that are under
the "/A/AA" directory, it would be a nuisance to have to keep writing "/A/AA"
for each file—and we'd be likely to make a typing error at some point. To
solve this problem, DOS keeps track of a *current directory*. So if we refer to
just a filename, without specifying the path to get to it, DOS assumes that it
should be in the current directory. We control where the current directory is,
with the change-current-directory command, CHDIR (which can be abbrevi-
ated CD). For example, to make "/A/AA" our current directory, we would
enter the command

```
CHDIR  /A/AA
```

If we wanted to change back to the root directory, we would use this:

```
CHDIR  /
```

To make things even handier, DOS keeps track of a *separate* current directory for each disk device it has. So if you have an A-drive and a B-drive, we
could set the current directories for them, independently, like this:

```
CHDIR  A:/DIR1/DIR2
CHDIR  B:/OTHER1
```

Then, whenever we referred to the A-drive, DOS would look in the "/DIR1/
DIR2" directory, while for any use of drive B, DOS would look in its
"/OTHER1" directory. If we did a global copy command, like this:

```
COPY  A:*.*  B:
```

then the files from the "/DIR1/DIR2" directory in drive-A would be copied to
the directory "/OTHER1" in drive B. No other files and no other directories
would be affected.

There are other ways to work our way around directory trees, besides
starting from scratch at the root directory. If we write out a pathname starting
with a slash, then we are telling DOS to start tracing the path from the root. If
not, then the pathfinding begins right where we are now, at whatever is the
current directory. So this pathname starts with the root

```
/XX/YY/FILENAME
```

while this pathname starts wherever the current directory is:

```
XX/YY/FILENAME
```

There are two special trick names to help us work our way around paths, and their names are "." and "..". These special names, one period and two periods, are used to refer to the current directory, and to trace back one level to the parent of the current location. As an example of using "." for the current directory, we could have written the last example as

```
./XX/YY/FILENAME
```

which is *just another way of writing the same thing;* the only difference is that it is a little more explicit.

The parent name, "..", is used if we ever want to trace our way backwards from the current directory. Let's switch back to our first example:

```
CHDIR   /A/AA
```

We're now in the "/A/AA" directory. If we want to find a file named ZZZZ that's in the "/A" directory, which is the parent of the current directory, we can path-find our way to it like this:

```
../ZZZZ
```

This business of using ".." to refer to the parent directory can be used for all kinds of sophisticated tricks—but they would be tricks, and anything that uses them is likely to be tricky and error prone. You'd be well advised to steer clear of the whole business. After all, if you had a complex pathname that traced its way forward and back, like this:

```
../../AA/BB/../CC/FILE
```

then you wouldn't be very likely to understand it and use it safely.

We mentioned that the CHDIR command is used to change the current directory. There is also a way to simply display the current directory. If you enter the CHDIR command, without specifying a new path, CHDIR displays the current directory instead of changing it. On some computers' versions of DOS, another command is used for this: PWD, which is short for Print-the-Working-Directory-pathname.

There is one more very interesting thing that we have to consider about how we find our way around the paths through the trees, and that is how we find programs and how we find data.

When programs and data are stored on disk, they are no different from one another—they are just disk files which contain one kind of data or another. But DOS uses a different method for finding programs and for finding other data. This seems puzzling at first, but there is a good reason for it and it turns out to be very handy for us.

When we tell DOS to go looking for a data file, DOS looks in only one place: the current directory. (If we specify a pathname with the filename, then DOS looks there rather than in the current directory—but it is still looking in only one place.) This is true whether we specify a particular drive to look on, or use DOS's default disk drive. Each drive has its own current directory (which will be the root directory, if it hasn't been set to some sub-directory with the CHDIR command). This is also true whether we are referring to a data file with a DOS command, like COPY, or whether a program we are using asks DOS to find a data file for it. If DOS is asked to find a data file, then DOS will look in only one directory—the current directory, or the directory in the pathname given with the filename.

For programs it is different. When we enter a command to DOS, we are telling DOS to find a program with that name and then to execute the program. The command program might be *internal,* as we discussed in Chapter 4, or it might be *external,* which means that the program to carry out that command is located on disk storage. When DOS goes looking for a program file to carry out a command, DOS does not look *only* in the current directory. Instead, if DOS doesn't find it in the current directory, it will search in as many other places as we have told it to. How do we tell DOS to do this *extended search* for command program files? With the PATH command.

The PATH command has a slightly misleading name—you might think that it has something to do with paths in general. But PATH sets the list of paths to be searched for command program files. PATH is a command to set-the-extended-program-search-paths. Remember that the search always begins in the current directory, but if the program file isn't found there, then the search goes on where the PATH command says it should. The PATH command can specify several paths, separated by semicolons, like this:

```
PATH /PROGS;/OTHER/PROGS;/
```

That PATH command would lead the search into four directories in this order:

- the current directory (automatic—regardless of the PATH)
- the PROGS directory, under the root (from "/PROGS")
- the PROGS directory, under the OTHER directory, under the root (from "/OTHER/PROGS");
- finally, in the root itself (from "/").

One of the most remarkable things about the PATH command is that the search paths can be located on different disks. So even if you don't use sub-directories, you can make good use of the PATH command to have it automatically search from disk to disk, looking for the right program like this if you had four disk drives, A, B, C, and D:

```
PATH A:;B:;C:;D:
```

If you want to discontinue the extended program search, this command de-activates it:

```
PATH ;
```

After that, only the current directory will be searched for command programs.

Why would we want to use the PATH command? There are two reasons, one for those who use sub-directories, and one for those who don't.

If your computer only has diskettes, and not a large-capacity hard disk system, then you are sure to have more programs than you can fit onto one diskette. You may have two different diskettes loaded into your diskette drives, each with programs on them. If you use the PATH command to search both diskettes, then you don't have to bother indicating which programs are on which diskettes—DOS will automatically go looking for them.

On the other hand, if you have a hard disk system, you are probably using sub-directories, and you probably have programs scattered around in various directories. Even if you follow my advice and try to keep all of your programs in the root directory, there will still be times when you need to have some programs in other directories. If you set the PATH command to search through all of the directories where you keep programs, then each and every one of your programs will be on tap for you, regardless of which directory it is buried in.

There is one rather obvious practical note you need to keep in mind about using the PATH search command: the more directories DOS has to search through, the longer it takes to find a command program. It speeds things up to put the most used program directories at the top of the list.

8.7 Other Commands Special to DOS-2

Besides the commands that we have looked at so far, DOS-2 has a number of other relatively minor commands, each with their uses. We'll take a brief look at them in this section.

There can be times when our programs need to have some general instruction which sets some basic ground rules. For example, the PATH command, which we covered in the last section, sets the ground rule for where command programs are to be found. DOS-2 contains a flexible, general-purpose method of doing this, something called DOS's *environment.* In the environment DOS keeps little equations, all in the form:

```
NAME=VALUE
```

The name indicates the subject matter that the equation concerns, and the value indicates how that subject is to be treated. Any programs which we run on our computers can check the environment to see if there are any equations that concern it.

The SET command is designed to set these environmental equations. We simply enter a command like

```
SET NAME=VALUE
```

and the NAME=VALUE equation is placed in the environment. If there was an old equation with the same name, it is replaced. If there is no value, as in

```
SET NAME=
```

then any old equation with that name is removed from the environment; not replaced with "NAME=", but actually *removed.*

This environmental equation scheme can be used for any purpose, and in fact DOS uses it for its own purposes. The search paths, set by the PATH command, are stored in the environment. In fact, the PATH command is just a specialized version of the SET command. If we enter the command

```
PATH xyz
```

the result is *exactly* the same as if we had entered this:

```
SET PATH=xyz
```

If any of your programs are specifically designed for DOS-2, they can make use of these environmental equations in any way that they find useful.

Since computers are used to store data that could be either commercially valuable or confidential, security can become an important issue. Some computer's versions of DOS-2 contain two security commands. The LOGIN command is used to control the basic use of the computer. The CIPHER command is used to scramble and unscramble data, together with the use of a security key code. A scrambled file can't be unscrambled without the same key that was used to code it. Under the right circumstances, these two commands can protect the use of your computer and the safety of your data. Under the wrong circumstances, these commands can mislead you into a false sense of security.

There are many ways that your disk data can be lost or damaged, and the whole subject of file recover is a very important one, which we'll go into in more detail in Chapter 14. DOS does not provide much in the way of file protection and file recovery, but there is one command, RECOVER, which does two limited kinds of file recovery.

If part of a disk has been damaged so that a file can only be partly read, the RECOVER command will remove the unreadable part so that you can use the rest. Depending upon the kind of file that it is, the recovered portion may or may not be usable. Generally this kind of file recovery works only with text files, which contain written material. To use RECOVER in this way, you enter the command followed by the name of the file it is to check for readable and unreadable parts.

The other kind of file recovery done by RECOVER is completely different than the first. Unfortunately it is easy to confuse the two. In the second kind of file recovery, RECOVER assumes that the entire directory of the disk is damaged and nonsensical. It throws away the *entire directory* and replaces it with a new one, which contains the data it found on the disk organized into files as well as possible. The new directory contains files with arbitrary names which RECOVER gives them—it is then your job to figure out what is what, as best you can. To use RECOVER in this way, you enter the command without specifying any filename. Remember that this form of RE-COVER wipes out your entire directory with very little warning. Be careful using it.

To assist in the printing of data, DOS-2 contains a PRINT command, which acts as a variety of *print spooler.* The job of a print spooler is to print information on your computer's printer, without tying up the use of the computer while the printing is going on. PRINT provides a limited capability to do this. It is not a particularly strong spooler, as Microsoft admits. For example, the information to be printed must be stored on disk so that any program that formats information for printing must send it to a disk file and not to the printer. (Most print spoolers intercept data that is being sent to the printer and accept it as fast as the generating program can send it. Later the data is slowly fed out to the actual printer, but DOS's PRINT command does not work this way.) Besides this inconvenience, the performance of PRINT is fairly modest. However, if you have no other way to run your printer and still use your computer at the same time, PRINT will do the job for you.

When DOS is ready for a command, it shows a prompt, which is normally the default drive, followed by a colon or a greater than symbol:

```
A:   or   A>
```

You can change the prompt to nearly anything, including a display of the current time and date. The PROMPT command allows you to set the prompt as you wish. The format and rules for setting a prompt are complicated, so you should see your computer's DOS manual if you want to use this command. For the most part, I think that it is a poor idea to change the prompt, unless you have a very good reason to do so.

When DOS is writing information to disk, it normally accepts the disk drive's report that all went well. This is generally OK because disk drives are quite reliable. But if you wish, you can ask DOS to check or verify all data that is written to disk. This is controlled with the VERIFY command, which can set verification on or off. DOS normally does not verify. If you are concerned, you can set verification on but it will add considerably to the time it takes to use the disks.

In the last chapter we mentioned the Control-C or break operation which will end any program you have operating. DOS-1 only checked for this break command under limited circumstances, while DOS-2 can check for it much more often. The BREAK command lets you instruct DOS-2 to either use the same rules as DOS-1 (BREAK OFF), or to check as often as possible (BREAK ON).

This brings to a close the miscellaneous commands that are available in DOS-2, but not in earlier DOS-1 versions. In the next chapter we'll take a closer look at how information is stored on diskettes, and the last section of that chapter will cover what is special about how DOS-2 uses diskettes with sub-directories and other advanced features.

What You Need to Know About Disks and File Formats

9.1 What's Inside a Disk

A storage disk is used to hold data that you need to preserve. A disk is like a filing cabinet—it's a safe place to keep information, and it has a large, but limited, capacity. Just as a filing cabinet has its contents organized into file folders, a disk has its data organized into files.

The files in a diskette are distinct and each file contains its own particular data. The files are identified by their filenames, which we'll learn more about in the next section. Within any one disk, each file must have a unique name; but on two separate disks there could be separate files with the same name. Since files are identified by their filenames, it is a very good idea to make sure that every file on every disk has a completely unique name, except when there is some good reason to reuse the same name. If a file on one disk exists solely to be a safeguarded copy of a file on another disk, that is a very good reason for having a duplicate file name; but even then it could be a good idea to give the files different names in order to distinguish the original or master copy.

Most of the space on a disk is devoted to storing our data, but some of the space is used by DOS for bookkeeping purposes, such as maintaining a directory of the files on a disk. In the directory, DOS keeps its record of everything that it needs to know about the disk's files, such as how to find their contents. Most of this information is of little use to us, but there are three things about a file that DOS will let us know.

The first is the filename itself. The second is the size of the file. And the third is a time stamp which shows when the file was most recently changed. If a file has not been changed since it was created, then the time stamp shows when it was created. These time stamps give both the date and the time (except that the time was not included in the first release of DOS, version 1.00).

There are several special things to know about the file time stamps. Although they are displayed to the minute, they are actually calculated to within two seconds of the exact time. When necessary, advanced programming techniques can be used to find the complete time stamp. If a copy is made of a file, the copy gets the same time stamp as the original. There is no way to tell if a time stamp is the original time the file was created, or the time the file was later changed.

These time stamps on files can be very useful in safely controlling your data. Looking at the time stamp you can answer questions like:

- Which of these files was I working on yesterday?
- Is my backup copy up to date with my master copy?

Because of this, it is very valuable to make sure that your system always knows the correct date and time. If your DOS computer needs to have you enter the time when it is turned on, I urge you to never be too lazy to key in the right date and time. The benefits of having the right time stamps on your files can be enormous; sometimes it can be as valuable as an insurance policy.

BOLINGER

And if your particular computer has a feature which automatically keeps track of the time when it is turned off, you are fortunate indeed.

There are actually three parts of overhead on a disk, including the directory. Since you may occasionally come across mention of them, it is worth knowing what they are. The first is called the "boot record," and it contains a very short program which is used to help start up the DOS operating system from the disk. Each DOS has a boot record on it, whether or not the disk contains the rest of DOS (if a disk has all of DOS on it, it is a *system* disk, which we'll come to in a moment). After the boot record, the next bit of overhead on the disk is a table which is used to keep track of the available space on the disk; this table is called the *File Allocation Table*, or just *FAT* for short. The FAT records where each file is located, so it is sort of an index to the disk; and it also keeps a record of the part of the disk's space which isn't in use. When the CHKDSK command reports on how much space is available on a disk, the information comes from the disk's FAT. The third and last part of the overhead on a disk is the directory, which lists all of the files on the disk. We've already discussed the directory since its contents are so important to us.

All together, the three overhead parts of a disk—the boot-record, the FAT, and the directory—take up very little of the space on a disk, typically only about two percent of the total. The rest of the space is used to store our data.

The overhead we talked about here is overhead that is intrinsic to the disk itself—the disk's own overhead—that uses up about two percent of the disk's space. But there is another potential overhead which can reduce the amount of disk space that is usable to us: the operating system. When DOS is started up, it has to be read into memory from a disk, and naturally this copy of DOS takes up some space on the disk. When we format a disk with the FORMAT command, we have a choice of whether we want DOS to be on the disk or not. With DOS on it, the disk is called a *system-formatted disk* or, for short, a *system disk*.

A system disk has the advantage that you can always start your computer system with it. If all of your disks are system formatted, then any of them can be used to start your computer, which can be a real convenience. On the other hand, having DOS on our disks uses up some of the space we might otherwise have for our own use. The amount of overhead for DOS varies according to the disk capacity and the version of DOS. In might be as low as 8 percent or as high as 25 percent. A typical figure is 12 percent. The space devoted to having DOS on your disks may, or may not, be important to you. I recommend starting out by putting DOS on all your disks, and then later deciding what is best. Chapter 13 covers some of the strategies you might use with your disks.

9.2 All About File Names

Files have file names, and the better you understand how they work the less likely you are to make a mess of them.

First, the simple mechanics of it. File names have two parts, called the filename (itself) and the filename extension. A filename can be up to eight characters long. Some examples?

```
A
LONGNAME
1234
AB_34
```

The filename extension is just that—an extension to the file name. Extensions can be up to three characters long. While a filename must have at least one character in it, the extension can be nothing at all. When a filename has an extension, the two parts are connected by writing a period between them. Here are some sample filenames with extensions:

```
JANUARY.84
PROGRAM.BAS
CHAPTER.2_3
```

There are some rules about what is a proper filename. The filename and the extension can be made up from any combination of the allowed characters, which consist of the letters of the alphabet A through Z, the digits 0 through 9, and a bunch of punctuation characters. The exact list of characters may vary slightly from computer to computer. This list is typical:

```
$ & # @ ! % ' ( ) _
```

You can use any of these symbols in any combination. It seems like a terrible idea to use the more exotic symbols, but some of these symbols work very nicely as a form of punctuation in a file name. For example:

```
JAN_MAY
```

You'll notice that there are a few common symbols that aren't allowed in filenames and extensions. These are the period (.), the colon (:), the hyphen (-), the slash (/), the asterisk (*), and the question mark (?). These five common symbols and four other less common ones—the vertical bar (|), the reverse-slash (\) and the greater than and less than symbols (> and <)—all have special uses so they are reserved. The period, as you've seen, is used to separate the filename and its extension; the colon is used to separate a device name from a filename, as in A:FILE. Either the hyphen or the slash is used to indicate command switches; which one is used for switches depends upon which computer you have. The slash or reverse slash are used in DOS-2 to indicate pathnames, which we covered in the last chapter. The greater than and less than symbols are used to control the movement of data, as we also saw in the last chapter. The asterisk and the question mark are used to specify wild cards, which we'll cover in Section 9.4 below.

Only capital letters are actually used in filenames. DOS, in a friendly way, lets us type in filenames in lower case if we want, but it automatically converts lower case to upper. This is why you'll find that DOS always lists files with their names in upper-case letters.

You may discover that there are some tricky ways to sneak illegal filenames past DOS. For example, it is possible to create a file that has a blank space in the middle of its name (like "AA BB.CCC"), or to create a file that has a lower-case name. Don't play that dangerous game; you are almost certain to regret it.

One of the very nice things that DOS does for us to make life convenient and easy, is that it lets us refer to parts of the computer, such as the printer, with simple names that are the same as filenames. These are called device names, because they refer to devices or parts of the computer such as the printer. In order to be able to do this, DOS has to reserve these names for their special uses. There is a short list of names that you can't use as your own filenames. The exact list may vary from computer to computer. Here is the usual list of names with what they are used for:

NUL	a null or empty file; if a program tries to read from NUL, it finds an empty file; data written to NUL is thrown away. This empty, or null, device can come in handy at times.
CON	the user console; input data is taken from the keyboard; output data is displayed on the screen.
USER	under some circumstances, this is an alternate version of CON;

USER can't always be used as a device name, but CON can. (Unless you know that USER will work, stick with CON.)

AUX   the communications line, or asynchronous communications port.

COM1   the first of possibly several communications lines; COM2 and COM3 are used to specify others; COM1 is the same thing as AUX.

PRN   the printer device.

PRT   the printer device (another device name for it).

LPT1   the first of possibly several printers; LPT2, and LPT3 are used to specify others; LPT1 is the same thing as PRN.

Some versions of DOS-2 have a feature which allows these device names to be used as file names—but that is generally an unwise thing to do, and it's an advanced topic anyway, not really something for this book.

With the exception of these special device names, you are free to give your files any names you wish, within the grammatical rules for filenames (one-to-eight characters, and so forth). It is almost the same with filename extensions, but not quite, and we'll cover that in the next section.

There are three more things to know about filenames, which we'll cover in the following sections and the last part of this chapter: what filename extensions are really about, what wild cards are in filenames, and some special DOS-2 items, such as disk labels and paths.

9.3 The Importance of Filename Extensions

You can give your files filename extensions as freely and arbitrarily as you can give them filenames—easier since there are reserved filenames, but there are no reserved filename extensions.

There is a distinct purpose for filename extensions—indicating the category and classification of files. Unfortunately, the importance and usefulness of filename extensions isn't emphasized much so many users of DOS don't fully understand it. In this section we'll explain what filename extensions are all about.

Filename extensions are intended to classify and categorize files, so that their purpose can be quickly and simply identified. The assignment of standard filename extensions is rather casual, and it is not explained fully anywhere that I know of, which leads to confusion about them.

Here are the main standard uses of filename extensions:

- Executable program files have extensions of EXE or COM; there are two formats for program files (which we'll go into in Section 9.5 below) so there are two filename extensions to distinguish them.
- Batch execution files have the extension BAT; we'll look into batch execution files in Chapter 11.
- Programming languages make use of several standard filenames, which we'll learn more about in Chapter 10. For source code, a different extension is used for each language: ASM for assembly, BAS for BASIC, COB

for COBOL, FOR for FORTRAN, and PAS for Pascal. For object code in any language, OBJ is the extension. For library routines, the extension is LIB. When BASIC uses BLOAD-format files, BLD is the customary extension.

- When a program creates printer-type output, but the output is stored in a file, LST is the customary extension. If there is more than one listing file being created at a time, other extensions may be used; compilers typically use COD for assembly-like object code listings, and the linker uses MAP for the map of the contents of a program. When practical, LST is the best extension to use for printer-type files.

- Editors and word processors use some standard extensions. When the old version of an edited file is preserved for safety reasons, it is given the extension BAK (for BAcK-up copy). Some word processors prefer to use TXT as the extension for the edited data. FMT may be used to hold the editing format.

- When a program uses a data file in its own format, DAT is often the extension.

- When a program needs a temporary work file, $$$ is most often used as the extension; occasionally TMP is used instead. The program fully intends to delete these temporary work files before finishing. If you ever find a file lying around with an extension of $$$ or TMP, that's a very good sign that something has gone wrong—and you ought to take the time to figure out what it was.

- VisiCalc uses VC for storing its worksheets in coded format, and DIF for data in the Data Interchange File format. Other spread sheet programs may use their own extensions following a similar pattern; for example, CAL.

To tabulate these most common filename extensions, here is the list in alphabetical order:

ASM	assembly source
BAK	text file backup copy
BAS	BASIC source code
BAT	batch processing files
BLD	BLOAD format for BASIC
CAL	Spread sheet calculation file
COB	COBOL source code
COD	object code listing, from compilers
COM	executable programs, in memory-image format
DAT	data files, in general
DIF	data interchange files, as from VisiCalc
EXE	executable programs, in relocation format
FMT	word processor format specifications
FOR	FORTRAN source code
LIB	library routines, for compilers
LST	printable listing files, in general
MAP	program maps, from the linker

OBJ	program object code, from compilers
PAS	Pascal source file
TMP	temporary work file
TXT	text files, for word processors
VC	spreadsheet data, from VisiCalc
$$$	temporary work file

The more closely you follow the pattern of these extension names, the easier your files will smoothly fit into the broad use of your computer. This is one of the many ways that you can safeguard the effective operation of your computer.

9.4 Wild Cards and Their Use

Connected with the subject of filenames is the subject of wild cards or generic file names. A wild card is a non-specific part of a file specification that can be used to match more than one particular file.

Every file has a specific, unambiguous filename (and extension), but you can refer to more than one file at a time by using wild cards in a file specification.

There are two forms of wild card—the question mark (?) and the asterisk (*). When a question mark is used in a file specification, for example as

```
THISNAM?
```

then it will match with any letter in that one particular position of the filename. So THISNAM? would match with any of these files:

```
THISNAME
THISNAM1
THISNAM$
THISNAM
```

This works so long as all of the rest of the positions of the filename match exactly. Wild cards, as you might expect, can be used in both the filename and extension parts of the complete name.

The asterisk form of the wild card is just a shorthand for several question marks. While a question mark is wild for the one single character position that it occupies in a filename, an asterisk is wild from that position to the end of the filename or the end of the extension. An asterisk acts as if there were as many question marks as there are positions left in the filename or in the extension. A wild asterisk in the filename stops at the end of the filename, and doesn't extend into the extension part. If you use the question mark form then you can be specific about the following positions in the name; with an asterisk you can't (if you try it, anything after the asterisk will be ignored, without warning).

A completely wild name would be either of these:

```
*.*
???????.???
```

and they would match any filename and extension. Note that they mean exactly the same thing, since an asterisk (*) is just shorthand for a series of question marks.

These wild card specifications are mainly used with four commands: the DIR directory listing, the DEL/ERASE file erase command, the REN/RENAME file name change command, and the COPY command. It also has a special copy-and-concatenate use with the COPY command (see the complete discussion of the COPY command in Chapter 5 for details). If "concatenate" is a new word to you (it was to me), it means to fit the two files together into one.

Other than the commands mentioned (DIR, DEL/ERASE, REN/RENAME, and COPY), most programs that require a file specification will not successfully use a name with a wild card, even if the wild card specification ends up matching only one single file. There are advanced programming techniques, though, which make it easy for a program to make good use of wild cards. DOS provides some special services to programs just for that purpose. It is a good thing for programs to make use of these services of DOS, so that when we use the programs we can give them filenames with wild card specifications. But not all programs do so, and we shouldn't be disappointed when they don't.

Beware. Use of wild cards can be very dangerous. Many a DOS user has erased files that weren't supposed to be erased by the accidental misuse of wild cards. Giving a wild card to a program which doesn't expect it can lead to other mishaps.

9.5 File Formats and What They Mean to You

It can help to understand what your disk data is like—how it is structured, what it looks like, and how it is stored. In this section we'll take a look at disk file formats.

First, how is data stored in disks? The scheme is simple and efficient. As DOS sees it, the storage space for data in a disk is made up of fixed-size chunks of space called sectors. The size of the sectors may vary from one type of disk to another, but within one disk the sectors are all the same size—typically 512 or 1024 bytes.

DOS manages the space on a disk by allocating sectors, or clusters of sectors, to any files that need them. If a disk has too many sectors to conveniently keep track of them one by one, then sectors are combined into logical units called clusters of sectors. Either way, space on a disk is allocated to files in uniform, fixed amounts. As a typical example, a single-sided 5¼ inch diskette might have its space allocated as individual 512-byte sectors, while a double-sided diskette might use two-sector clusters, so that its space is allocated two sectors at a time—which would be 1,024 bytes for each cluster.

While this is interesting to learn about we don't need to know this information at all, and that is one of the beauties of DOS's way of storing data on disks. DOS reads and writes disk data in fixed-size sectors and allocates that space one or more sectors at a time. We don't see these fixed-size sectors at all.

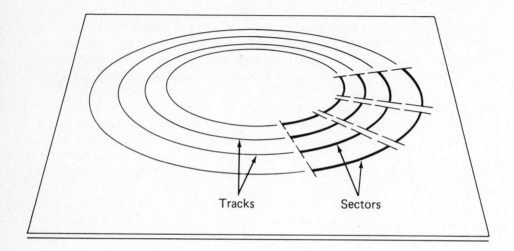

Tracks   Sectors

Instead, DOS lets us store our data in any size that is convenient to us. DOS worries about fitting our data into the fixed-size sectors, and does it so efficiently and so quietly, that we never have to concern ourselves about the mechanics of how the data is stored. Shoe horning our data into fixed-size sectors is work for DOS, not for us or our programs. This is a very good thing because it makes a clean division of labor: DOS worries about where and how to store our data, and all that our programs have to worry about is how to use the data.

There are more or less four file formats that are used to store our data on disks—three special formats and a sort of catch-all format.

Two of the three special formats are used to store executable programs. The formats are known by their standard filename extensions—COM and EXE. COM files are used to hold programs that are completely ready-to-execute; this is a memory-image format, which means that what's on disk is identical to what is in the computer's memory when the program is executed. The EXE format is more sophisticated; EXE programs require some last minute fix-up work to be done as they are loaded from disk into memory. This fix-up mostly

BOLINGER~

involves placing the program into the right part of memory, and letting the program know where it has been placed. The EXE format is mostly used for the more complicated type of program that is produced by compilers. Because of the extra overhead, EXE format programs are bulkier when they are stored on disk; inside the computer's memory, they can be just as compact as COM-type programs.

There is nothing about these two special program file formats that is of much practical consequence to us. In fact, the main thing worth knowing about COM and EXE program files is just their filename extensions. By looking for COM and EXE files, we can see which are the executable programs on a disk.

The BASIC programming language is an exception to many rules, and that's also true when it comes to program files. If you have BASIC programs that are run with the BASIC interpreter, then those programs are stored in files with the extension BAS. You may think of these as executable programs, and from our point of view they are. From the point of view of DOS, a BASIC program in a BAS file is just data that the BASIC interpreter reads in order to find out what to do. This is a technical point but one that is worth knowing. As DOS and the computer see it, the BASIC interpreter is a true program and a BASIC

BAS file is just data; that is why the BASIC interpreter is stored in a COM file—because it's a true program.

That covers the two special program file formats. The other special file format—one that is particularly interesting to us—is the ASCII text file format. This is the format that is used to store our text data, such as correspondence, reports, and the source code form of programs.

There are various terms used to talk about this file format—sometimes it is called a text file, or an ASCII file, or a word processing file. We'll usually call it an ASCII text file. ASCII text files use a format that is very flexible and is adapted to serve many purposes. It is probably the most widely used format for computer data; it is certainly universal to small personal computers. (ASCII refers to the code scheme that computers use to recognize the letters of the alphabet, and so forth, that make up a file of written text; ASCII is short for the American Standard Code for Information Interchange—it's the standard code used for computer characters. In layman's terms, the letters ASCII mean written material as the computer sees it.)

An ASCII text file consists mostly of a stream of written information—the alphabetic letters, numbers, and punctuation that make up the types of things that we people write. What you are reading in this book is typical of the contents of an ASCII text file. These very words are stored on a disk in an ASCII text file in my home. Besides the words—or text—an ASCII text file contains some formatting information that helps make the text more useful. At the end of an ASCII text file is an end-of-file format marker (this is the ASCII character number 26, which is also sometimes called Control-Z; Control-Z is discussed, along with some other special characters, in Section 7.3).

Inside an ASCII text file, the text is marked into lines by having two formatting characters placed at the end of each line; these two characters are known as carriage return (ASCII character 13) and line feed (ASCII character 10).

This is really all the formatting that is normally placed in an ASCII text file—carriage return and line feed at the end of each line, and end-of-file at, naturally, the end of the file. ASCII text files normally don't have any more format punctuation in them—there normally aren't paragraph or page markings. In the definition of ASCII there are formatting characters which can be used for this kind of marking and more.

(We've been mentioning some special characters by their ASCII codes. For example, ASCII 13 is the carriage return character. Everything inside a computer works like a number, so every character has a numeric code, whether it's a letter of the alphabet, like capital A, which is ASCII 65, or whether it's a special character, like end-of-file, which is ASCII 26. If you know or will be learning the BASIC language, BASIC refers to these numeric character codes like this: CHR$(26).)

The kind of programs that we call editors, or text editors, all work with ASCII text files. DOS itself comes with a simple but powerful text editor called EDLIN. We discussed EDLIN a little in Chapter 6 and we go into more detail about it in Chapter 19. Word processors, too, usually work with ordinary ASCII text files. However, sophisticated word processors, like the popular WordStar, need more complex formatting information than what ordinary ASCII easily accommodates, so they augment and bend the rules a bit to get the kind of data that they need. As a consequence, WordStar text files are a little different than ordinary vanilla-flavored ASCII text files. Yet, underneath the trappings of a WordStar file there is a simple ASCII text file.

What's particularly interesting and important to us about ASCII text files is that they are the most common and most interchangeable of all file formats. That means that if we have one program tool that uses ASCII text files, then we should be able to move data from it to other programs that use ASCII with a minimum of fuss and difficulty. This can be a tremendous advantage in flexibility. Because of this, it can be to our advantage to have as much data in ASCII format as possible.

If you are programming or having programs designed for you, you should consider using the ASCII text file format, even if it is not the most convenient for your programs. In the long run, the benefits can be considerable.

After these three special file formats—COM program files, EXE program files, and ASCII text files—we come to the catch-all format of the general data file. Unless a file has a special format, it consists simply of data stored on a disk. Usually data files are made up of fixed length parts called records. The records can be as short as a single byte, or as long as you like. To read or write

Lines as we see them:

(Mary had a little lamb,)

Its fleece was white as snow.

And everywhere that Mary went,

The lamb was sure to go.

Data as it is in the file:

(Mary had a little lamb,) <end-line> Its fleece was white as

snow. <end-line> And everywhere that Mary went, <end-line>

The lamb was sure to go. <end-line> <end-file>

such a data file, a program tells DOS the basic information about the file, such as what the record size is, and DOS does the work of finding where each record is, and in what part of what disk sector.

There is one special thing worth knowing about files that are made up of fixed-length records. Since the records are all the same size, a simple arithmetic formula can be used to calculate where each record is stored. This means that it is possible for a fixed-length-record file to be accessed randomly, skipping arbitrarily from one record to another. A fixed-length record file can be processed either sequentially, one record in order after another, or by random skips. This is one tremendous advantage over an ASCII text file, which must be read and written sequentially, from front to back in proper order.

When you think about files, and consider what can be done with them, you should keep in mind the special random access capability that a fixed-length record file has.

9.6 Diskettes and Other Animals

There are more creatures in the forest than you or I might imagine. Just when we think we've seen them all, up pops another furry critter. So it is with disk storage. For whatever computer you have that uses DOS, you probably know the particular options that are available for disk storage. It's worthwhile to know a little about the full range of disk storage formats.

There are three main species in the disk forest, with lots of variations and a few hybrids thrown in for variety. The three main types are floppy diskettes, hard disks, and electronic disks.

Floppy diskettes have been the most common form of disk storage for small personal computers, although they are rapidly being supplanted by newer, more advanced storage media.

Floppies get their nickname because they are made of a flexible plastic, and they can be easily and harmlessly bent. A classic floppy comes in a black, square-shaped protective cover. In the cover is a hub opening where the diskette is grabbed and spun, and another slotted opening where the diskette surface is read and written on magnetically.

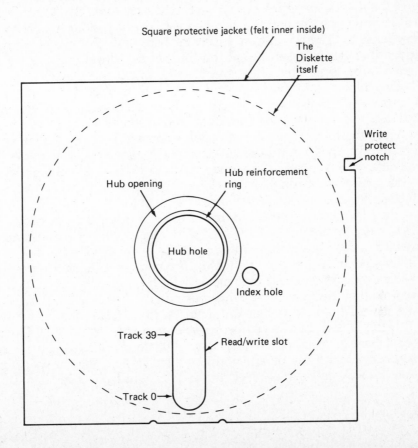

Square protective jacket (felt inner inside)

The Diskette itself

Write protect notch

Hub reinforcement ring

Hub opening

Hub hole

Index hole

Track 39→

Read/write slot

↘Track 0→

The original floppies were eight inches in diameter. Later, 5¹/₄-inch mini-floppies were developed, and they have been the most common size used in personal computers. There are lots of variations in diskettes besides their size. They can be recorded on one or both sides, and the recording density can be in what is called single, double or quadruple density, which are recorded at 24, 48, or 96 tracks-per-inch density. Also, diskettes can be hard or soft-sectored, depending upon whether or not the formatting of the diskette into sectors is fixed or variable under program control. One of the most common forms of diskettes, especially for DOS computers, is double density soft-sectored. But every possible variation is used on some computer somewhere.

Typically a diskette holds somewhere from 100,000 bytes to 500,000 bytes of data or more, but the full range of capacities is much wider than that with all of the formats that are available.

Hard disks are a higher-capacity storage media than floppies. Hard disks are made of a rigid platter coated with magnetic recording material. Usually they make use of a technology that was first code-named Winchester, so hard disks are also called Winchester disks. Their capacity is dramatically higher than floppies. The minimum capacity is around 5 million bytes, and some can hold as much as 50 million bytes. A true Winchester disk is completely sealed against the outside air and dust so it isn't removable—you don't change these disks like you can swap floppies, but then with the high storage capacity, there is less need to. There is also a variety of hard disk that has a removable cartridge that can be taken in and out of the disk drive, just like a floppy. Chapter 16 discusses some of the special needs of hard disk users.

As something of a hybrid between floppies and hard disks, there are micro-disk formats. Micro-disks are around 3 inches in diameter, and are enclosed in a rigid case, like the removable cartridges used in some hard disk systems. The design and the technology of micro-disks combines features of both floppies and hard disks. One unfortunate development in micro-disks is that over half a dozen different incompatible sizes and formats of micro-disks sprang up before any widespread standardization was done. That will probably keep micro-disks from being used as widely as they otherwise might be.

The third completely different format of "disk" storage is the electronic disk, or RAM disk. An electronic disk isn't disk storage at all, but a combination of memory and computer program that produces a simulation of a disk storage device in random access memory (RAM). The point of using an electronic disk is to adapt the speed of electronic memory to the operating standards of disk storage. With an electronic disk, numerous programs and their associated data can be moved from conventional disk to electronic disk, and then used at much higher speed than would be possible on a true disk device. Electronic disk operations are perhaps ten times faster than floppy disks, and twice as fast as hard disks, which can be an enormous advantage. There are special problems and considerations in using electronic disks, which are covered in Chapter 16.

9.7 Special Things About Disks in DOS-2

Disks are used in a richer and more complex way in DOS-2. We've already learned most of what is special about DOS-2 and disks when we covered sub-directories and paths in Chapter 8. Let's do a quick review and relate it to what we now know about disks.

All disks have a directory of the files that belong to them. With DOS-1, this is the only directory that there is. With DOS-2, the disk's main or root directory can have *sub-directories* under it, and each of those can also have any mixture of files and sub-directories under it.

Where do these sub-directories come from? As they are stored on the disk, sub-directories are just files like any other file that we keep on the disk. Sub-directories are specially marked so that DOS-2 can treat them as part of the directory structure and not as other files are treated. But as to how they are stored on the disk, sub-directories are like any other file. This has some interesting and important consequences for us.

First off, a sub-directory can grow in size, just as any file is allowed to grow. There is no arbitrary limit to the number of entries that can be placed in a sub-directory. This is a major advantage over each disk's root directory—because a root directory is fixed in its location and size, so there is a definite upper limit to the number of files that can be placed in a root directory. Sub-directories can grow without limit (except for the limit of space on the disk).

The second practical consequence of sub-directories being stored like any other file is that it takes longer to get to them, because DOS-2 has to hunt around the disk for them. A disk's root directory is located at the very beginning of the disk, next to a table which keeps track of the available and used space on the disk. When DOS processes a file that is in the root directory, all of the information needed to find it—the directory entry for the file and the information of where the file is stored—is located close together, where it can be gotten to quickly. With sub-directories it is another matter. To work with a file that is kept in a sub-directory, DOS has to hunt through the path of sub-directories that leads to the file; and each sub-directory is stored on the disk some distance away from the space table. Tracing through the directory path, and going back and forth from the directories to the space table, adds a lot of overhead to the work that DOS must do. If a disk is fast—as most hard disk systems are—and if the path is short—and I recommend that you keep all your paths short—then there isn't much problem. But with a slow diskette device or with complicated paths, the extra work can slow your computer down considerably.

DOS-2 adds one more feature to disks that DOS-1 does not have—disk labels. When you format a disk with DOS-2, you have the option of adding a label. Whenever DOS reports on a disk for you, as with the DIR, CHKDSK, and TREE commands, DOS will check for a label and report it to you. This can be handy in helping you keep track of your diskettes, so I highly recommend that you label your diskettes, provided you *do* have something useful to name them. Incidentally, the disk label is stored in the disk's root directory, similar to the entry for a file or for a sub-directory; but the label entry is specially marked, and doesn't use any of the disk's working data space.

10

What You Need to Know About Programming Languages

Even if you don't do any programming, there are some important and interesting things you ought to know about programming languages. How programming languages operate affects the way your computer works for you, and the performance of your computer is deeply affected by choices that are made about which language is used, and how that language is used. If you program, or have programming done for you, it is very important for you to understand what programming languages are all about.

10.1 What Are Programming Languages?

Programming languages are the way that people talk to computers in order to tell them what to do. A programming language is used to record, in an exact way, the instructions that the computer is to carry out. There are many programming languages, and even if you are a newcomer to computing you probably know the names of some of the most common ones: BASIC, COBOL, FORTRAN, and assembly language. (Assembly language is also called assembler and sometimes it's called "machine language"; these terms mean roughly the same thing.) Less common ones that you might have heard about are Pascal, Forth, C, PL/I, and Ada. There are many more.

What sets them apart from each other? Several things. One is what is called level. A low-level language, like assembly, is oriented more to the computer than to the people who are programming in it. High-level languages, like BASIC and Pascal, are more people-oriented. What does that mean? It means that in a high-level language our programs say more directly what work we want the computer to accomplish, while in a low-level language much of the program will be occupied with details that have little to do with what we actually want to accomplish. The difference between a high-level and a low-level language is similar to the difference between giving a carpenter a detailed blueprint of what you want built (high-level), and telling him where to put every screw and nail (low-level).

Another difference between languages is their intended purpose: COBOL is for business programming, FORTRAN is for engineering, and BASIC and Pascal are for general-purpose use. Finally, there is how "structured" a language is. "Structured" is a technical programming term that refers to some principles and techniques of programming which help make programs more reliable and easier to fix and change. Modern structured languages, like Pascal and C, help produce reliable, easy-to-maintain programs; less structured languages, like BASIC and FORTRAN, resist efforts to write programs of good quality. Later in this chapter we'll take a closer look at why this is important to you.

Computers don't work directly with anything you or I would recognize as civilized speech. They take their marching orders in a form known as machine language or machine code; it is also sometimes called absolute. Machine language is usually very intricately coded, and is very hard for a human to make sense of—it is designed for the convenience of computer circuitry, not for our convenience.

When machine code is displayed for us to look at—and heaven forbid that we should have to look at much of it—it is normally shown in the numbers and letters of hexadecimal notation. An example:

`83 06-0AAA 03`

This particular machine language instruction tells the computer to add (83) the value three (03) to whatever number is stored at a certain memory location (06-0AAA). A typical machine language instruction has three parts—an operation (add in our example), a source operand (three in our example), and a destination operand (the memory specification 06-0AAA).

People don't write programs in machine code even when they want to work on that level. Instead, they use a symbolic equivalent known as assembly language. The key thing to know about assembly language is that it substitutes symbolic names for the detailed numbers of machine language. To write our sample instruction in assembly language, we would write ADD instead of 83; the assembler takes care of the work of substituting the proper operation code for the word ADD. An assembler does a lot of things that make the programmer's work easier, but fundamentally all it is doing is translating meaningful symbols (ADD) into machine codes (83). An assembly language programmer writes out every detailed instruction that the computer will perform.

Assembly language is a low-level programming language—in fact it is the lowest—because programs in assembly contain all the tedious details necessary to produce a working program. Every instruction that the computer will perform in carrying out the program appears, in symbolic form, in the assembly program.

Fortunately for us all, there are higher level languages that take care of many of the tedious details for us. High-level languages, like BASIC, are called high level because each command in the BASIC language is translated into many instructions in machine language. But this many-for-one translation isn't the important thing about high-level languages. The important thing about high-level languages is that most of the tedious details of instructing the computer are taken care of for us; in a high-level language we tell the computer what to do, in a broad sense, and the programming language translates our commands into the narrow, detailed instructions.

Example: In BASIC we might write

```
LET TOTAL.PAY = HOURS.WORKED * HOURLY.RATE.OF.PAY
```

while the machine language equivalent might be a dozen—or even several hundred—instructions.

But don't make the mistake of thinking that with a high-level language we can just tell the computer what we intend to have done. We have to tell the computer how to accomplish what we want done. This, in fact, is what programs are—a statement of all the steps that have to be performed to accomplish some purpose. A program is an "algorithm," a statement of the strategy and tactical details needed to perform some work. The difference between high- and low-level languages is in how tediously the details must be spelled out. In either case, the details of the work must be specified in the program and not just the intended result.

There are two main ways that we write our programs to get them translated into instructions that the computer can use—called compiling and interpreting. Since the common language BASIC uses both methods, we'll compare them in the next section where we discuss the two kinds of BASIC.

10.2 The Two Kinds of BASIC—Interpreted and Compiled

For a computer to carry out what our programs ask it to do, the programs must be translated into machine language in one way or other. There are two ways that this is done, known as interpreting and compiling. Most programming languages come to us in one form or the other; BASIC is unique because Microsoft provides both interpreted and compiled versions of BASIC for DOS.

(Assembly language programs are translated by a process called assembling but that's really just the same thing as compiling. It's just traditional in the world of computers to call the translation of assembly language *assembling*, and the translation of high-level languages *compiling*.)

There is a simple way to understand what interpreting and compiling are. An interpreter does its translation on the spot as the program is run, while a compiler does its translation in advance before the translated program is used. There is a simple human analogy to this: an interpreter works like the simultaneous translators at the United Nations, while a compiler works like a scholar who translates Homer from ancient Greek into modern English. Necessarily, the on-the-spot interpretive translation will be rough-and-ready, while the compiled translation can be quite polished.

It wouldn't matter to us whether or not a program is interpreted or compiled except that it influences how we interact with programs. First there is the matter of speed.

Compiled BASIC—or any compiled language—runs much faster than interpreted BASIC for three reasons. First, an interpreter does its translation work while the program is running each time the program is run. So while you are using an interpreted BASIC program, the translation work is done while you are waiting. With a compiler, the translation overhead is done in advance, only once; whether the overhead of compiling is large or small, it has already been done before we use the programs—so that compiled programs run faster. Following the analogy of a book translator and a UN interpreter, it doesn't matter how long it took to *write* a book (compile a program), we can *read* the book (run the program) as quickly as we wish. When we listen to a UN interpreter, we can't listen any faster than the interpreter speaks.

A second reason why compiled programs run faster than interpreted programs is that programs usually execute their subroutines many times, and with interpreted BASIC that means the same part of the program is translated over and over again. If a speaker at the UN repeats himself, the simultaneous translators work that much longer. Finally, a compiler gets to look at the whole program before writing up the translated version; this gives the compiler an opportunity to do a polished translation—to optimize the finished result into an excellent translation. But the UN's simultaneous translators don't get to polish their phrasing; what's said now is translated now, even if it leads to a poor choice of words. And that makes interpreted BASIC very slow. How slow? My own tests with Microsoft's interpreted and compiled BASIC showed speed differences of between 50 and 75 to one—a breath-taking difference.

Don't be seduced by dreams of speed, though. Many programs spend their time waiting for data to come and go from disks; a faster-running compiled BASIC program won't speed that up. Many BASIC programs run fast enough in interpreted mode. It is only if an interpreted BASIC program is taking too long while it is computing that there would be any speed advantage in having it compiled.

There are other interesting and important differences between interpreted and compiled BASIC. The most important difference is that with an interpreted program, you can change the program while it is running. You can stop a program, make corrections to it, and then tell the interpreter to carry on. When programs are being developed this is a tremendous advantage, because it makes much more efficient use of human time in writing and testing programs.

There is one more important difference between compiled and interpreted BASIC. Due to some technical details in the way that DOS computers manage their memories, there are different restrictions on how much memory can be used. For interpreted BASIC, the combined total of the size of the program and the size of the data is limited to 64K, or 65,536 bytes. Compiled BASIC programs can use that entire 64K for data alone, while the program may grow to any size without reducing that space available for data. (What we've said here has to do with designed-in limits on BASIC programs and data; naturally the amount of memory available in your computer puts another practical limit on the size of data and the size of programs.)

10.3 How Compiled Languages Work in DOS

There is a certain conventional way that compiled languages work in DOS, and its worthwhile to understand the main points even if you will never do any programming.

What we'll be describing here is the customary way that Microsoft's compilers work. Compilers from other companies may work in curiously different ways from Microsoft's, or they may be the same. Either way, the basic principles that we'll cover here still apply.

Programs as people write them are called source code. Source code programs are ASCII text files, which we covered in Chapter 9 on file formats. There is a convention for the file name extensions used for source code, and it is a good idea to follow it. By this convention, the filename extension indicates the language the program is written in. The extension names used for the most common languages are these:

BASIC	.BAS
Pascal	.PAS
Assembly	.ASM
COBOL	.COB
FORTRAN	.FOR

One warning about BAS files. BASIC is often an exception to the rules in computing, and that's true here. While our BASIC source code programs all have filename extensions of BAS, not all BAS files have the same format. BASIC uses three different file formats for source programs. One of them is the standard ASCII text file format, which all compilers use. In addition, BASIC has two special formats which only interpreter BASIC uses. The first of these is a compressed "tokenized" format that consists of a BASIC program translated into the format that interpreter BASIC uses internally. This tokenized format takes up about 23 percent less space than the normal ASCII text format, and interpreter BASIC is able to read and write it faster as well. The other special format is the protected form of BASIC programs. When a BASIC program is protected, it is encoded in a way that resists efforts to reveal the program source code.

Interpreter BASIC can work with any of these three forms of BAS files, but the BASIC compiler, like all other compilers, needs to have its source programs in the standard ASCII text format. Interpreter BASIC can store any of the three formats, and they are selected through an option in the SAVE command. If

"SAVE filename,A" is used, then ASCII text format is written. If "SAVE file-name,P" is specified, the protected format is written. And if neither the A option nor the P option is used, then BASIC uses its tokenized format.

Compiled (or assembled) languages all work the same way in DOS. Preparing a program for execution involves two main steps after the program has been written. These two steps are called compiling (or assembling, for assembly language) and linking.

How a compiler works varies from language to language. In some cases, like the Microsoft BASIC compiler, the compilation is a simple one-step process. In other cases, like the Microsoft macro assembler, the translation appears to us as a one-step process, but behind the scenes the translation actually takes two steps, and the source code is read twice by the assembler program. For some of the most advanced compilers, like the Microsoft Pascal compiler, two fully separate steps are performed. In the case of Pascal, the first stage of the compiler reads the source code and translates it into a semi-digested form. Then the second stage of the compiler gobbles up the semi-digested program, chews on it for some time (performing numerous internal steps that do different things),.and then spits out the compiled result.

The more sophisticated the compiler, the more able it is to produce compact, efficient, fast-running machine code. A really advanced compiler is able to detect all sorts of unnecessary duplication of work and produce highly optimized machine code.

The job of a compiler is to translate source code into machine language in a standard form called an object file, or object code. Object code is the fully translated program in machine language. But object code isn't quite ready to be used—it still needs some work done on it called linking, or link editing, which we'll get to in a moment. Object code is stored in files with the standard filename extension of OBJ.

Why isn't the object code ready to use? There are two closely related reasons, both having to do with incorporating other programs into the compiled program. These other programs can be subprograms that we have written, or they can be part of the programming language's standard library.

When our programs ask the computer to do something—such as displaying a number on the screen—as often as not what we've asked the computer to do is something quite common, yet laborious, to carry out. in the example of displaying a number on the screen, two quite standard operations need to be carried out—first to convert the number from its internal computational form into a display format that people can read, and second to actually place that display format onto the screen. Each of these operations is done a lot, and each requires quite a few machine-language instructions to carry it out.

It would be silly for a compiler to generate all the necessary machine-language instructions each time we did such a common operation. Instead, compilers have a library of subroutines that perform these common tasks. So when the compiler comes to that part of a program, instead of generating the lengthy machine-language code needed to do the task, it just generates a brief "call" to one of its library routines—and the library routine is prepared to do similar work for any part of our programs.

The task of patching together different programs is done by the link editor, or linker, called LINK. Having a linker makes the whole process of preparing programs much more flexible, since it means that compilers can use libraries of routines, and programmers can write their programs in separate parts and later combine those parts into complete programs. The linker takes in object files (with file name extensions of OBJ) and libraries (with file name extensions of LIB) and combines them to produce a finished working program. For more about the LINK program command see Chapter 6.

A library is nothing more than a collection of object files with a built-in table of contents to tell what's where. Each programming language comes with its own specialized library. When the linker goes to work on a program's object files, it checks which subroutines each needs from somewhere else, and also which subroutines each file can supply for others to use. All the cross connections are made, and any library routines that are needed are gathered together. The result is a machine-language program, with all of its parts supplied and converted from object (OBJ) format into the format of a ready-to-run program (EXE).

Some versions of DOS include a library maintenance program, called LIB, which allows you to control the modules in a library—adding them, removing them, replacing them, and even building your own libraries from scratch. LIB is discussed in Chapter 6.

Ready-to-run programs can have two forms in DOS, and they are known by their filename extensions as EXE-files and COM-files. The difference between the two is technical, and the details aren't of much interest to us. In essence, a COM-file program can be loaded into memory as is, while an EXE-file program has some last-minute preparation work done on it as it is loaded into memory. The linker always produces EXE-type programs but under the right circumstances they can be converted to COM-format. There are DOS utilities to convert from EXE to COM and, beginning with DOS-2, from COM to EXE. Compiled programs usually must be in EXE-format.

There is one more important thing that you need to know about compiled programs in DOS, and that's the subject of run-time support. Compiled programs need library routines, as we've already seen. There are two ways that

OBJECT FILE 2

LIBRARY

OBJECT FILE 1

READY-TO-RUN PROGRAM

these library routines can be provided. The first way is from a regular library. When they are supplied this way, then the resulting link-edited program is self-sufficient, and doesn't need anything else to be run on our computers.

The other way to provide library routines is through a run-time module. A run-time module is a separate file of subroutines which is connected to our programs not when the program is linked but when the program is run. In effect a run-time module is a last minute, help-you-on-the-spot form of library.

Whether or not a run-time module is needed depends on how the compiler for that language was written. One company that sells compilers might produce a COBOL that uses a run-time module, while another compiler company might make a COBOL that doesn't. Among the Microsoft compilers, Pascal and C don't use run-time modules; COBOL and FORTRAN have to use them. And straddling the fence is BASIC, which can be compiled so that BASIC programs are either self-sufficient (getting all their routines from the library) or dependent on the run-time module.

Run-time modules are easily identified by their file names. For example, BASIC's is named BASRUN.EXE and COBOL's is named COBRUN.EXE.

There are some practical consequences involved with run-time modules: size, speed, and expense. If you have twenty programs in stand-alone format, then they will contain twenty individual copies of the most common subroutines—

which can take up a lot of storage space on your disks. If the same twenty programs used a run-time module, then one copy of the subroutines could service them all for a sizeable saving in disk space. A typical size difference is ten or fifteen thousand bytes for each program.

Run-time modules tend to take longer to use, because some of the work of making connections has to be done over and over again; this makes them partially analogous to interpreted programs. One test that I performed with a compiled BASIC program ran one-third faster in stand-alone form than in the form which used BASIC's run-time module. When speed matters, a program that uses a run-time module is at a disadvantage.

Stand-alone programs can usually be distributed without any special permission or licensing agreement from Microsoft (or whoever else produced the compiler). Normally the run-time modules must be purchased separately for every computer that they are used on. This involves not only extra expense, but a real administrative nuisance as well. If you are selling programs that need the run-time module, you may have to ask each of your customers if they already have the run-time module or if they need to buy it. The alternative is to include the module in the cost of every copy of your programs, forcing some of your customers to unnecessarily buy a duplicate copy of a module that they already have. Even if you aren't selling programs but are just distributing them within your organization, the same problems arise. So programs that require a run-time module can be a real headache.

10.4 Choosing a Programming Language

If you are going to program—or have programming done for you—then it has to be done in some programming language. All too often, the choice of programming language is made casually or by default. It shouldn't happen that way. The choice of a programming language can deeply affect the quality of your programs—how fast they run, how easy they are to update, and even how well they are built. Under some circumstances the programming language should even be a factor in choosing which of several competing programs to buy. This is particularly true for accounting programs.

If you are a user and not a writer of programs, you might be puzzled as to why the choice of programming languages should matter to you. Think of it this way. If you owned a business, and were about to have a new factory built, it would matter a lot to you whether that factory was built out of wood or steel and glass—because you would have to live with the heating bills and the cost of fire insurance. You would probably leave the decision to a professional engineer; but you'd want to be reassured that the decision was made right— you might even want to have the final say yourself. And you'd make absolutely sure that your factory wasn't being built out of adobe mud. But there are an awful lot of mud-built programs on the market. More than you might imagine possible.

There is no completely simple guide to making a wise choice among programming languages, but here we'll give you an idea of what the main factors are in making an intelligent choice.

Let's start by considering the language level. There are three levels to choose from: low, high and extra-high. The high-level languages are BASIC, Pascal, COBOL, FORTRAN, C, Forth, and a host of others. These, of course, are the mainstream of programming languages, and we'll have quite a bit to say about how to choose among them. But before we go into that, lets consider the alternatives of low-level and extra-high level.

Low-level means assembly language. Assembly has the advantages of compact program size and fast running speed, but some enormous disadvantages. It requires highly skilled programmers to write, it is much more time-consuming to write and to test, and when changes are called for it is enormously more difficult to update. The only people who should use assembly language already know why they need it. If you are reading an introductory book like this, neither you nor anyone who works for you should ever consider assembly language. On the other hand, if you are buying programs, the advantages of assembly programs look very attractive—fast speed and compact size. This advantage is a sound one to go for if the product is mature and well tested. If you buy a newly introduced program that was written in assembly, then you are running a higher risk that the program will have errors in it and that the errors won't be easily corrected.

What are extra-high level languages? Some of the most sophisticated programs for computers are, in effect, programmable themselves. How could a program be programmable? By being so flexible that it accepts commands and instructions that take on some of the characteristics of programs, such as logical decisions and controlled repetition.

There are two main categories of these programmable programs. First are the spreadsheet programs, such as SuperCalc, Microsoft's Multiplan, and the granddaddy of them all, VisiCalc. Second are data base programs, particularly dBase II. Programs of this type are sophisticated enough to act as their own (specialized) programming languages. Here are two examples of how they can be used: if you are looking for an income tax program, you can find ones that work on their own or ones that are templates—that is programs—for VisiCalc. If you want a mailing list program, you can get a stand-alone one or one that works through dBase II.

What are the advantages and disadvantages of using extra-high level programming? There are two main advantages. The first advantage is a magnification of the benefit of using a high-level language: programs are quicker to write and test, easier to adapt, modify, and improve, and the programmer is relieved of more tedious details, particularly the details of data and file management. The second advantage is that the programs and data are easily integrated with other programs and data (provided that they are developed using the same extra-high level tools; mixing different dBase II data may work dandy, but mixing dBase II and Multiplan may be a disaster).

The main disadvantage of using an extra-high level language is that it tends to lock you into the use of one proprietary tool, dBase II, VisiCalc, or whatever. This can reduce your future options and the mobility of your data to other systems. A lesser disadvantage is that extra-high level languages tend to be slow, sometimes awfully slow; this problem grows smaller over time as extra-high level tools improve and as computers become faster. Extra-high level languages are generally interpreted rather than compiled.

My personal opinion is that the disadvantages of extra-high level programming languages are slight and that the benefits are enormous. As a general rule, I think that you should always choose to use an extra-high level programming language whenever you have the choice.

Most programming is done in ordinary high-level languages; they are the mainstream of programming languages. So let's take a look at the principal high-level languages and see what matters about them.

There are six main languages to be considered: BASIC, C, COBOL, Forth, FORTRAN, and Pascal. The greybeards in this list are COBOL and FORTRAN, so let's consider them first.

Both COBOL and FORTRAN were among the very first programming languages to be developed, and they have been the mainstay of traditional, large-system computing. COBOL was designed for business-oriented programming, while FORTRAN is oriented to engineering-style calculations. The principal advantage that these two languages have for use on DOS computers is that there are many programmers available who are fluent in them; this is particularly true for COBOL. At times it has seemed that COBOL programmers were a dime a dozen, and wise programming managers chose COBOL as a language since COBOL programmers were more readily—and cheaply—available.

There are some strong reasons against using COBOL and FORTRAN, even though they have been so widely used in traditional computing. COBOL and FORTRAN programs and programming skills don't necessarily transfer well to the smaller and more interactive environment of DOS computers. But there is an even more important reason for avoiding them. Since the days when COBOL and FORTRAN were developed, a great deal has been learned about what makes a good programming language, and what techniques lead to safe, reliable, and easily maintained programs. Most of these techniques sail under the banner of structured programming. Older programming languages are not oriented towards structured programming, and they may resist attempts to use them in a structured way. FORTRAN is particularly bad in this regard.

Because FORTRAN is archaic, is difficult to structure, and also because it is relatively easy to translate FORTRAN programs into BASIC, I would recommend against using FORTRAN. (My private opinion is that FORTRAN programming on a DOS computer is inexcusable.) While COBOL has many disadvantages as well—again, it is archaic and its implementations are usually inefficient, bulky, and slow running—there is less reason to avoid COBOL. There are much better languages than COBOL, yet COBOL is reasonably easy to structure, and it doesn't translate easily into another substitute language. COBOL is not a language of choice, but if you have good reasons to want to use COBOL—existing programs or existing programmers—then by all means use it. Unlike FORTRAN, COBOL isn't a language to avoid, it is just not a language to choose.

For microcomputers, BASIC is the first and foremost language (thanks mostly to Microsoft). BASIC is not a good language for structured programming—in fact it is as bad as they come. Even so, BASIC has some tremendous advantages that have made it the first choice of many program developers for microcomputers. First, it is the most widely available language for microcomputers, which means that programs you write and buy are likely to be more readily transferred to other computers. This should improve the salability of your own programs, and reduce the cost of programs that you buy. This gives BASIC a strong plus. Also, BASIC programming skills are the most widely available among experienced microcomputer programmers, which is another argument in favor of BASIC.

The strongest argument in favor of BASIC is that it is uniquely available in both interpretive and compiled versions. Microsoft provides both for DOS. Thanks to these dual versions, you can have the best of both worlds by programming in BASIC. You can develop programs in interpretive BASIC getting all the advantages of interactive program development. Then, after a program has been thoroughly tested, it can be compiled for fast running speed. This is a unique advantage that makes BASIC very attractive for program development. (Two warnings though: if you intend to develop interpreter-BASIC programs, and then later compile them, pay close attention to the subtle differences between what the two versions of the language allow. It is a good idea to start test-compiling early in the process of developing a program to avoid a nasty surprise later. And you shouldn't assume that you will be able to compile interpreter-BASIC programs that you have bought; converting them into compilable form may be a difficult task and the programs may be in protected format, which can't be compiled.)

Among programming languages which facilitate modern structured programming techniques, Pascal and C are highly regarded. These two languages both provide all the features that are needed to write effective, fast, safe, and reliable programs for DOS computers. Pascal and C are similar, and the main difference between them is that Pascal emphasizes safety at some sacrifice of power, and C emphasizes power over safety. Both are very fast. (If you have heard that Pascal is slow, you've heard about the "p-System" Pascal, which is interpreted; DOS uses a fast compiled Pascal.) Either Pascal or C is an excellent choice for programming DOS computers. Between them, Pascal may be the better choice since Pascal emphasizes safe programming, and many computer science college students are well-trained in Pascal. In fact, Pascal was developed specifically as a language for teaching good programming practices. Incidentally, Microsoft does most of its own program development in C, though that doesn't make it a better or worse choice of language for you.

If you don't understand why I have been emphasizing the terms structured programming, safety, reliability, and ease of maintenance, then you have been lucky to avoid the agonies that many traditional computer users have suffered in recent years. In the past, a great many poorly engineered programs were written with little thought to the importance of sound design principles in programming. Later, this lack of good design and engineering came back to haunt large computer shops. The ugly task of maintaining poorly written programs has come to eat up the majority of time and money at many computer sites. There is no excuse for this expensive mistake to be repeated in the modern world of personal computing, but unfortunately many people who program microcomputers are taking a very shortsighted and amateurish approach to their computers. A major contributing factor in the production of bad programs has been the use of the BASIC language, regardless of BASIC's many virtues.

There is one odd language left in our list of mainstream languages: Forth. Forth is a curious and quirky language which has the unusual distinction of being designed for efficient interpretation. This means that Forth, like BASIC, gets the benefits of both interpretation and speed—but Forth gets to have both virtues at the same time (only compiled BASIC is faster). Because Forth is so unusual in its form and is known by so few programmers, I can't particularly recommend it. But if you are drawn to Forth, for whatever reason, I see no reason to avoid it.

Besides the languages we've gone over here, there are a host of others. I think that it is unwise to even consider any of them. Would you buy a car you can't get parts for? Should you use a language that few programmers know how to maintain? Should you use a language that is unlikely to be updated to match new computer features? Not unless you like to suffer.

There is one more factor to consider. You don't really use a programming language, you use an implementation of that language. If your programs are in Pascal then they must be compiled by a Pascal compiler, and you may have a choice of more than one compiler. The quality of the compiler should influence your choice between different compilers, and perhaps even between different languages—it is better to have a well compiled COBOL than a poorly compiled Pascal.

In this regard, Microsoft has a huge advantage that should bias you in favor of using Microsoft compilers. Microsoft started out in the language business— they wrote the first BASIC interpreter for microcomputers—and it has been their main specialty. Generally we can expect Microsoft compilers to be of good quality (but check the reputation of any particular one you are considering). Microsoft has two other advantages that should make you want to choose one of their compilers. Since they are the authors of DOS, we can expect that their compilers will be well integrated into the operating system, and will be updated quicker and more thoroughly than those of any of their competitors. And as one of the biggest and most successful software producers, you don't have to worry about Microsoft going out of business.

This shouldn't prevent you from considering using other companies' compilers. Often a company that specializes in producing one product—such as one compiler—can do a much better job than a large company with many products. You might find, for example, a COBOL compiler whose reputation is much stronger than Microsoft's COBOL. You must weigh the risks and benefits.

Let's end with one final warning. No matter how standard a programming language is, different compilers usually provide different features when you get down to the details, and programs are often dependent upon these details. This tends to be truer on small microcomputers than it has been on traditional large-scale computers. Just because your programs are written in COBOL don't assume you'll be able to switch from compiler-R to compiler-M if you later want to. The usual experience is that once you begin using one particular compiler you are stuck with it. Migrating to another compiler may not work at all. *Beware.*

11

Batch File Secrets

Batch processing files are one of the most useful and powerful features of DOS, and we'll take a look at them in this chapter. First, we'll cover the simple idea of what a batch file is, and then get into some of the fancier tricks of using batch files. Finally, we'll finish the chapter with some suggestions and examples to help you get the most out of batch files.

11.1 Introducing Batch Processing—REM and PAUSE

The basic idea of batch processing is simple and ingenious: if you need the computer to perform a standard task, why should you have to key in the details of the task? Instead, let the computer be told what it is supposed to do by reading its commands from a file. With a batch file, DOS doesn't perform our commands extemporaneously—it reads from a script.

There are some interesting details on what a batch file can do, but first let's see the elemental part. Batch processing is always done with a "batch processing file," which must have the filename extension of ".BAT". The file must be an ASCII text file (which we described in Chapter 9), and you can create it with any ordinary text editor, such as the EDLIN editor that comes with DOS. You can also use a word processing program to create batch files, though you should be sure to check if your word processor needs any special instructions to create an ordinary ASCII text file.

Inside the batch processing file are ordinary DOS commands, just as you might enter them on the keyboard. There can be one or many commands in the file with each command on a separate line.

You put a batch file to work by entering its filename without the BAT extension (although you could key that in if you wanted). This works exactly the same way that you use a program—you type in the name of the program, or the name of the batch file, and DOS goes looking for it. Whenever DOS's command processor encounters a command that isn't internal, it searches the appropriate disk for a file to carry out the command. The file could be a program file (with an extension name of COM or EXE), but if it turns out instead to be a BAT batch processing file, then DOS starts executing the commands held in that file.

FOR BATCH FILES, DOS READS FROM A SCRIPT.

Let's take a look at a very simple batch file to get an idea of how it works. Let's suppose we've created a file with a name of D.BAT. Notice that it has the proper extension of .BAT. Since the filename itself is "D", then "D" is all that you would need to type in to invoke this batch processing command. Now the contents of this batch processing file might be something very simple, such as a single line that reads:

```
DIR
```

which, you probably remember, is the name of the directory command that lists the contents of a disk.

With this batch processing file set up, what would happen if we keyed in "D" and pressed *enter*? DOS would search for this batch file, and then start executing it. DOS would find just the one command, DIR, so it would just give us a directory listing.

This example is about as silly and as short as you could imagine. You might be thinking that it is a completely artificial example with no practical value. Surprisingly, no. There is a use for batch processing commands like this. What this command does, in effect, is let you use D as an abbreviation for DIR; that may not seem like a big deal, yet it cuts the keystrokes you have to type in half, from four to two (counting the enter key). This is one of the main purposes of batch files—to simplify the typing you have to do to get your computer to do some work for you. One of the best uses of batch files is simply to provide convenient abbreviations of commands.

One of the rather clever things that DOS does is to keep track of where it is working in a batch file. When the file has more than one command, DOS knows how to carry on. When each command is finished, DOS searches for the file, reads past as many command lines as it has processed, and then starts the next command.

Why would you want to have batch processing files? We've already seen one reason—to create an abbreviation for a command name. There are two other good reasons, even before we get into the advanced stuff.

The reason for using batch files that you have probably anticipated is the most important one: grouping several commands into one functional unit. Very often you need to do several things to carry out one task. For example, to write the very words you are reading, I used a batch file which has four steps: the first runs my text editor program, so that I can type in these words; the

BATCH FILES TURN MANY COMMANDS INTO ONE COMMAND.

second checks what I have written for spelling errors; the third runs my editor again so that I can correct the spelling errors; and finally, the fourth makes a backup copy of what I have written onto another disk.

I could, if I wished, do each of these four steps separately; however, I chose to run them. But putting them all into one batch processing file has done two very useful things for me. First, it has saved me the trouble of invoking each step by itself. Second, and more important, it has established a standard operating discipline: each time I write, I will check my spelling and I will make a backup copy. Laziness won't keep me from doing those two important tasks.

So the most important reason for using batch files is to gather together, under one name, all the separate steps needed to perform a unified task. The reason for doing that is as much for uniformity and completeness as it is for convenience and ease.

Finally, there is one more key reason for using batch files, besides abbreviation of commands and combinations of commands. That reason is safety. If you don't know it already, there are some maddeningly dangerous commands available to us in DOS. These are the commands that can wipe out our data in the blink of an eye. There are three such dangerous commands: DEL/ERASE which discards data, COPY which can overwrite good data with bad, and FORMAT which can wipe out the entire contents of a disk, beyond all hope of recovery. Batch files can reduce the danger of using these commands.

Let us suppose that we routinely need to ERASE a file called DATA.OLD, while preserving the file DATA.NEW. If you have to type in the command:

```
ERASE DATA.OLD
```

there is just a little chance that one day, absent-mindedly, you will type in NEW rather than OLD. Wouldn't that put you in a pickle? But if you had a batch file with that ERASE command in it, you won't have to worry about that kind of mistake. In fact, you might have a batch file which safely and reliably ERASEd all sorts of files without a worry—because if you got the batch file built right, then the commands would go right each time. Never a slip. You might even name that batch file something evocative and easy to remember, like KILL-OLD. Remember, that if KILL-OLD is to be a batch command, then the file that defines what it does must be named KILL-OLD.BAT.

There are some commands built into DOS that are there just to make batch file processing better. Two of these are the REMark and PAUSE commands. REMark, of course, is intended to let you put comments into a batch file, which can be very useful as a reminder of what is going on in the batch file— the REM comments can say, "this is what I'm doing." The PAUSE command is just another form of the REM command, but is suspends the operation of the batch file until a key is struck.

The PAUSE command is good for two purposes—one is to keep some useful information from rolling off the screen. With a PAUSE command, you have a chance to look at what is on the screen for as long as you want before the computer carries on its work. The other use is for safety. If a batch file is about to do something that might endanger some of your data, then a PAUSE to check that everything is in order is a very good idea. This can be particularly valuable before a command that might ERASE or COPY over your data.

BOLINGER—

*PAUSE STOPS A BATCH FILE WAITING FOR OUR
INSTRUCTIONS.*

If you use the PAUSE command in this way and decide that you don't want things to carry on, how do you stop them? The break command, also called Control-C, will stop the operation of the batch file so that it will not carry on to whatever it was going to do. On some computers there is a special key for the break command, while on others it is just entered by holding down the control key and pressing the C key. Either way, Control-C or *break* is what you use to stop a batch file from carrying on—and the PAUSE command gives you the opportunity to do it at the right moments.

Here is a dummy example of how PAUSE might be used for safety:

```
COPY DATA.NEW    DATA.OLD    make a safe copy of our old data
PROCESS          DATA.NEW    use a program that creates new data
DIR              DATA.NEW    check the directory for info on new
                             data
PAUSE  If all is well, delete old data, otherwise, press BREAK
DEL              DATA.OLD    discard old data
```

This example is, as we said, a little artificial, but the ideas are ones that you will probably want to use. Notice that DIR is used to take a quick look at the new data—it will show us both the size and the time stamp on the new data file, which ought to be enough to tell us if the PROCESS program was successful in creating the new data. If everything looks good, we proceed from the PAUSE statement to clean things up by deleting the copy of the old data. If things *aren't* all well, then we *break* at the PAUSE so that the old data isn't deleted, and we can try to fix whatever went wrong.

What we've seen so far makes batch files look very useful. But what you can do with them is even richer and more useful than you have seen so far, as we'll see in the next section.

11.2 Slightly More Advanced Batch Processing

You'll remember that I mentioned that I used a batch file to help me write this chapter. The name of the file might be WRITE.BAT, and, simplifying things a bit, the contents of that batch file might be like this:

```
EDIT    CHAPTER.11
SPELL   CHAPTER.11
EDIT    CHAPTER.11
SAVE    CHAPTER.11
```

But there is something drastically wrong with this batch file: it only works for Chapter 11. I would need to change it to work on any other chapter, which would be pretty stupid. The solution? Parameters. When I invoke the batch file, instead of just entering the batch command

```
WRITE
```

I would give a parameter, indicating what chapter I wanted to work on:

```
WRITE 11
```

Meanwhile, inside the batch file WRITE.BAT, everywhere the chapter number was needed, the batch file would have a special symbol, "%1", which would tell DOS to substitute the parameter that I had entered. Our batch file would look something like this:

```
EDIT    CHAPTER.%1
SPELL   CHAPTER.%1
EDIT    CHAPTER.%1
SAVE    CHAPTER.%1
```

There can be more than one parameter, so a digit is used after the percent sign (%), to indicate which parameter is used. %1 is used for the first parameter after the command name, %2 for the second, and so on, for up to nine parameters. (If you need anywhere near that many, you're probably making things much too complicated.) Parameter number zero, %0, is used to get the name of the batch command but there isn't much point in that.

There are some more things to know about batch files in general, before we go onto the extra features of DOS-2's batch processing. Inside a batch file are commands—which could be program names or other batch file commands. If the command is a program, then when that program is done we can carry on with the batch file. But if the command is the name of a batch file, then control never comes back to the original batch file. In technical terms this means that batch files are *chained* but not *nested*. If batch file A invokes batch file B, when B is done things stop; they don't carry on where A left off.

One of the batch commands that could be in a batch file is the file's own name. A batch file can invoke itself starting an endless repetition of the same work done over and over again. This can be very useful when you have to repeat some operation. The *break* command, commonly called Control-C, can be used to break out of this endless repetition. Putting a PAUSE command just before the repetition starts can be a good idea.

It is also possible for a program to control its own destiny by writing out the contents of a batch file that will be executed when the program is done. This is a very clever mechanism that makes it possible to use the full, rich logical capabilities of a programming language to decide what commands are to be carried out next. This is done is like this: we create a batch file, let's call it A, which runs our program; following the program, our A batch file tells DOS to carry out a batch file named B. But the program that is run by the A batch file itself creates the file B.BAT—so the program decides what is to be done when it finishes. The program in the A batch file creates whatever exact instructions are to be performed in the B batch file.

If you go in for this sort of trick, test your work carefully and beware of certain traps. For example, it is much safer for a program to create the next batch file that will be executed than try to change the batch file that is currently being performed.

11.3 *Even More Advanced Batch Commands—ECHO, SHIFT, GOTO, IF, and FOR*

DOS-2 has many more advanced features in batch processing. So advanced, in fact, that understanding them pushes a little at the outer edge of what an introductory book like this should cover—but we'll make sure that you have some understanding of their capabilities, at the very least.

When DOS is working its way through a batch file, it shows the commands that it is executing on the screen, just as if you had typed them in. This is good and bad—good to show you exactly what is being done, bad to display extraneous information. After all, one of the points of a batch file is to turn several commands into one unified operation. When you run a program, a listing of the program doesn't appear on your screen, so why should a listing of a batch file get displayed? This little conflict is resolved by the ECHO command. ECHO is used to tell DOS to display, or not display, each batch file *command* as it is executed. With command ECHO on, each command appears on the screen as DOS processes them; with command ECHO off, the commands aren't shown. The ECHO command itself controls command echoing like this:

```
ECHO   ON
ECHO   OFF
```

Any commands performed between the ON and OFF will not appear on the screen. That is, the *command itself* won't; if the command program generates any display output, that will continue to show on the screen.

One of the things that ECHO OFF will suppress is the display of comments from the ordinary batch file commands REM and PAUSE. But we might want some comments to appear on the screen. To make that possible, there is a third option to the ECHO command besides ON and OFF. If the command name ECHO is followed by anything other than ON or OFF, then what follows ECHO is displayed as a comment on the screen. The command is entered like this:

```
ECHO   message
```

ECHO OFF SILENCES DOS.

and it works with any message that doesn't begin with ON or OFF. ECHO's messages appear whether command echoing is on or off, and it has one real advantage over the REM command. When we use the REM command, the REM itself appears on the screen, which doesn't do anything to clarify the message. With the "ECHO message" command only the message appears, which is cleaner and clearer.

One of the enrichments that DOS-2 provides is a logical capability within batch commands. This means that batch command files can react to developing situations in a scaled-down version of the kind of logic that can be used in a computer program. There are four batch commands which are related to this logic capability—SHIFT, GOTO, IF, and FOR. As we mentioned before, the full glory of these commands is really an advanced topic beyond the range of this book, but we'll give you a sketch of what these commands can do.

Let's start with the SHIFT command. If you have a batch file which uses several of the % replacement parameters, the SHIFT command lets you move the parameters over, one by one, to make it easier to process the parameters. When a SHIFT is done, the parameter symbol %1 takes on the value that used to be %2, and %2 gets the value that used to belong to %3. So all the values are shifted over one place. This makes it more practical to have one batch file process a number of files fairly easily. The process works with one filename, taken from the %1 parameter, and then SHIFTs the list over to deal with the next filename. The real use of the SHIFT command comes when we use it with the GOTO and IF commands, which we'll explain in a moment. But to help you understand what SHIFT does, let's create an artificial example.

Suppose we want to create a batch file which will COPY a list of files. Let's say, for simplicity, that we want to be able to give it a list of any three filenames, and have it copy them from drive A to drive B. If the name of the batch file is 3COPY, and our file names are X, Y and Z, we want to copy them by just entering the command

```
3COPY  X Y Z
```

Here is what our "3COPY" batch file might look like using the SHIFT command:

```
COPY    A:%1 B:
SHIFT
COPY    A:%1 B:
SHIFT
COPY    A:%1 B:
```

Since each shift command moves the parameters over, the second and third COPY commands find the filenames Y and Z in the first parameter, or %1, location. It should be obvious to you that this example is a little artificial, since we could have just used %2 and %3 in the second and third COPY commands. But we are setting the stage for something more complex, where SHIFT makes more sense.

Will the example we showed copy exactly three files? What if we would like it to copy more files without a limit? In that case, we can set up a program *loop,* which will SHIFT and COPY forever. To do that we use the GOTO command, which will make the batch command loop around in circles. This time, let's see an example before the explanation:

```
:ONWARD
COPY A:%1  B:
SHIFT
GOTO ONWARD
```

The first line we see here, ":ONWARD" is a *label,* which is needed so that we can loop around in circles. The label begins with a colon to identify it, and it can have any symbolic name we want to use. I chose ONWARD but we could have used any other short name. The label, by the way, must be on a line by itself, just as we show it. Following the ONWARD label are our familiar COPY and SHIFT commands; the COPY does the work and the SHIFT command moves the % parameters over one, ready for the next COPY command. Then comes the GOTO command. The GOTO tells DOS to find the label that follows the GOTO command, and then to pick up processing from there. Since we GOTO ONWARD, DOS will go back up to where the ONWARD label is and continue from there.

What we have here is a loop, something that will make DOS go around in circles. Each time around, another file will be copied and then the parameter list will be shifted over one. As we have it in this example, this could go on forever, but naturally at some point we'll run out of filenames to copy. But the batch processing file will continue looping forever—with the copy command complaining that we aren't giving it any names to copy.

To keep this batch file loop from going on forever, we can use the IF command. The IF command will test some logical condition, and then if it is true it will carry out one command. One of the things that we can have the IF statement test for is if a file name exists. We might replace our GOTO ONWARD statement with this:

```
IF EXIST %1  GOTO ONWARD
```

This IF statement will test to see if there is a file with the name that the parameter %1 gives—if there is such a file, it will loop around to the ONWARD label and we'll continue merrily along. But if we've run out of filenames, then the IF won't loop back and the batch file will end.

There is more to the GOTO and the IF than we have seen so far. Our example of a GOTO skipped to a label that was earlier in the batch file, but it could just as easily have been later after the GOTO statement. Skipping to an earlier point in the file will set up a loop, while skipping forward will bypass some commands. Depending upon our needs, either direction of GOTO will work.

The IF statement can test for things other than the existence of a file. It can also test for two other conditions: one is to check to see if any program has reported trouble by signalling an *error code* to DOS. We test for these like this:

```
IF ERRORLEVEL 1 GOTO SOMEWHERE
```

The other kind of condition is a string comparison, which we can use to test for some particular parameter value. For example:

```
IF %1==FINISH  GOTO  SOMEWHERE
```

For all three kinds of IF conditions, there is a corresponding IF NOT condition.

There are more complicated details to the IF command that we can go into here—it becomes quite an advanced subject when you look at everything that IF can do. When you are ready for all the complications, check your computer's DOS manual for all the details.

There is one more advanced batch processing command which gives us another way to repeat commands: the FOR statement.

FOR lets us create a list of filenames, for example, and then repeat a command with each of the names in the list. It involves a symbolic variable, marked with two percent signs, "%%", and that variable is set to each of the items in the list in turn. Here is an example:

```
FOR %%NAME IN (A,B,C,D,E) DO  COPY A:%%NAME  B:
```

In the example, the COPY statement will be repeated with each of the names in the list—A,B,C,D,E—substituted for the symbolic variable %%NAME. In effect, this FOR command is translated into five separate COPY commands:

```
COPY A:A  B:
COPY A:B  B:
COPY A:C  B:
COPY A:D  B:
COPY A:E  B:
```

If you are ingenious, you can create some very clever batch processing files using the FOR command. It is also quite easy to create a mess with it since the whole process is rather tricky.

All of the advanced batch processing commands that we have covered here have their uses, but they certainly aren't for beginners. And there is some question about how useful they *really* might be for advanced users when everything is considered. A lot depends upon how much taste you have for trying complicated tricks. If it suits you, don't let me discourage you at all from trying it—just be careful.

11.4 Suggestions and Examples of Batch File Tricks

In this section we're going to show you some examples and tricks in using batch files. Let me warn you right away that some of the examples are a bit complicated, and it's possible that you might get lost as we go over them. If so, back off from them for a while and keep your own use of batch files simple and straightforward. Later, when you are ready for some of the messier tricks, you can come back to the more complicated examples.

Let's start this discussion of the uses of batch files with some philosophy— the philosophy of the black box. Roughly speaking, there are two ways of using a personal computer: expert and dumb-dumb. Experts know what they are doing (or think they do), and they usually enjoy being involved in the mechanics of how work gets done. Us dumb-dumbs don't really know what's going on, and probably don't care—we want the results and don't care to get involved in the mechanics of how it's done. For dumb-dumbs, computer operations need to work like what is called a black box; we don't need to see how the box gets its work done, as long as we are confident it is doing the work correctly. While it is very nice to have an expert's technical knowledge, for most users of computers the more the computer is a trustworthy black box, the better.

One of the features of DOS which can help make it work like a friendly black box is batch file commands. My reason for explaining this so elaborately is to instill in you the idea that batch files are more than just a convenient, efficient, and safe way to direct the computer's operations. Batch files are also a key way of building black boxes to help make the use of your computer less technical. When you understand this idea, it can guide you into making the best possible use of batch files. The key thing in making batch files work like black boxes is to write them in a style which makes them work as smoothly and as unobtrusively as possible.

Several features of DOS-2 help make this unobtrusive operation possible. One is the ECHO command, which lets you suppress the display of the commands that are being carried out. Another is the re-direction of output. Sometimes you need to include a command in a batch file, but really don't want to subject the computer user to whatever output it displays. A prime example of this is the CHKDSK command, which can clean up messy file allocation, left over from some programs. If you want to CHKDSK, but hide its report from the screen, the output can be re-directed like this:

```
CHKDSK >NUL
```

Notice that we sent the output of CHKDSK to the null device so that it is thrown away. This is a handy way to get rid of extraneous display output. On the other hand, it might be better not to throw the information away completely—if something has gone wrong, you might want to come back and look it over. So you might use a little catch-all file to store this information in, like this:

```
CHKDSK >CATCH.ALL
```

Two of the most useful things you can put into batch files are remarks and pauses, using the REM and PAUSE commands. It is surprisingly easy to lose track of exactly what you are doing. That sounds really dumb, but it's true— especially if you are doing the same thing over and over again. If you are, say, working your way through a list of files, then you might lose your place in the list. That problem can be solved by using the REM command to show you the parameters that your batch file is working with. Example? All my batch files that run my text editor end with this REM:

```
REM  Was editing the file named %1
```

And, of course, the parameter %1 shows me the file name.

The same thing can be done with the PAUSE command, but PAUSE has some extra advantages. If you are running something lengthy and automatic through a batch file, PAUSE can be used to suspend the operation so that you see the current screen display, and also decide whether or not to proceed with the rest of the batch file. If you don't want things to proceed, the *break* key will shut down the batch file command.

Pausing for approval to continue is a very important part of any batch file that does anything potentially dangerous. For example, you might have a series of programs which deliberately leave their work files on disk so that you can recover the data if anything goes wrong. In a batch file like this, you could have the last step of the batch file ERASE the files and then you could put a PAUSE just before the ERASE, giving you a chance to check that everything was all right before the files were destroyed.

On the subject of the ERASE command, if you use ERASE/DEL in a batch file it's a good idea to put a DIR command right before it so that you see a list of the files that are about to be erased. This is a nice safety feature since it keeps you in the know.

There are some commands in DOS which are very useful to use that are a nuisance to type in. With batch files, you can use them liberally with no effort at all since the batch file does all the work for you. One of the most important is the check disk command, CHKDSK. CHKDSK is useful to put in your batch commands for two reasons. First, it lets you know how much working space is left on your disk—and it is useful to see that often, so that you get early warning about running out of space. CHKDSK also inspects the disk for some logical damage (meaning scrambled data but not physical damage) on the diskette, and it's a good thing to do that frequently even though the scrambling isn't a common occurrence.

It is also quite handy to add the DIR command to most of your batch files. You can put in a specific command (indicating what files you want to know about) to see things like the file size and the files' date and timestamp. Examples: DIR %1 DIR *.BAS. You can also use the show-me-everything form of the DIR command just to see what's on the disk you are using. If you usually have a lot of files, the "-W" or "/W" switch, which is an option of the DIR command, will list them across the screen so that they take up fewer lines. Example:

```
DIR *.*
DIR *.* -W
DIR
```

With DOS-2, you can get the listing sorted so that they appear in alphabetic order which makes for easier reading. This is done with a pipeline combining DIR, SORT and MORE:

chg data Drive
p. Shop

DIR | SORT | MORE

There is a very simple, but very handy, batch file that I call BAA because of what it does with the default disk drive. Probably the most common set-up for DOS computers is to have two disk drives, A and B. And the most common and efficient way to use those drives is to dedicate drive A to holding programs, and drive B to holding data on which the programs work. Since it is usually more convenient for a program to use data from the default disk drive, the BAA batch file is designed to temporarily switch the default to drive B, execute the program (from drive A), and then switch the default back. For a program which we'll call XXX, the batch file would look like this:

```
B:        (switch the default to B)
A:XXX     (run XXX from drive A, but use B as the default data drive)
A:        (switch the default back to A, ready for the next task)
```

Naturally you would set up one of these batch files for each program that you wanted to use it for. The natural name to give the batch file would be a handy abbreviation of the name of the program. (You can't give the batch file the same name as the program since DOS looks for programs before it looks for batch files. With both a program file and a batch file with the same name— but different filename extensions—when you enter the name as a command, DOS will execute the program and bypass your batch file.)

On the other hand, if you prefer to use the name of the program as the command name that you use to activate a batch file like the BAA batch file, then you can use the RENAME command to change the program file to an alias name and then use the original name for your batch file.

Before we finish with the BAA batch file, we should note that you can easily set up a generic BAA file which uses a parameter to specify the program name. In this case, the BAA batch file would look like this:

```
B:
A:%1
A:
```

You could do this if you wanted to, but the main point of batch files—and of computers in general—is to make your work simpler and easier. It makes more sense to set up a separate batch file tailored to the needs of each particular program that you run. In fact, it is likely that each program's batch execution file will have more in it than the BAA file shown above; what else will be in there depends upon what you need to help you best use your programs.

Closely related to the BAA batch file is a trick that you can use to make it easier and more convenient to make backup copies of your data. The most common operating style, for computers with two diskette drives, is to use the A drive for diskettes full of programs (and batch files); the B drive is dedicated to data that the programs work on. Now, how do you make backup copies of that data? The only sensible way to do it is to leave the data diskette where it is, in drive B, and change the program diskette in drive A for the diskette you use to back up the data in drive B. Now there are two convenient ways to use batch files to supervise this backup copying: one is under manual control and the other is fully automatic.

The manual control way of making backup copies is to place a batch file on the backup diskette. The only task of this batch file is to copy from B to A like this:

```
COPY    B:*.*    A:*.*
```

This is the straightforward backup operation; you might give it a command name of SAVE or just S for short. When the computer is being used by someone who knows when a backup copy of the data is needed, then this simple method is best. But there is a more elaborate method, which adds an element of idiot-proofing to the backup operation. This is the fully automatic backup procedure mentioned above.

The automatic method makes use of batch-file chaining so it gives us an opportunity to see how chaining is done. Let's set the stage with a little explanation, seeing what we want to do, so that you can better understand the chaining trick. For the backup method mentioned above, the knowledgeable computer user removed a program diskette from drive A, replaced it with a backup diskette, entered the command SAVE, and then switched back to the program diskette. But our user had to know what steps to follow. To idiot-proof the backup operation (as much as we can), we'd like a batch file to lead us by the hand in the steps to be done, and that's what we'll explain here.

The first part of this scheme, the first link in the chain, is the batch file that was already being used on the program diskette in drive A. (Recall that the point of this operation is to backup new data after the end of a program operation—so we can assume that our computer user was using a program, and naturally we expect that a batch file was being used to run the program.) At the end of that batch file, we place a command to switch over to another batch file that is located on the data diskette in drive B, which will be the second link in our chain of batch files. That batch file has to have a command name (which is the filename minus the.BAT extension), so we'll call it AUTO-SAVE. The last line in the batch file that was being used on the program diskette will switch control over to AUTOSAVE, like this:

```
B:AUTOSAVE
```

Notice the "B:" part, which is important. The current default drive at this point should be drive A, so we have to specifically tell DOS to look to drive B for the AUTOSAVE command.

Now, why are we chaining to another batch file? Why don't we just continue using the batch file in drive A for whatever we need to do? For one simple reason: we're about to remove the program diskette from drive A, and DOS wouldn't be able to find the instructions inside the batch file. So, temporarily, we switch our base of operations, the location of our batch file, over to drive B. This is the heart of our chaining trick.

What will be inside this AUTOSAVE batch file? Two things: one is the working part, a COPY command to copy the data from the master data diskette in drive B to the backup diskette in drive A. The other thing that will be in the AUTOSAVE batch file is the idiot-proofing, in the form of simple instructions to the computer user of what to do; this we do with PAUSE commands. Our AUTOSAVE batch file looks like this:

```
PAUSE Place the data back-up diskette in drive A
COPY  B:*.*  A:*.*
PAUSE Replace the program diskette in drive A
```

To match your particular needs, the comments in the two PAUSE statements can be more specific; they can use your terminology for the particular diskettes to be used with drive A. For example, they could say "accounting data back-up" and "accounting programs," or whatever is appropriate.

What happens after the second PAUSE statement in this AUTOSAVE command file? Since the default drive is A, DOS gives the prompt for drive A, and our computer user at the keyboard can enter the next command. On the other hand, we could add a third link to this chain of batch files by putting the name of a batch command as the fourth and last line of AUTOSAVE. Then DOS would take off executing that batch file, and things would be even more automatic. If we wanted to, the name of this command on the last line of AUTOSAVE could be a parameter (like %1), so that the command line that invoked AUTOSAVE would also indicate what was supposed to be done when AUTOSAVE was done. With this trick of passing the name of the next command as a parameter to AUTOSAVE, you could have one universal form of AUTOSAVE batch file that you could use with every one of your program and data diskettes. If you wanted to, you could write a custom AUTOSAVE batch file for each different use—or you could use the universal form with its parameter. Use whichever technique better suits your operation.

This example of chaining batch files for the purpose of backing up data should give you an idea of how command chaining can be used to add more automation to your computer operations. Commands can be chained from diskette to diskette (as we did in setting up AUTOSAVE), or they can work on the same diskette. There is less reason to chain commands when you are not switching diskettes, since any command that you chain on the same diskette could be included in one command file. But that's a matter of taste and style. Some people might prefer to do lengthy operations as a chain of commands, and others might prefer to use one large command file. The result is the same. But where batch file chaining really pays off is in allowing you to switch diskettes and still keep operating under the automatic control of batch files.

Besides all the handy things that you can put inside of batch files, there are some very useful things you can do outside them—that is, how you name and organize them.

One of the handiest of these is what I call the A-B-C trick. Many of the things we do with our computers have a logical series of steps. For example, if you are writing programs, the first step might be to use your text editor to do the writing, while the second and third steps would be compiling the program and then testing it. Another example is when you are writing a letter or report. There the first step is composing the letter, and the second would be to check its spelling; the third step would be to re-edit it for corrections. For each of these steps you'll set up a batch file to supervise it. You could give each of these steps meaningful names like EDIT, COMPILE, and TEST. It is a very good idea to give batch files simple meaningful command names. But on the other hand, for quick convenience, we could just as easily name these steps A, B, and C, or 1, 2, and 3. There are two advantages to the A-B-C trick: the command names are shorter and quicker to key in, and it is easier to combine them and remember the names of the combinations. There is a logical progression to the steps we go through, and our batch files can simply number the steps 1, 2, 3 or letter them A, B, C. If our edit step is named A, and our compile step is named B, then a batch file to do both edit and compile would be named AB, which can be easy to remember and key in. There is one obvious disadvantage to the A-B-C trick: you have to remember that A means EDIT (or whatever), and so forth. This can be confusing to your co-workers, or even to yourself. But when you won't have any trouble keeping track of the meaning of the steps, then A-B-C is a good way to go.

To show you how far this can go and how useful it can become, take a look at what I do when I write Pascal programs. There are actually five separate steps to creating a Pascal program (for your interest, they are edit, 1st stage compile, 2nd stage compile, link edit, and then test run the completed program). I have separate batch files for each step (which I happen to name 1 through 5 because it suits me), and then lots of different combination batch files. Depending upon the kind of program I'm writing, it makes sense to use different combinations of the five steps. Sometimes I do step 1 by itself, and at other times I combine steps 1 and 2. Other combinations are handy at other times. By having a batch file for each step by itself, and as many combinations as I find useful, I'm in full control of what is going on when I write these programs—and its all quick and convenient for me. The same idea can be applied to any multi-step operation that you do. The more complicated the steps, the greater the advantage in setting-up A-B-C type batch files to supervise them.

There is one further handy thing you can do with A-B-C, and that is to create parallel batch files for tasks that are similar in general, but different in detail. To use the example of programming again, I happen to write programs in three languages—Pascal, assembly, and BASIC. For each of them, I have the same set up of batch command names—so that for me editing a program is always done with the command named 1, and the compile or assemble is always begun with the command named 2. What the command "1" actually does is different in each case, but what it means to me is always the same—it means let me use my text editor to write a program. The same thing applies to writing a letter or to writing this chapter. Everywhere, the first step, which I call "1", is to use my editor to compose something—a letter, a program, or a part of this book. The next step after that is step "2" and it's quite different depending upon what I'm doing—for writing, step "2" is a spelling check, while for programming, step "2" runs a compiler or assembler. But *as I use them*, these numbered batch processing steps make perfect sense, since they follow the natural progression of whatever work I am doing.

Another handy trick with batch files is to have different versions lying around in waiting. Why would you want to do that? Let me use my programming as an example again. Sometimes I do my programming work on ordinary diskettes; other times it is handy for me to move everything onto an electronic disk. And finally, when I work on my biggest programs, I need to use both an electronic disk and ordinary diskettes. So I keep three versions of my main programming batch files. Now there are two ways to handle this, and one of them I think is a really nifty trick.

The first way is to have all three versions active at once, under slightly different names. For example, my step one, named "1", could have its diskette version named "1D", and the electronic disk version named "1E". While this puts them all on tap at once, it means that I have to remember which version I'm using and keep entering that form of the command name. That's clumsy and error prone. But the second way uses a foxy trick to solve the problem.

The trick is to keep all three versions around under the same command name, but with an alias for a filename extension. So my electronic version of the "1" command would be in a file named 1.ELE. Now, as you know, batch files have to have the extension BAT, so this ELE file can't be used as it is—but it can be moved into place very easily. With a simple COPY command, all ELE batch files can be activated:

```
COPY *.ELE  *.BAT
```

does the trick. Each of my three versions of my batch files is kept with its own distinct extension name. Then each set is activated by an appropriate COPY command, which makes it the current working version and overrides whatever version was working before. And I don't have to use any different command names—the names stay the same but different versions take effect. Naturally I don't type in the COPY commands—another series of batch files do that for me.

Since the real magic of using batch processing files comes from tailoring them to your own needs, our suggestions and examples can only scratch the surface of the possibilities, and can only hint at some of the things that you can accomplish on your own through the creative use of batch files.

There is almost nothing in the use of DOS that will reward your efforts like the rewards of speed, convenience, and safety that you can gain by making full use of batch files.

12

Odds and Ends You Need to Know

In this chapter we'll cover an assortment of useful and interesting things to know. Some of them will be new topics, and some of them will be new perspectives on items that we have already looked at before.

12.1 Finding Out What's at Your Command

It isn't always obvious what your computer can do for you, especially when you are first getting to know it. So here is a quick summary of what *commands* you can ask your computer to carry out at any given time.

Recall that as DOS sees things there are two kinds of commands that it can be asked to carry out—what DOS knows as *internal* commands and *external* commands. The internal commands are built right into DOS so they are always ready for us to use. The external commands are performed by programs which are kept on disk, so they are only ready for us to use when we have a disk mounted which has a copy of the command program.

While the internal commands are always ready for us to use, there is one very minor disadvantage to them, at least for the beginner—there is no simple, straightforward way to have your computer tell you what their names are. With external commands there's a simple way to learn their names, which we'll come to in a moment, but not for the internal commands.

Here, for reference, is a list of the internal commands that you can expect to have on tap at all times. The exact list varies with the specific version of DOS and also varies somewhat from computer to computer, but this is the basic list. For all versions of DOS:

COPY	makes copies of disk files
DATE	displays and sets DOS's record of the date
DEL	deletes (erases) disk files
DIR	lists the files on a disk
ERASE	erases (deletes) disk files
PAUSE	used in batch files to stop and display messages
REM	used in batch files to display messages

REN   renames files; changes their filenames
TIME   displays and sets DOS's record of the time
TYPE   displays the contents of a disk file on the display screen

DOS-2 versions only:

BREAK   controls how often DOS checks for break, Control-C
CHDIR   changes which directory is the current one on each disk
CLS   clears the display screen
CTTY   puts DOS into remote control by re-directing the "console"
ECHO   turns command echoing on and off and displays messages
FOR   used in advanced batch files to work through a list of files
GOTO   used in advanced batch files for looping and skipping
IF   used in advanced batch files to test for logical conditions
MKDIR   creates a new sub-directory on a disk
PATH   tells DOS where to search for external command programs
PWD   displays the current working directory name

REMEMBER THE DIFFERENCE BETWEEN EXTERNAL
AND INTERNAL COMMANDS.

RMDIR	removes a sub-directory from a disk
SET	sets environmental equations that can control programs
SHIFT	used in advanced batch files to work through the parameters
VER	displays which version of DOS is being used
VERIFY	makes DOS double check all data written to disks
VOL	displays the volume identification label from a disk

In a sense we have to memorize the list of internal commands that are available, because DOS doesn't have a simple way of displaying their names for us. Of course this isn't much of a problem, since we have the use of this book and our computer's manuals to give us a list of the internal commands. Also, any commands that we'll be using much, we will learn quickly. But it is nice to be able to display a list of what commands are available, and we can do this with the external commands.

You'll recall that the external commands, which reside on our disks, are either true programs or else they are batch file commands, which are files that list a series of commands that we want carried out together. We can identify programs and batch files on our disks by their filename extensions. (For a review of filename extensions, see Chapter 9.) Programs are stored on disks in two forms, known by their extension names as *COM* and *EXE*. Batch files always have an extension of BAT. Together, these three extensions cover all the ground on the commands that can be on a disk.

If we have a disk in one of our computer's drives, for example drive B, we can find out the commands on that disk by doing three DIR-directory listings. We need to do the DIR command three times if we want to see all of the commands that might possibly be on that disk. Here is how to do it:

```
DIR B:*.BAT
DIR B:*.COM
DIR B:*.EXE
```

In our example we looked at the B-drive, but we could have specified any of the computer's drives; or we could have used DOS's current default drive. In each of the DIR commands we used an asterisk (*) for the filename part, because we wanted to see any and all names which matched the extension that we were specifying.

If you have a diskette—one you have made up or one which you have been given—and you are not sure how you can use it, these three DIR commands are very good to give you a quick peek at what commands are set up on the diskette. In the next chapter, by the way, we'll go over some advice on what you should do about setting up commands on your diskettes.

There is one special case which you will run across when you get a listing of the COM-program files. There is a special COM file, named COMMAND.COM, which is actually part of DOS itself and not a separate command that you can execute. If you list the COM files on a disk and see COMMAND.COM among the program command files, *don't* try to enter COMMAND as a command—you may throw DOS into a tizzy. Incidentally, COMMAND.COM is a program file that contains all the internal commands, such as COPY and

DIR. In the next chapter we'll learn some practical things about COMMAND
.COM.

Before we finish with this section, there is one loose end we should take care
of. You know that external commands are invoked by using their filename. But
there are three different filename extensions that could be used with a command file: BAT, COM, and EXE. With the different extensions, you could
possibly have three different command files, *each with the same filename* and the
same command name. Of course we shouldn't have two or three command files
with the same command name. That would be a rather stupid thing to do. If
you do, though, DOS will only find and carry out one of them. You might
expect that DOS would simply use the first one it finds, with any of the three
extensions, but as far as I know DOS sets a priority among the three—first
COM, then EXE, then BAT. You shouldn't play around with this, though.

12.2 Throwing Things Away and Other Information on Devices

We've mentioned a few times earlier in this book the devices that DOS works
with other than your disk drives. Devices are parts of the computer which can
be *talked* to—that is, which can send data, or receive data, or both. In this
section, we'll look a little more at devices and what you can reasonably do with
them.

The easiest way to understand what devices are on your computer is to
consider the computer's keyboard, and its display screen. If you think of them
separately, the keyboard is something that the computer can take information
from; DOS can "read" what we type on the keyboard, so from the computer's
viewpoint the keyboard is an *input* device. The display screen is just the
opposite. The computer can "write" information onto the display screen, but it
can't read from it. So the keyboard is a model example of an *input* device, and
the display screen is an example of an *output* device. If we put the two together
and think of them as *two halves of one device*, we have a model of a two-way
input and output device.

The disks in your computer are quite different. While the computer can both
read and write information on the disk, the disk isn't really *one* single place to
read or write information—because a disk can have any number of files stored
on it, each of which can be read or written. So a disk is quite different from our
keyboard or our display screen. A disk is something with many independent
sources of input and output, but all of them connected in one logical way—
they all are accessed through a *disk drive*.

This short explanation gives us a working idea of what *devices* are, and can
be, to DOS. A device is some part of the computer which can be read from or
written to. If it is like a disk drive, with many potential data paths in it, then
DOS calls it a *block device*. Block device is a technical term which really doesn't
concern us here. All other devices are called *character devices*, because DOS can
read or write characters to and from them *in the name of the device itself*. For a
disk, a block device, DOS has to find a file on that device to do any reading or
writing of information. But with a character device, DOS can talk directly to it.

According to the way that DOS works, all disk-like block devices are identified by a letter of the alphabet, followed by a colon, such as "A:" and "B:". This is the way we refer to our computers one or more disk devices.

Usually our computers have a *real* disk drive for every block device that our DOS uses, but it doesn't have to be that way. As we saw in Chapter 4, if your computer has only one disk drive, the A-drive, then DOS will create an imaginary B-drive, mostly so that you can copy files from one diskette to another and keep the two diskettes distinct. When DOS does this, your one real diskette drive is treated as the A-drive and then the B-drive alternately. Every time DOS makes the switch from one to the other, it tells us to change the diskettes so that they are kept distinct.

There are other ways to have more working disks than there are real disk drives on our computer. One way is for the computer to use part of its memory as a simulated disk drive; this is usually called an *electronic* disk, or a *RAM disk* (meaning a memory disk). The point of an electronic disk is that it works as fast as the memory in our computer, which will be five or ten times faster than an ordinary diskette. We'll cover some of the interesting and practical points about electronic disks in Chapter 16.

Besides the disk-type block devices, DOS has a number of character devices which we can use. Some of them are really there, just as our disk drives are really there, and some of them are valuable trickery like the B-drive on a computer which has only one real disk drive. Let's see what some of these character devices are, and what we can do with them.

One of the most interesting character devices is a fake one called NUL. NUL is a dead-end, or black hole device, that is used to swallow up data that we want to throw away. Why would we want to throw information away? Well, a program may be generating some information that we just don't need, and we don't want it cluttering up our display screen or our computer's printer. If we wrote the program ourselves, we could make the program just not generate the information in the first place; but most of the programs that we use, we didn't write—so someone else set the rules for when data is generated and when it is not. If a program generates data, *and if the program gives us a choice of where to send the data,* we can tell the program to send the data to the black hole called NUL. DOS creates this phantom device called NUL for just this purpose—as an easy way to discard information. So whenever you need to discard data that a program is generating send it to NUL.

DOS-2 users will recall from Chapter 8, that standard output from a program, which normally goes to the display screen, can be re-directed by using the ">" symbol. If you want to make this information just disappear, you can send it to the NUL device by specifying ">NUL". It will disappear without a trace.

We mentioned before that character devices can be read from for input, or written to for output, or they may have both input and output ability. The phantom NUL device is actually an input/output device. If a program must read data from somewhere, and you want to give it *no data at all,* then you can tell it to read its information from NUL. When a program reads information from any character device, the program is prepared to get an end-of-data or

DATA DISAPPEARS INTO THE BLACK HOLE OF NUL.

end-of-file signal at some point. We discussed the end-of-file marker on disk files in Chapter 9, and we discussed how it can be signaled from the keyboard in Chapter 7. When any program tries to read data from the NUL device, all it gets is an end-of-file signal.

As you can see, the NUL device can be very useful for discarding output information or creating a dummy and empty set of input data. You are likely to find times when you want to use NUL as a destination for your output data; but don't be surprised if you rarely have any occasion to use NUL as an input device—but even if you don't need it, you should know that it is there. DOS-2 users will see a similarity with their use of re-direction; re-directing output is fairly common, and re-directing input is much rarer. Both ways of working are there for us to use if we need them.

NUL is a dummy, or phantom device, but our computers have real character devices as well. The most important one is called the console, or CON. The CON device is the man-machine interface—it's the combination of our keyboard (for input) and our display screen (for output). The CON device is the one that DOS uses all the time to talk to us. Many programs take their input

YOUR PRINTER IS PRN OR LPT1; YOUR TELEPHONE IS AUX OR COM1.

from the CON keyboard and write out their output to the CON display screen, and they do this without asking us for permission. Sometimes programs let us choose where data is to come from or go to. These are the occasions when we can direct it to the NUL device, as mentioned above, or direct it to the CON console.

If we tell a program to send its output to CON (instead of to our printer, or to a disk file), then it will appear on the display screen. Likewise, if we tell a program to read its data from CON, then it will take in whatever we type on the keyboard. Remember, by the way, that programs usually expect an end-of-file signal to tell them that there is no more data to be read. If we are entering data on the keyboard, we can key in an end-of-file signal by entering the Control-Z code—we hold down the *control* shift key and press the Z letter key. This gives the program an end-of-file indicator.

While the CON is the character device that we use the most, it isn't the only one. If we have a communications adapter on our computer, it will have a device name. Several different names are used for this: AUX (short for auxiliary device) is most often used; another device name for the communications line is COM1 (for communications line number 1). If our computer can have more than one communications line, they would be referred to as COM1, COM2, and so forth. Usually there is only one line but there could be more. Like the console, the communications lines, AUX, COM1, and so forth, can be used for both input and output.

Computers commonly have printers attached to them to make a permanent written copy of any information we need. Like the communications line, the printer has several names. The universal name is PRN (short for printer), while LPT1, LPT2, and so forth are used when you have more than one printer line; LPT is short for line printer, which for us means the same thing as a printer. Naturally the printer is a one-way output device and it can't be used as an input device, unlike the CON console and the AUX communications line.

There are two common ways to connect a small computer and a printer. These two ways are known as *serial* and *parallel*. The difference is technical, and has to do with whether data is sent to the printer one bit at a time (serial), or with several bits that make up a character all sent out at once (parallel). The difference concerns us for only two reasons. One is when we buy a computer and a printer, we have to make sure that we get the right compatible combination. The other is that *serial* printer connections usually talk to the computer's communications device, whose name is AUX, or COM1. The practical significance is that you may have to refer to your printer as the AUX device, *not* as the PRN device. It will work just the same, but you may have to use another name for it. If you don't know which way your printer is hooked up, you can probably find out by simply experimenting—send some data to PRT and to AUX, and see which appears on your printer.

12.3 The Importance of Where You Are

Sometimes you need to know where you are and sometimes you don't. On your computer, where you are really means the current disk location that DOS is working with. There are two different senses to this, one which applies to all versions of DOS and one which applies only to DOS-2.

In all versions of DOS, DOS keeps track of the *current disk* or *default* disk drive. The current default disk drive is where DOS goes looking for disk files, unless it is specifically told to look elsewhere. If we enter a command like this:

```
EDLIN
```

DOS will look on the current disk drive for the command program file to carry out that command. On the other hand, if we specifically want it to look somewhere else for the command, we can tell DOS this way:

```
B:EDLIN
```

This rule, that DOS goes looking on the current disk drive unless told otherwise, applies to both programs that we invoke by entering their names as commands and also to the data files that those programs use.

The practical significance of this is that many programs will work or won't work, depending upon whether you have the default drive set to where the program's data is located. Once you have worked with a program for a while, you will learn what it needs and whether it follows the direction of the current default drive, or whether it demands that its data be on certain specific disk drives. Incidentally, programs that specify which drives their data must be on can be a real nuisance because they reduce the flexibility of your computer operations. (We'll see more about this in Chapters 16, 17, and 20.) If you have the source code for a program, then you may be able to remove any references to specific disk drives. Often this is possible with programs written for the BASIC interpreter since their source code is usually available. Even for other programs you may be able to remove the use of specific disk drives, as we'll see in Chapter 20 on the DEBUG command.

For DOS-2 the same idea applies, except that it is enriched by the idea of a *current directory.* You'll recall from Chapter 8 that when DOS-2 goes looking for data files, it not only looks on the current disk it also looks in just the current directory on that disk. For many practical purposes, each sub-directory on a disk acts very much like a completely separate disk; if a data file isn't in that directory, it won't be found, even though it is somewhere on the same disk.

The main thing we have to say here is that it can matter to your programs where the current disk location is, so it should matter to you. To help you keep track of where the current default disk is, the prompt that DOS displays gives the drive letter. For example:

    A: or A>   or B: or B>

As you'll recall, you change the default drive by entering a drive letter (and the colon that goes with it) as a command by itself. DOS will acknowledge the change by responding with a prompt that has the new drive letter in it.

For DOS-2, we aren't automatically told the current *directory* over and over again, as we are told the current drive. To find out the current directory, we use the CHDIR or PWD commands. If your version of DOS-2 has the PWD command (not all of them do), then PWD will display the current directory location. Otherwise, the CHDIR command will show it; CHDIR really serves two functions: one is to change the current directory, if we specify a new one. The other is to display the current directory name, similar to what PWD does; to use CHDIR to display the current directory, rather than change it, we enter the CHDIR command, with no directory parameter.

You will find that the current disk location is significant with more programs than you might expect. If you have something like an accounting program, you naturally expect that it will be using data files, so it may make use of the current directory. But many complex programs also use data files to hold supplements to the program, such as help screens and a kind of program fragment called an overlay. So even if a program doesn't use data files that you know of, it may be looking to the current disk for some of these supplementary files.

When you start using a program that is new to you, you should expect that there will be a learning period during which you not only find out how to

DO YOU KNOW WHERE YOUR DOS IS ?

work with the program, but you also learn how to make the program work effectively with your computer. Integrating a new program into your computer operations really involves a two-way fit—fitting yourself and the program together, and fitting your computer and the program together. Part of this process of fitting new programs into your computer's operations involves things like where the programs expect to find their data (and where you would prefer it to be). Be prepared for this adjustment period; if you don't expect it, or if you try to take shortcuts around it, you may make things worse for yourself. We'll see some more about this in the next few chapters.

12.4 Programs You Ought to Have

You probably have a pretty good idea of the main programs that you need for your computer. These are the application programs that take care of the tasks that you want to perform on your computer. You don't need me to tell you to get those programs—you already know about them. But there are other programs which you might not know about but that you almost certainly need for your system.

One is a selective copy program. This kind of program is like the COPY command that comes with DOS, but with an interesting difference—it can select what it copies. One of the main reasons for using a program like this is to copy only the files which have been changed. The heaviest use that we are likely to make of the COPY command is in backing up our data from a master disk to a backup disk. With a lot of data, this operation can be more time consuming than necessary, particularly when only some of the data has been changed. A good selective copy program can check the time stamp on each file, and only bother to copy the files which have been changed. For my work, I use the JET program from Tall Trees Systems, which works on the IBM Personal Computer. Similar programs ought to be available for your computer. You should look for a selective copy program that operates on your particular DOS computer.

Other important kinds of programs that you need to get are file recovery programs. These are programs which restore disk files that you have lost, due to erasure (a horrifyingly common problem) or damage to the diskette. DOS-2 includes a RECOVER program which will re-construct a garbled disk direc-tory, which is quite a bit of help for damaged diskettes, but RECOVER is not all that you need. Since erasing files is the biggest problem, you should be sure to get a program to recover erased files. For my work, I use my own program, called UnErase, which works on the IBM Personal Computer; there are also other programs for undoing an erasure, and you should be sure to get one that works on your DOS computer.

You may be puzzled at the idea that an erased file can be recovered, but it can be. The reason is simple—when a file is erased, the data isn't destroyed or overwritten, it is simply "thrown away." This is analogous to taking a file folder out of your filing cabinet and tossing the pages in the waste basket. If the waste basket hasn't been emptied, you could dig through it to find the pages from the file folder. It works the same way with disk data. When a file is erased from disk, the disk space where the data is stored is taken away from the erased file and placed in the pool of available space on the disk. If no other file has used that space, then the data is still there and it can be recovered. If you use an "un-erase" program right after an inadvertent erasure, you should be able to completely recover all of your data.

The first line of defense for your data is to make backup copies, and the second line of defense is to be very careful about operations which can destroy your data (erasing, formatting, copying). But an essential third line of defense is file recovery programs, such as an un-erase program, and other file recovery tools. So look for this kind of program, and be sure to get them before you need them. File recovery programs are like insurance policies—you have to get them before you need them, not after.

In general, you shouldn't be stingy in acquiring programs. Besides the pro-grams that you know you will need, there are probably plenty of handy auxiliary programs that can make your work easier or more efficient or, as in the case of file recovery programs, safer. It is probably a worthwhile investment to buy any auxiliary programs that you think might be useful to you, provided you can afford them. After all, you have invested a significant amount of money in a computer to augment your work, and you would be foolish to pinch pennies on programs which can help with that work. Some of the pennies you spend on auxiliary programs will be wasted—but the real value to you of the programs that turn out to be useful will make up for it.

13

Handy Tricks

In this chapter we're going to look at some things you can do to help make your use of the computer easier and smoother. Tricks of the trade, if you will.

13.1 Setting Up Your Disks and DOS

One of the most important things you will do in learning how to make effective use of your computer is to figure out how to get your disks organized. If you do it right, your work will be smooth and the operation easy and sensible. If you do it wrong, it will add a large measure of clumsiness to how your computer works for you. In this section and the next we're going to look at the main tricks of being effectively organized in your disks. There are two main parts to the business of organizing your disks—how you fit DOS into them, and how you organize the rest of your files.

Whenever we mentioned the FORMAT command in Chapter 3 on getting started, and in Chapter 5 on elementary DOS commands, we noted that there are two ways you can FORMAT a disk—with DOS or without. Our general advice was to always include DOS in the formatting, but now it's time to get down to the details of what that means.

DOS breaks down into two parts: all the commands that DOS gives us (like the FORMAT command) and *DOS itself*. The core of DOS, or DOS itself, is loaded into memory from disk when we start up, or "boot," the system. On disk, DOS itself is kept in not one but three distinct files. It is these three files which make the difference between a *system-formatted* disk and an ordinary disk. We can start up DOS with a system-formatted disk, but we can't with an ordinary disk. When we use the FORMAT command to prepare a disk, we use the S-switch, written "-S" or "/S", to indicate that we want system formatting, that we want the three files of DOS itself on the disk.

What are these three files? They are two hidden system files and one ordinary, visible file which is named COMMAND.COM. The two hidden system files have special names (which differ from computer to computer), which we really don't need to know since we can't even see the names because they are hidden from us.

Why there are two hidden files and not just one isn't of any practical importance to us, but the reason is interesting. There are parts of DOS which are quite universal, and which apply to every computer that uses DOS; there are other parts which have to be tailored to the exact specifics of each particular computer. To make it easier to create and maintain DOS, the two parts are separated into distinct program files. In technical terms, the universal part provides the DOS services, and the computer-specific part provides the BIOS services. There is one reason why we need to know that there are two different hidden files: when we use the CHKDSK command to report on a disk's condition, it will report the two hidden files, if the disk is a system disk. So CHKDSK is an easy way to see if a disk is system-formatted; if there are two hidden files the disk is a system disk, and if not, it's not.

DOS-2 users have an opportunity to create a third hidden file, if they use the V-switch to put a volume label on the disk when it is formatted. So, with DOS-2, there are four possibilities in the number of hidden files that CHKDSK will report:

Number of hidden files	Labeled?	System disk?
0	un-labeled	non-system
1	labeled	non-system
2	un-labeled	system
3	labeled	system

The third of the files that make up DOS itself is COMMAND.COM, which is the command processor. The command processor has the smarts to interpret the command lines that we enter on the keyboard, or that are read from a batch file. The command processor also contains the programs that actually carry out each of the internal commands. (The external commands, as you recall, are carried out by programs which have to be loaded from disk each time they are used.)

There is a very special reason why the command processor COMMAND .COM is an ordinary file, and not a hidden file like the two other parts of DOS itself. To understand why, we need some background information. When all three parts of DOS are loaded into memory, they take up quite a bit of memory space. For computers which have plenty of memory, this isn't very important, but for computers which are short on memory this can be a significant problem—it might leave too little room for some of our larger programs.

The solution to this problem is to make part of DOS only provisionally resident in memory. The command processor is needed when we are entering commands, but it is not needed after DOS has loaded a program and the program is running. So the command processor is made provisionally resident in memory to free some memory space, while the rest of DOS stays permanently resident. What does "provisionally resident" mean? It means that if the space is needed, the command processor is erased from memory and the space is used for other programs; but if the space isn't needed, then the command processor is left in memory ready to be used again.

But what happens when the command processor is kicked out of memory? The command processor is needed again after the end of the program that took up its space. This means that DOS has to get a fresh copy of the

USE CHKDSK TO SEE HOW YOUR DISKETTES ARE FORMATTED.

command processor back into memory—so it goes looking to its disks, to find the COMMAND.COM file, in order to reload the command processor.

This all boils down to one practical significance—we may have to have a copy of COMMAND.COM on many of our disks, *even if those disks aren't system-formatted disks.*

Does all this sound confusing? Let's step through it again, and then we'll get down to the practical recommendations.

First, to *start* DOS you have to use a *system-formatted* disk. That system-formatted disk will have copies of the two hidden system files and also a copy of COMMAND.COM. After DOS is running, we won't need a system-formatted disk again. How do we identify a system-formatted disk? If CHKDSK reports that a disk has two (or more) hidden files, then it is system-formatted.

Second, when we run our programs, we may or may not have plenty of room for them and all of DOS as well. If we *do* have enough room, then we'll never need anything special on our working disks. But if we *don't* have enough room, the command processor, COMMAND.COM, will be kicked out of memory. When the program that swept COMMAND.COM out of memory is done, DOS will have to load the command processor again—and that means that we'll need to have COMMAND.COM on our disks, *whether or not* the disks are also system-formatted.

With this information at our command, we can work out what the practical details of maintaining our disks are. The handiest thing, if it is otherwise practical, is to have every disk system-formatted. If every disk is system-formatted, then any disk can be used to start DOS and every disk will have COMMAND.COM on it, whenever DOS might need it.

There is a reason why it may not be practical to make every disk system-formatted. Having DOS on a disk can take up a sizable fraction of the disk space—even as much as 25 percent; usually it's a smaller proportion, perhaps 10 percent, but it still is a good chunk of disk space. When we load up our disks with what we want on them—and we'll come to advice on that in the next section—we may run out of room. Not having the disk system-formatted may provide just enough extra space to make room for what we want.

So here is our advice so far: start out with every disk system-formatted. Later, as your experience grows, decide on which ones can afford the space. If you have some disks system-formatted and some that are not, then you will probably be better off doing one of two things: either have *one* single "master boot" disk, which you use only for starting up DOS, *or* try to have every working disk system-formatted, and then specially mark the ones that aren't, so you won't try to "boot" DOS from them.

If you create disks that aren't system-formatted, put a copy of COMMAND .COM on each of them, unless you know that you have enough memory to not need it. How much memory is enough? Here is a simple rule of thumb: 64K is *not* enough; 512K is enough and 256K is very likely enough; 128K or 196K may or may not be enough, depending upon the size of the programs that you use. Experience will show you if you actually have enough memory, or if you need COMMAND.COM on your disks. If DOS goes looking for COMMAND.COM and doesn't find it, then DOS will complain to you with a message such as "Insert COMMAND.COM disk." This message will tell you two things: one is that you don't have enough memory to keep the command processor resident, and the other is that your disks don't have COMMAND .COM on them. The way to tell if DOS looks for COMMAND.COM when it is there (and there will not be an error message) is if the disk is used briefly between the end of a program and the appearance of DOS's command prompt.

After that comes our practical advice on what to put on our disks, and how to treat data differently from programs, which we'll cover in the next section.

13.2 More On Setting Up Your Disks

The next thing we want to look at is what to put on your disks—and this raises two special issues: how many disk drives you have, and the distinction between programs and data.

When we're doing something on our computers, we want to have everything that we need right at hand. This means all the programs that relate to what we are doing, and all of the data as well. That much is clear enough, but how do we organize the programs and data? That depends upon how many disk drives we have.

If our computer has only one disk drive, then we need to squeeze all the necessary programs and data onto one disk in order to have it all accessible to the computer. It is very unwise to have only one disk drive on a computer, for many reasons, and it is likely that yours has two or more. (If it doesn't, I hope it's likely that you will dash out and get another disk drive—you'll be glad you did.) If you do have only one disk drive, here is the special approach you need to take: a real shortage of disk space will be your greatest problem. To help alleviate this problem, you should make the subject matter of each disk as small as possible. Give each disk some functional identity, a subject matter, and gather together the programs and data needed to cover that use. Since it is likely that you will be cramped on each disk (and since you need some growth room on each disk), you should try hard to keep the requirements small. If you

PROGRAM DISKS AND DATA DISKS: KEEP THEM APART.

can, keep perhaps a third of each disk's space open for the growth of the data you use with the disk. On the other hand, if it is not possible for you to squeeze both programs and data together on one disk, then you will have to work as though you had two disk drives, which will mean that you will have to switch your disks back and forth.

When you have two disk drives, it is best to distinctly divide your disks into program disks and data disks. The program disks are placed in your computer's A-drive, and the data disks are placed in the B-drive. In fact, you will find that most programs are oriented to working in this pattern so they will fit in nicely with this way of organizing the disks, and they will tend to fight back if you use them any other way.

Among the many practical reasons why it is best to keep programs and data files on separate, distinct disks is that your program disks are fairly stable—once you work out the right combinations of programs, you seldom make changes to the program disks. However, the information on the data disks will be changed as often as you update your information. Since you should keep duplicate backup copies of your data, it will be cleaner and simpler with the data completely isolated from other files.

Most DOS computers have no more than two disk drives, but if your computer has three or more, then you have a more complex choice of how to get the best use of those drives. If you tend to have more programs than data (which is a common experience), then you should probably devote all but one of the drives to holding program disks, and just one to holding a data disk. On the other hand, if you ever use more data than will fit onto one disk at a time, then you will want to spread the data onto several disks, mounted in different disk drives. One strategy that you can use in this situation, to simplify your backup procedures, is to place the stable files on one disk, and the volatile ones on another.

When you have disks that are devoted purely to holding data, and not programs, then the general advice that we gave, of having each disk system-formatted, does not apply. Pure data disks have no use for a copy of the DOS system files, so you should format those disks without the system.

Now the question comes up, which programs and what data to place on your disks? The answer, basically, is to organize the disks by usage, that is by the subject matter that you use them for. If you write programs, then you will have a disk with your program development tools on it. You will probably have a word processing program disk with your writing tools, and several data disks to use with it—perhaps one data disk just with correspondence and another one for less casual writing. The key thing is to gather together all of the program tools that are used in connection with one kind of working task. Then your use of the computer's disks becomes much simpler and better organized.

What about the external DOS commands? What disks should you put them on? You can decide about them on a program by program basis: which ones you need where—just as you will with all other programs. But as a general piece of advice, you don't need many of the DOS commands on most of your program disks. I would advise that you keep a special DOS command program disk, which has everything on it that DOS provides. When you need to use FORMAT or DEBUG, then you can switch to that disk. But for your ordinary program disks, there isn't much among the DOS commands that you are likely to need often. The main one, which ought to be on all of your program disks is CHKDSK, which checks your disks for available space and logical damage. Since it is wise to use the CHKDSK command often, it should be on every disk.

For DOS-2 users, there are three special command programs which you should also include on all of your program disks—the filter commands SORT, MORE, and FIND. Since these three are used in pipelines, you should have them at your command at all times.

There is one other thing that is a candidate for every one of your program disks, and that is an editor program such as DOS's editor, EDLIN. The reason for this is simple. Even if what we are doing isn't writing, we often need to use an editor program in connection with our work. For example, you need an editor program to set up batch processing files—and if you are good at making effective use of your computer, you will be creating and changing your batch execution files often, *probably several times a day*. So having EDLIN, or another editor, on each program disk is very handy. If you have a compact, easy-to-use editor, put it on your disks. If your only editor, besides EDLIN, is a bulky word processor, then just put EDLIN on your disks and learn to use EDLIN just enough to be able to build batch files.

Beyond what we've said here, you should think fairly regularly about how your main working disks are organized, and whenever you have a better idea about them, take the time to reorganize. This effort will pay off handsomely, especially in the early months of your use of the computer.

13.3 Making Commands More Convenient

Most of the commands and programs that we use have names that describe what they do: COPY, FORMAT, TIME. These names are nice, and their straightforward quality makes it easier to remember them and use the right command name.

But if you are using a command over and over again, it can be tiresome to keep typing the name in. So you might want to consider giving your commands some *aliases*, or other names. You might want to change the names entirely, but the most common and reasonable thing to want to do is to shorten the name of the command, perhaps to a single letter so that the keystrokes you have to press are as few as possible.

There are three ways that we can give programs aliases. One is simply to create a batch file, under the alias name, which turns around and performs the proper command. This is the slowest and least elegant way of creating an alias, but it will work with *any* command, internal or external. The other two ways of creating an alias work only with external commands.

For external commands, we can make copies of the command program file, with a different name. This is quick and easy with the COPY command. For example, if we want to give the FORMAT command an alias of F, we can make a copy with the new name, like this:

```
COPY FORMAT.COM F.COM
```

The only disadvantage of making an alias this way is that the command program now takes up twice as much space on our disk.

Another way to give an external command a new name is to rename the program file with the RENAME command. For example,

```
RENAME FORMAT.COM F.COM
```

This has one great disadvantage, though. After renaming a command, it can only be used under its new name, and not the old name as well. For our convenience the new short name may be terrific, but it means that the command can't be used in standard operations, or by other people, under the standard name. So I don't recommend using this method for giving commands aliases, *except when your purpose is safety,* which we'll discuss in the next chapter, on danger areas.

13.4 Some Tricks For DOS-2

In the line of handy tricks, there is one exceptionally useful one that DOS-2 provides. Often we need a list of some of our files because we are going to copy them, or erase them, or just print them out. Or whatever.

With DOS-1, whenever we want to do something with a list of files, we have to key in the filenames, which is a laborious and error-prone process. But with DOS-2's ability to re-direct output, we can have the DIR command store a list of files into a data file. For example, to get a file which contains a list of all of the BAT, COM, and EXE files on a disk, we can do this:

```
DIR *.BAT >LIST
DIR *.COM >>LIST
DIR *.EXE >>LIST
```

You'll recall that ">", used in the first command here, sends its output to a file, replacing whatever was in the file before; and ">>", used in the last two commands, adds onto an existing file. These three DIR commands together create one list file, which contains all three lists.

After we have used output re-direction, we can use our editor, such as EDLIN, to do whatever we want with the list. The most common thing is to turn it into a functional batch processing file. With our editor we would first remove any extraneous information, then change the list to be just the files we want (our purpose, for example, might be to erase just some of the files on a disk), and then finally add onto each file in the list the name of the command we want to perform on the file—erasing it, copying it, or whatever. Finally, after we have used our editor to turn the list into a usable batch file, we can execute the file and the commands, acting on the list of files, will be carried out.

While this operation may seem a little elaborate, it is much easier and more accurate than typing in an entire batch file with a list of files in it. Output re-direction has made the work simpler, more accurate, and safer.

You will probably have more use for this trick than you might imagine. It is quite common to need to copy, erase, or print out a list of files.

14

Danger Areas

In this chapter we're going to look at some of the ways you can make a dangerous mess of things, and lose a lot of your data. These are danger areas, where just the wrong moves could wipe out a lot of valuable information—so we'll show you the sources of these dangers, and what you can do to avoid them.

14.1 Mixing Your DOS's

One subtle and insidious danger to your data is through mixing up your versions of DOS. There are more versions of DOS than you might imagine. For example, I have four different *official* versions of DOS and another three unofficial versions. Because the parts of DOS work very intimately together, it is important to not get them mixed up. If you do get them mixed up, then it is very unpredictable what will happen—but one thing that can happen is the loss of an entire disk's worth of data. I've helped rescue two Hollywood writers who lost their data this way.

To avoid this danger, you need to know how it can happen to you and what you need to do to prevent any damage.

Changes are made periodically to DOS, to revise it, extend it, improve it. As we've been seeing in this book, there are two major versions of DOS, the 1-series, which we've been calling DOS-1, and the 2-series, which we call DOS-2. In addition, there are minor revisions within each series. Even if your computer currently has only one single version of DOS, it is almost certain that there will be new ones in the future.

You might encounter different versions of DOS three ways. One is that you simply received a new improved version; this is the safest situation since you are aware that you have two versions. Another way that you can encounter a second version of DOS is by exchanging disks with colleagues—they might be using a different version than you are, and in exchanging disks you might unintentionally be mixing your DOS program files together. The third way this can happen is when you buy a copy-protected program.

The customary situation when you receive a copy-protected program is that you must use it from the disk it is distributed on, and the disk is prepared to accept a copy of DOS onto it. Copy-protected disks like that are supposed to

MORE THAN ONE DOS CAN CONFUSE YOUR COMPUTER.

be formatted *as if* they have the DOS system on them, but they are not supposed to actually have it on them (we're supposed to transfer DOS onto a reserved blank space on the disk). But sometimes it isn't done this way, and the disk already contains a copy of DOS—a copy which might not match yours.

In both of these last two situations, exchanging disks with friends and receiving copy-protected disks, you can encounter another version of DOS *that you are unaware of,* and you can accidentally start mixing it up with your own version. The problem is insidious since you don't really know that it is happening. And things might work just fine for you for a while, until you get just the wrong combination of programs and operations and—bang—you've lost a disk's worth of data.

How can you prevent this from happening? First, be aware that there are three different parts to DOS—the two hidden system files (these count as one part), the command processor (COMMAND.COM), and the various DOS command programs, such as FORMAT. (For more on the hidden system files, see Chapter 13.) For DOS to work properly, all three parts must match—all must be from exactly the same version of DOS.

For COMMAND.COM and the various DOS command programs, it is relatively easy to check to see that you have a matched set, thanks to the date and time stamp that is placed in each disk's directory. To find out the date-and-time marking of your DOS, take your original master disk of DOS (or an unaltered copy of that disk), and do this DIR command:

```
DIR *.COM
```

You should see COMMAND.COM, FORMAT.COM, and numerous other program files listed. The dates and times on all of them should match, and this gives you the official reference point for checking any other disk.

With that in hand, you can check any other disk to see if the visible DOS program files match that version. With DIR commands to list all of the COM and EXE files (since some DOS programs are the EXE type), you can see all the DOS files on your disks and check their dates. When you do this, you should only be checking the DOS files, which will be COMMAND.COM, and COM and EXE files which have the names of DOS commands. Any other program files, which aren't an integral part of DOS, can safely have any date and time on them.

If you find that there is any mismatch of dates and times, you should copy a coordinated set of program files onto the disk so that there is no question of a mixup.

So far, we've shown you how to check for, and fix up, a mismatch in the *visible* DOS files. But there are also two hidden system files which are used when DOS starts up, and we have no ordinary way to check to see that they match the rest of our DOS. While we can't check them, we can force them to match our master DOS version. Here is how it is done.

First, we have to see if a disk even has the two hidden files. We do this, as explained in Chapter 13, by using the CHKDSK command. If it reports two (or three) hidden files, then the disk has these two DOS hidden files. We don't know which DOS version they are from, but we can make sure that they match our version of DOS. This is done with the SYS command, which was discussed in Chapter 5. The SYS command is designed to transfer these two hidden files from one disk to another; the COPY command can't be used, because hidden files are invisible to the copy operation—but SYS has a special X-ray vision, that gives it the ability to copy these two files. To make sure that a disk with the two files has the version you want it to have, use SYS to transfer the files from a disk you are sure of (such as a copy of your master DOS disk) to the questionable disk.

With this as background, we see what we need to do when we change to a new version of DOS, or when we receive a new disk which we want to match our version of DOS. For each disk that you need to update or confirm:

- First, check for the hidden files with CHKDSK;
- Second, transfer the hidden files, as needed, with SYS;
- Third, check for the presence of COMMAND.COM and other DOS files with DIR;
- Fourth, if any DOS files have the wrong dates, COPY the right version to the disk.

This operation involves enough looking and deciding that you must do it more or less by hand, but it is still possible to reduce the work involved by setting up repetitive batch files.

What if you want to have two different versions of DOS? This is all right, as long as you take care to not mix them up. If you do set up two versions of DOS, for any reason, you should carefully mark your disks as to which version they contain (or if they don't contain any part of DOS). Then you should keep the use of those disks distinct. Remember, as we discussed in Chapter 13, DOS will sometimes reload COMMAND.COM from a disk. So if you have started DOS from one disk version, and then insert a disk that has another version of DOS, there is some danger that the wrong COMMAND.COM will be loaded. Fortunately, this is one error that all versions of DOS are good at checking for, so the worst that will happen is that DOS will complain that you have the wrong COMMAND.COM on the disk.

Fortunately for DOS-2 users, these versions of DOS contain internal checks to avoid a mismatch in any of the parts of DOS. This provides us with some partial protection against a mix-up, but it is far from completely solving the problem. So you cannot, and should not, rely on DOS-2 to protect you from the dangers of mixed versions.

14.2 Disastrous Interruptions

One of the things that can destroy your data is to interrupt the writing of disk information when it is incomplete. There are several ways that this can happen.

One way is if the power goes off on your computer while something is being written. A similar result can happen if you remove a disk while it is being written to, or if you use the *break* command, Control-C, to tell DOS to interrupt the operation. If your computer has been interrupted in mid-operation, there might be some harm to the disk data; on the other hand, just because your disks were spinning, doesn't mean that the computer was writing—it might have been reading from the disk when it was interrupted, and that can't do us any harm. Only if we were writing, could any damage be done; even then we might get off scott free.

In general terms, any of the interruptions which we have mentioned run the risk of damaging one file, but there is less risk that everything on the disk is messed up. Sometimes no harm is done and we are lucky. Occasionally one file, the file that was being written, will be messed up. Very rarely will there be more harm.

How do you tell if there has been harm to a disk? The first and best way is with the CHKDSK command. CHKDSK will tell you if there is any logical scrambling of the disk for one file or any others. If CHKDSK gives no error messages, then you know that the disk as a whole is OK, and also that the one file that was being written might be all right, but we don't know yet. The next check is to use the DIR command to look at the file's directory entry. If you know which file was being written, ask for it; if you don't, then ask for the full directory listing (DIR *.*).

When you see the directory listing, the main thing to check for is a reasonable size for the file (or for all files). If a file size is given as zero, then the creation of the file was cut off in mid-stream, and the data that was being written (or any old data that the file had before) has been lost. Sometimes files are created under a temporary working name, and then only given their official name when the creation process is finished. If you suspect that a file was cut off as it was being created, you should check for unusual file names; common possibilities are names with extensions of $$$ or TMP.

There is one kind of interruption of the computer's writing to disk that can do much more harm. This happens if you switch disks in the middle of an operation. The problem relates to the disk's record of its used and unused space, which we discussed in Chapter 9. After a file is written, a record of the space the file occupies is written to the disk—but this record applies to every file, and not just one. If this space table, called the File Allocation Table or FAT, is lost or damaged, then *every* file will be damaged or permanently lost.

This problem can occur in quite an innocent way, and I know of many people who have had it happen to them. You think that you are just beginning to write out a file, and DOS reports that something is wrong with the disk—so you substitute another disk. DOS finishes writing out the file, *and* the File Allocation Table. However, DOS doesn't know you switched disks, so it writes the FAT that was read from the first disk onto the second disk. Every file that was stored on the second disk is now lost. Ugh. DOS-2 has more protection against this problem built into it, but the danger still exists. The way to protect against this danger is simple—whenever DOS tells you that there is trouble with a disk, *never switch to a disk with good data on it.* Either fix the one disk, or switch to a blank disk, or abort the operation. But don't put in a good disk with existing files, because they may all be lost.

14.3 Ordinary Ways to Lose Your Data

So far we've talked about the more interesting and exotic ways that you can lose your data. Now we'll get down to the dull, prosaic, and common dangers.

There are exactly three ordinary ways to lose your disk data: by copying over it, by erasing it, and by—gulp—re-formatting a disk.

Of these three dangers, the least frequent is to copy old or bad data onto new, good data. Although there are a million ways we could do this without meaning to, the most common is when we intend to make a backup copy of our data, but we copy in the wrong direction—instead of copying from our newly updated original to the backup disk, we copy from an old backup, overwriting our latest data. Oh, my.

There are several ways that you can protect against this problem. One is to follow a strict physical pattern in the way that you copy data—for example, the original *always* in drive B, the backup copy *always* in drive A. Another is to keep using the same disk as your original, instead of rotating between the original and the backup. Another is to keep more than one backup and rotate them (perhaps one backup disk for odd numbered days, another for even).

Another is to never make the copies manually, but instead use a batch execution file to make sure that the copy is made correctly. Among the advantages of a batch file is that you can have it display the file dates before any copying is done as a precaution—if the dates don't look right, you can stop and check why.

The next problem, and probably the most common destroyer of data, is the DEL/ERASE command. It is incredibly easy to accidentally erase files that you didn't mean to erase. This happens most often through the unintended or misguided use of the asterisk wild card, which will match any filename or any extension. DOS does contain one small precaution against this: if we enter the complete wild card name, "*.*", then DOS will pause to ask us for confirmation. That's not a lot of safety.

There are two things that you can do to protect against losing files through erasure. One, as we mentioned in Chapter 12, is to get an "un-erase" program, if one is available for your computer. The other is to avoid using the DEL or ERASE command manually. If you have any routine need to erase files, *don't* do it by entering the command by hand; instead, build a batch execution file which will then have the names of the files being erased specified correctly. If you use a batch file, instead of manually entering the erasure command directly, you guard against an accidental mistyping of the names to be erased (provided you get it right in the batch file).

The last of the dangers we are going to cover is the danger of re-formatting a disk that has valuable data on it. This is the goriest of all the dangers to your data, because it is completely unrecoverable. If you erase your data, you may be able to unerase it. If you copy over your data, some of it may still be left on the disk. But when you format a disk, everything that was on that disk is gone. Every part of every file is gone, beyond any hope of recovery. You can't unformat a disk the way you might be able to unerase a file. It's tough.

The best way to protect against formatting over your data is to only use the FORMAT command through a batch file—and have that batch file first check the disk for any files that are there. Here is an example of what such a batch file might be like:

```
REM       About to format a disk-check for files
CHKDSK B:
DIR B:
PAUSE     Are there any valuable files? If so, BREAK, don't continue
FORMAT B:
```

By doing all of your formatting with something like this batch file, you add a measure of protection to your data.

Beyond all these things, the best protection for your data is simply meticulous care. Be careful to always label your disks, indicating what is on them. Be careful not to do physical damage to your disks. Be careful about the specifically dangerous operations of copying, erasing, and formatting.

15

Coping with Copy Protection

One of the most exasperating things in the job of effectively organizing the use of your computer is coping with the special troubles of copy protection. It is a messy and annoying area, and we can't make it much better for you. But in this chapter we'll give you as much help as possible.

15.1 Tricks of the Trade

Copy protection is intended to prevent copies of computer programs—or other computer data—from being copied. Copy protection became necessary because it is so easy to "steal" valuable software: one legitimately purchased copy could be passed around to dozens or even hundreds of people, and each could easily keep a working copy of the program. This problem arose long before the days of DOS, before small personal computers started being used by serious professionals and businesses. In the old hobby-oriented world of personal computing, stealing software became a game.

To protect themselves, software developers began to copy protect their programs. But as soon as that started, pirate programmers began to develop copy busters, which would copy anything. Well, almost anything. The protectors developed more sophisticated protection schemes, and the busters tried to match them. The battle was on, and it's a battle that continues.

In the war between the protectors and the copy busters, the busters usually win, because whatever schemes the protectors can think of, the busters can figure out as well; and the busters have the advantage because a copy protected diskette is full of clues about how it is protected. The only advantage the protectors have is that they get to invent the new protection schemes, and then they are safe for a short while, until it is decoded by the copy busters.

As with most wars, it's the innocent bystander who gets hurt the most. All of the honest software users have to put up with the problems of using copy protected programs.

For your interest, you might want to have a little idea of how copy protection is done to better understand your computer, and what is going on with it. Part of the story of how copy protection is done is very important to us, as you will see in a minute.

Before diskettes can be used they have to be formatted. Formatting a blank diskette is analogous to drawing lines on a blank piece of paper—it provides a framework on which information will be written. The hardware of the diskette drives can do this formatting in many ways, but for simplicity the operating system software (that's DOS) uses only some of the possible formats. If a program creates a nonstandard format, then DOS usually cannot read that part of the diskette. So nonstandard formatting is one of the most common ways of doing copy protection. By having at least some of the diskette formatted in a way that DOS can't work with, the disk can't be copied by the ordinary tools that DOS gives us, COPY and DISKCOPY.

There are two completely different ways that this nonstandard formatting can be done to accomplish copy protection, and there is a tremendous practical difference between them. In one style of protection, the programs are not directly protected—so DOS can read and load them into memory.   Then, when the program begins running, it checks its diskette for copy protection, usually by reading from the unconventionally formatted part of the diskette. If all is well, the program continues; but if anything is wrong with the protection, then the program refuses to work. This kind of copy protection doesn't interfere with DOS, which is nice for us. But the other kind is not so nice.

In the other style of copy protection, DOS can't load the protected program—it has to load itself, which normally means restarting or re-booting your system before and after using the program. This, of course, is a real disruption to the work flow in your computer.

There are basically three problems with copy protection—three ways that copy protected programs make it harder for us to use our computers effectively. The first problem is copying copy protected diskettes for backup and safety purposes. This is the problem that people talk about most when they complain about copy protection; frankly, this is the least of our worries. Getting backup copies of a protected diskette is not very much trouble; the program's developers normally make them readily available, and you can always turn to a copy busting program to make your own backup copies.

After you are experienced with personal computers, you learn that damaged diskettes are a rare occurrence. All the worry and hullabaloo about losing your only copy of an expensive copy protected diskette is mostly nonsense. For an example from my own experience, in eighteen months of very heavy continuous use of two, and sometimes three, computers, my office has never damaged even one diskette. This is not to say it can't happen, only that it is rather rare. Diskettes are seldom damaged and backup copies are available, so this isn't such a big problem. An inconvenience, but not a problem.

The real problems come from two other areas. One is the transfer problem. Hard disk systems—and also electronic disks—are being used more and more and for good reason. For the serious use of a computer system, high-speed and high-capacity disk systems are essential. And the history of traditional computing makes it clear that users of small DOS computers will find their dependence upon their computers always growing. This makes it very important that programs can be transferred from diskette media to other media, such as hard disks and electronic disks. Unless some special trick is used, copy protected programs can't be transferred, and that is the problem.

The last of the three problems with copy protected programs concerns the ones that don't run under the DOS operating system but load themselves instead. When your use of the computer is casual and sporadic, it hardly matters that you have to shut it down and start it up just to use some program. But when your use of the computer becomes regular, you just can't afford the disruption—and the annoying effort—to switch your system back and forth between DOS and programs that won't run under DOS. If you think that this is small potatoes, think again. Imagine if the telephone company announced that from now on all telephones would be outdoor payphones, so that every time you needed to make a call, you had to run outside with a handful of change. You couldn't fit the use of the telephone into your work or your social life very well could you? It would be more than an inconvenience— for most businesses it would be an impossible difficulty. And so it is with copy protected programs that don't run under DOS.

It seems likely that there will emerge copy protection mechanisms that serve the needs of both program sellers, and program users—for example, the use of hardware serial numbers, which make it possible for a program to be freely copied, but only run on the one computer which has the right serial number. When we talk about copy protection here, we're not talking about any such nice schemes—we're talking about the traditional copy protection schemes, the ones that cause the problems we covered above.

What can you do to cope with copy protection? The snappy answer is, don't buy copy protected programs. In fact, we can expect to suffer less from the nuisance of copy protection in the future, for the simple reason that copy protected programs are less useful to serious professional computer users, and competitive forces will give nonprotected programs an advantage in the marketplace. But just saying don't buy copy protected programs doesn't do you much good. Sometimes you don't have a choice. Sometimes you are stuck using a copy protected program.

What you can do is fourfold. First, don't make the problem worse by being a villain; if almost no one made illicit copies of programs, we wouldn't have copy protection on so many programs. Second, vote with your pocket book by avoiding copy protected programs as much as you can. Third, vote with your pen—by complaining to the producers of programs which interfere with the smooth use of your computer. And finally, there are some things that you can do to make copy protected programs fit into your system more easily.

The key to the easy use of copy protected programs is batch execution files. Even if you have to use a copy protected program, you can make it easier with the right batch files. What sort of batch files you'll need depends so much on the program, and the way your computer is organized, that we can only give you some suggestions. One of the main things to consider is which drive is the most convenient one to place your copy protected diskette in; another is where you want any working data to go—sometimes it's convenient, or even necessary, for the data drive to be the current default drive. Finally, is it practical or safe to place your own batch execution files onto the copy protected diskette (usually it is, but sometimes not). Here are some examples.

If your computer has two diskette drives, and nothing more—which is one of the most common setups—then you are probably using your A-drive exclusively for programs, and your B-drive exclusively for data. In this situation, the best thing to do is to treat the copy protected diskette like any of your other program diskettes. This means putting any necessary batch files on it, plus the DOS file COMMAND.COM and any other program tools that you might need. Candidates for inclusion on the diskette are FORMAT, CHKDSK, and the editor you use, which might be DOS's own editor, EDLIN. You can only do this, of course, if the copy protected diskette is in a format that allows you to transfer files to it, and if there is enough room on the diskette.

One batch execution file which will make it easier to work this way is the BAA file, mentioned in Chapter 11. To conveniently use a program, which we'll call XXX, on drive A, and work with data on drive B, the BAA batch file temporarily switches the default drive. BAA is like this:

```
B:
A:XXX
A:
```

The first line switches the default to drive B, and the third switches it back to A. In the second line, the program named XXX is executed (from the A-drive), but any data files that it uses will be found on the B-drive, since B is the current default drive. The natural name to give a batch file like this is some abbreviation of the program name. Or, on the other hand, you could use the RENAME command to give XXX some alias, and then XXX can be the name of the batch file. (If the batch file has the same name as the program file, then when you type in the name as a command, DOS will execute the program directly and not use your batch file.)

If you have a hard disk system, which imitates a number of diskettes (some hard disks work this way, even though DOS discourages it), then the kinds of batch files you need are similar, but they are built a little differently. For example, your main programs and batch files might be on disk partition A, while D might be your customary data work space. B might have your permanent data, and F might be your only diskette drive, which is where the copy protected diskette would have to be loaded. In a case like this, you might want to use a batch execution file that is similar to this outline:

```
COPY      B:*.XXX  D:*.DAT   (move your data to the work drive)
D:                           (change the default to the work drive)
F:XXX                        (run the program)
COPY      D:*.DAT  B:*.XXX   (move the data back to permanent
                              space)
DEL       D:*.DAT            (clear it off the work drive)
A:CHKDSK D:                  (clean up any mess)
A:                           (switch the default back to normal)
```

If you can understand the thinking that went into that batch execution file, then you should be able to custom tailor your own batch files to suit your particular needs.

15.2 Something Worse Than Copy Protection

What could be worse than copy protection? Another operating system.

DOS isn't the only operating system around. There are many others, and two are in widespread use and are likely to be available for your DOS computer. One is known as CP/M-86, and the other is the UCSD p-System (often just called the p-System).

Whatever the virtues of any other operating system are, it is very, very inadvisable to be using more than one operating system on your computer. Why? It would be like trying to run an office where half the workers spoke only French, and the other half spoke only English. A mess. As a general rule, each operating system is totally incompatible with each other one—neither

DIFFERENT OPERATING SYSTEMS DON'T GET ALONG
VERY WELL WITH EACH OTHER.

programs *nor data* can be shared. Even worse, from our point of view, the skills and familiarity that we gain using one system won't work on another.

Due to these problems, you will probably not choose to use any other operating system than DOS. But one may sneak up on you. Some programs are sold with a working copy of their operating system; this is particularly true with the p-System, although it can happen with CP/M-86.

If you buy such a program, it is no different than if you had bought the kind of copy protected program that requires restarting your computer. To use a p-System program, you will have to shut down DOS to use the program. In some ways using one of these programs is worse than a copy protected program, because a p-System or a CP/M-86 program will probably force you to deal with at least some part of its operating system.

If you are considering buying a large expensive program, be sure to check if it is one of those which comes with its own operating system. If it is, then you need to consider if the advantages of the program outweigh the disadvantages of its not working under DOS.

You may wonder what are just the right questions to ask about a program, to see that it will fit into your working environment. If you are not a technical expert on computers, you may be concerned that you won't know the right questions to ask. To be sure that you don't encounter the kind of difficulties that this chapter has been discussing, here are the right questions to ask about a program you consider buying:

- Is it copy protected?
- If it is and you use another media such as hard disk, can it be transferred to another media, even though it is copy protected?
- Does it run under DOS?
- To ask the same question another way, does it require "re-booting" your system?
- What are the program's hardware and software requirements? (If it doesn't require DOS, it doesn't run under DOS.)

16

Special Tricks for Hard Disks and Electronic Disks

Personal computers are usually based upon floppy diskettes for their storage needs—storage that is relatively slow and small. But many small computer systems take advantage of the special capabilities of hard disks and electronic disks. In this chapter we'll consider their special needs. Before we get into the details, though, we need a little background information.

16.1 A Little Background

The practical use of a computer centers around its storage. That may not seem sensible—after all, the computing power of a computer is what you use a computer for. Beyond that, the features of your computer that you are probably most interested in are likely to be the quality of the display screen—can it do graphics? is it easy to look at?—or of the printer. While we may think the most about our machine's computing speed, or its display formats and printing quality, storage is the element that the entire *use* of the computer centers around.

The widespread use of personal computers and their operating systems, such as DOS and CP/M, was based upon the floppy diskette—and for good reason. Diskettes are cheap, reliable, and flexible in more ways than one. Their technical flexibility made it easy to design them into all sorts of computers. Their flexibility of use—easy to put in and take out, easy to store, easy to mail—greatly enhanced how practical it was to get things done with a small computer.

But floppy diskettes have two severe disadvantages—slow speed and small storage capacity. Let's explain a little about each.

A computer consists of a collection of components, all working together. Each part has an effective speed of how quickly it accomplishes its own task. In a rough sort of way, the separate speeds of the different parts can be compared, so that we can get an idea of whether they are appropriately balanced. If the parts of the computer are well matched, all is well. Let's consider what happens if one part is made much faster or much slower. Suppose that the working of one part of our computer takes up exactly 10 percent of the total time needed to get some work done. If we replace that part with one that is ten times faster, then it will get its job done in only 1 percent of the old total time—and our whole computer will run 9 percent faster. One part is improved ten times, but the whole is improved less than 10 percent. Then, if we replace that part with one ten times slower than the original it now takes 100 percent of the original time just to do that one part of the work. The whole computer now runs 90 percent slower, almost halving its effective speed, thanks to just one slow component.

The moral here is that there is little advantage in having one part of the computer disproportionately fast, but there is a huge disadvantage in having one part disproportionately slow. The question is one of balance, and of bottle-necks. If one part is slow relative to the rest of the computer, it is a bottleneck which can cripple the entire computer.

In most personal computers, the greatest bottleneck is floppy diskettes. This statement is not absolutely true, just generally true. How true it might be for you depends upon two things—first the relative balance of speed in the parts of your own computer, and second the relative balance of how *your* work utilizes *your computer's* parts. If you and I had identical computers, but you used your disks hardly at all, they couldn't be a bottleneck for you; if I use mine very, very heavily, mine are certain to be a bottleneck. So there are no absolutes here. But for most users of most personal computers, the disks are clearly the bottleneck, the limiting factor in the entire computer's working speed.

Let's look at some representative numbers so that you can see what we are talking about. The computer that this book was written on has all three kinds of storage—floppy diskettes, a Winchester technology hard disk, and an electronic disk. In my own practical speed trials, I found that the hard disk was roughly five times faster than the floppy diskettes, and the electronic disk is twice as fast as the hard disk, or ten times faster than the diskettes. But these speed tests were for purely disk operations, not for the whole computer. What did they mean in practice? Is there a bottleneck? I tested one of the most time-consuming things I do with my computer—checking something that I have written for spelling errors. I knew that my spelling checker did lots of computing, and a fair amount of disk work, but I didn't know about balance; I didn't know where the bottlenecks were for that particular computer task. I tested a large chunk of spelling to check, using each of the three storage media. Using the floppy diskette, the operation took about three minutes. Then I tried the hard disk, which, for disk work alone, is five times faster. When I used the hard disk for spelling checking, the time was down to about two minutes.

Aha. A dramatic improvement—a full third off the time. Was disk access still a bottleneck, or was it now in balance with the rest of the computer? A test with the electronic disk answered that—only 6 seconds came off the time. So

DISKETTE   HARD DISK   ELECTRONIC DISK

THERE ARE THREE DISK SPEEDS.

even though the electronic disk was twice as fast—in pure disk operations—as the hard disk, the total benefit was very little.

My own speed trials rather dramatically demonstrated both sides of the speed question. Up to a certain point a faster disk can help you, but beyond that, speed is not the problem. Your own speed needs or problems are uniquely yours, but typically they will be similar to mine: for most personal computers, ordinary floppy diskettes are *somewhat* a bottleneck, and anything which promises to be several times faster will eliminate that bottleneck.

Now let's look at the other side of storage: capacity. There are many formats of disk storage, so there are many different capacities. Diskettes alone can range from a low of about 100 thousand bytes to a high of over a million bytes. Typical capacities are around 200 to 400 thousand bytes. This is much less than the total amount of storage that we need.

There are three problems with using diskettes that won't hold all of our data. First, there is the nuisance of shuffling diskettes around, putting in one set for one kind of work, and another set for other work. Not only is this inconvenient, but also the physical handling of the diskettes greatly increases the danger of damage to our data. The second problem is that we may want to have more data on tap than will fit into our diskette drives at one time. It is hard to correlate the information on three diskettes when you have only two diskette drives. The third problem is that diskettes set a low limit on how big our biggest single file can be—since no file can be bigger than the disk that holds it.

While electronic disks do nothing for our storage capacity problems, hard disk systems do, and they solve all three problems with the limits of diskette capacity. They eliminate diskette shuffling, they allow the simultaneous use of large amounts of data, and they allow single files to grow very large.

You may be wondering how much you might need a hard disk system, or what size will do for you (after all, if you get one that is too small, again you have the problems of the diskette world). If you can estimate your data storage needs, fine. But if not, here is my suggested rule of thumb. For a computer in personal use, or professional use without large amounts of data, a hard disk with five million bytes capacity is likely to be enough. For a professional user, or for a business with moderate amounts of records, ten million bytes might be right (ten is what I have, and for me it's just barely enough). For extensive business records, or a large research data base, or anything similar, twenty million bytes and up might be needed. If you are choosing a hard disk, it is safer to get larger rather than smaller. But if you know that you can add more later, then you can safely start small.

With this general information about the needs for and uses of hard disks and electronic disks, let's now move on to the special things you need to know about each.

16.2 The Special Uses of Electronic Disks

To know how to use electronic disks, we have to understand a little of what they are about. Our programs, including DOS itself, expect to read and write information that it keeps in files on a storage medium called disks. That is really all that our programs need to know—that they can read or write files from storage.

Clever folks in the world of computing noticed, though, that an enormous increase in speed could be obtained by not actually reading and writing files from a disk, but instead holding the data in the computer's memory. The program which used that data would not know that the data was being held in memory and wouldn't use it directly in its memory copy. Instead, our programs would request that data be "read" or "written," presumably from disk. But actually, the data would be transferred in memory from the simulated disk to the program which is using it. The working result would be the same, but the speed would be much faster—in the neighborhood of fully ten times faster. This little trick is what is known as an electronic disk, or a memory disk, or a RAM (Random Access Memory) disk; other exotic terms are used, such as flash disk—it all refers to the same thing.

To create an electronic disk, two things are needed: the spare memory to hold the data, and an appropriate program to do the work of simulating disk operations in memory. There are several strategies for providing them, and you may find that your computer has several kinds of electronic disk available for it. One kind might use dedicated memory, which is only intended to be used as an electronic disk. Another might share part of your computer's main memory, giving you a useful flexibility about how much memory is used for the electronic disk, and how much is used for ordinary memory. (Mine happens to be of this adjustable kind, which I sometimes find very handy.)

Whatever the case, to create an electronic disk on your computer you will need some special software—which does the disk simulation—and plenty of memory. If you are using DOS-1, the special software is likely to involve a modification to your operating system, which may reduce your ability to use other exotic software, or tie you to one particular version of DOS. With DOS-2, though, electronic disk programs can be integrated into DOS in a safe and flexible way that does not interfere with DOS or other software, which is a real advantage. So, if you consider getting an electronic disk, you should be aware that the potential problems are greater with DOS-1 than they are with DOS-2.

When you have an electronic disk, you have a fragile and vulnerable storage medium. If something goes wrong with your computer, or if the power goes off, the data stored in your electronic disk will be lost. A diskette is a pretty safe place to store your data, because it is unlikely that it will be damaged. But data stored on an electronic disk is dependent upon the continuing operation of your computer to preserve it; if the computer goes out, the data is lost. Even if an electronic disk has some protection against a power outage, the danger still exists.

So an electronic disk is not a place to actually store data—it is a place simply to *use* it. The normal way of working with an electronic disk is very temporary. At the beginning of a working session, your data can be transferred from its permanent storage location, probably a diskette, to the electronic disk. There it is worked with by your programs. Afterwards, any new or updated data can be transferred back to the permanent, safe storage. When you work with an electronic disk this way, your only danger is that you might lose one session's work.

You will have to judge for yourself how great the dangers are for you with an electronic disk. It will depend upon how reliable your computer is, how steady your power supply is, and how great the loss would be if some work was destroyed. My own experience, even with constant exposure to corrosive salt sea air, and a power supply that jumps with every passing storm, has been good. In fact, the only work I have lost in my electronic disk has been through my own stupidity and not through the fault of the disk.

When you set up to use an electronic disk, you should create batch files which will easily and reliably transfer your data into and out of the electronic disk. If you are concerned about the reliability of your disk, take break points often to copy your new data back to diskette.

To give you an example, here is a batch file which will transfer the entire contents of a diskette to an electronic disk, and switch your operation to the electronic drive. For this example, our batch file takes D as the drive identifier

AN ELECTRONIC DISK MIGHT VANISH INTO THIN AIR.

of the electronic drive, and assumes that the A-drive holds the diskette we want to copy from:

```
REM Transfer up to the electronic drive
COPY A:*.* D:*.*
D:
```

You can have a similar batch file to return the data when you are done. The pair of batch files might be called UP.BAT and DOWN.BAT, or whatever you thought were good names. This example is very simple—you can add your own elaborations to transfer only the files needed.

One aid that can make an important difference in the speed, convenience, and safety in the use of an electronic disk is a fast selective copy program, of the kind I mentioned in Chapter 12. A common way of using an electronic disk is to copy quite a few files into the disk but only change a few of them. It is good to have a copy program which is smart enough to save back to real disk storage only the ones which have changed (which can be told by the files' time stamp).

When you set up to use an electronic disk, you will probably not have enough room on the disk for all of the program and data files that you will be using. You must decide which files to place on the fast disk. Under most circumstances that means your data files, but not always. Sometimes you run one program and it reads or writes large amounts of data—in this case, the data ought to be in the fast electronic disk. In other situations it is the programs themselves that are being read all the time. Most accounting programs and most large programs written in BASIC repeatedly read parts of themselves into memory from disk. This is also true of many word processing programs, spread sheet programs, and especially multi-function programs (which we'll be discussing in Chapter 17). If you know that your programs use overlays, or load help-screens from disk, then it is likely that they would operate much faster if the programs themselves were loaded into your electronic disk.

If you can fit everything you need onto your electronic disk, fine. If not, you should decide which files to load and that usually means deciding between data files and program files. There are two reasons for choosing to put the program files into electronic memory. One, mentioned above, is that sometimes the program files are the ones used the most, so they are the most deserving of a speed advantage. But there is another reason: if you put your programs but not your data into the electronic disk, then your data is not exposed to the dangers of being lost that an electronic disk creates. If something goes wrong with the electronic disk, you have lost nothing but a copy of your programs—no data and no work is lost.

In general, you want to put the files used most into electronic disk; after that, you want to use the electronic disk for files that don't change—program files or data that is only read, not written. You don't always have a free choice of which files can be placed where, though. This is a problem that electronic disks share with hard disks, so we'll discuss it in a separate section at the end of this chapter.

16.3 The Special Uses of Hard Disks

In this section we'll cover what's particular to the use of high-capacity hard disk systems, used together with the features of DOS-2. Although it is possible to have a hard disk system with DOS-1, and many DOS computers have had hard disk systems installed, DOS-1 does not really have the features necessary to make full and proper use of a hard disk system. Often, when hard disks have been installed on DOS-1 computers, it involved many compromises and gerry-rigged elements. There is no consistent philosophy guiding the use of hard disks with DOS-1 but there is with DOS-2.

The heart of the successful use of a hard disk system with DOS-2 is the intelligent use of the directory tree, which we described in Chapter 8.

The main problem with using a tree-structured directory is figuring out when to separate files into distinct sub-directories, and when to keep them together in one main directory.

There are probably as many strategies for the effective use of directory trees as there are people using DOS-2, and I certainly can't claim to offer

SO, LET'S DISCUSS THIS COMPULSIVE NEED YOU HAVE...

A HARD DISK NEEDS A DIRECTORY TREE.

definitive advice about the best way to use them. But some things seem clear to me, and that is what I will try to explain here.

The main reason for creating any sub-directory is to keep track of the files in it. If you don't have a strong reason for needing to keep track of some files as a distinct group, then you shouldn't have them in their own directory. What are good reasons why you would want to keep track of files as a group? One reason is for "parallel" or "generation" backup. If you have some data that is changed regularly, for example your accounting files, you might want to keep some old versions, or generations, of the files in case you make a mess of the current version. With accounting data, that might be the end-of-the-month data for each of the last few months. The reason for using a separate directory for this kind of data is mainly so that the file names can be kept the same. If there is an easy and sensible way to use alternate names for previous generations of your data, then there is no strong need to use a sub-directory, although it still might be a real convenience. Any time you need to keep more than one version of the same data under the same name, you have a good reason for using a sub-directory.

Another reason why you might need to keep track of files in a distinct sub-directory is simply so that you can keep track of them. DOS may do a very good job of keeping track of hundreds of files in one directory, but we usually can't. To manage our files well, we need to be dealing with a reasonable number of them at a time—which means that we should group them into sub-directories in ways that make sense to us, and that are small enough for us to comprehend the entire list of files. If there are a hundred files in a sub-directory, you aren't going to know what they are all about, and you won't readily be able to identify anything wrong with a list that big. If a file is missing, or damaged, or extraneous, or out-of-date, how would you know if it were buried in a list of a hundred other files? One of the strongest reasons for creating sub-directories is simply to keep the file lists in a manageable size.

On the other hand, the files that we don't need to keep track of we might as well place in one main holding area—either one catch-all sub-directory or the disk's root directory. The main candidate for these files is all of our programs: the DOS command programs and our other programs as well. Also, there is little reason not to have all of our batch execution files in the same main directory. So, unless you have a reason to do otherwise, place every program file, every file with an extension of BAT, COM or EXE, in your main directory.

If you literally have all of your executable files, all of the BAT, COM, and EXE files in one place, then you can have DOS always look there for its programs. As you'll remember from Chapter 8, the PATH command is used to tell DOS where to look for command files. If all of our command files are in the root directory, then the PATH command to tell DOS where to look would be like this:

```
PATH /
```

where the slash (or reverse slash on some computers) tells DOS to look in the root directory. If our command files are not in the root directory, but in a sub-directory, say with the name "COMMAND.DIR" then our PATH command would look like this:

```
PATH /COMMAND.DIR
```

To make effective use of the sub-directories that you create, you should create batch files which switch your operation to them. As an example, if we have a sub-directory to hold our correspondence, which me might call LETTERS, then we could create a batch file which would switch the current directory to the LETTERS sub-directory. This batch file might be named LETTERS.BAT, so that its command name was LETTERS, or we might just make it L.BAT, to give us a short, one-key command name. The working contents of this batch file might be very simple:

```
REM             Switch to correspondence directory
CHDIR /LETTERS
PATH /LETTERS;/
```

This batch file does three things: it has a remark which tells us what it is doing (a *very* good idea in all batch files), a change of the current directory, and a change of the path. Now if my advice on command files was followed strictly, the PATH command would be unnecessary—all the commands would be in the main command directory. But, most likely for one reason or another, you will have some command files located in each of the sub-directories. And, if you do, then you need to use a PATH command like the one shown to tell DOS to look to that directory for commands and then to the main directory. Naturally, if you have the commands you'll be using scattered among several directories, then the PATH command should refer to them all, in the order that you want them to be used. (I say that it is a bad idea to have your commands scattered around, but you may have your own reasons. Wherever your commands are, be sure that you get access to them with a PATH command which goes looking for them all.)

Each of our main operations should have a batch execution file for it, similar to the example shown here. The batch file should set the context of operation by performing a CHDIR command and a PATH command, first and foremost. Second, it should show you anything you need to know like the message relayed by the REM command, which just reminds us of what we are doing. Another useful bit of information would be a listing of the files, using the DIR command, so that we can see the names, size, and time stamps on our files. A third thing that these commands might do is to begin the necessary operation—by executing a program, or by copying files to a backup directory, or whatever. Anything you need done when you switch to a new subject matter could be performed by the batch file which takes you to the sub-directory.

If you have a batch file to take you *into* each sub-directory area, you ought to have one to take you out again. For example, I have a batch file, named ROOT.BAT, which returns me to my root directory no matter which sub-directory I have gone to.

There are reasons why you might put your command files into various sub-directories, besides doing it because you feel like it (which is reason enough). One reason is that you may have several versions of a batch file or even a program (some programs can be "patched" to custom tailor them, and you might keep several different tailorings around for different purposes). You should naturally make sure that your PATH commands take this into account.

As we've mentioned before, some programs read parts of themselves into memory after they have started operation. This is done with complex programs which have "overlays," and it is also done with interpretive BASIC programs.

Generally these program parts are treated as data and not as *programs,* which means in practical terms that DOS will go looking for them only in the current directory (set by the CHDIR command), and not through all the defined program paths (set by the PATH command). This means that the subsidiary parts of a program must be located in the current directory. If you use a program like this on data that is located in several different sub-directories, then you will need copies of the program's subsidiary parts in each directory. There are two ways that you can deal with this problem. One is to simply keep separate copies of the parts in each directory in which they are used. This will waste some disk space (since there will be multiple copies of the files), but it makes for fast and convenient use. The other approach is to keep one master copy of the parts and then copy them into a sub-directory as needed. A batch file which executes the program can copy the program parts into the right directory before the program starts, and delete the parts after it is done. For an example of how this is done, we'll say that we are working with WordStar (which uses overlays) in our LETTERS correspondence file:

```
REM   Switch to writing LETTERS using WORDSTAR
CHDIR /LETTERS
PATH  /LETTERS;/
COPY  /WS*.OVR /LETTERS/WS*.OVR
WS    %1
DEL   /LETTERS/WS*.OVR
CHDIR /
PATH  /
```

This example has more elements than might be necessary and, just to be clear, it makes some things explicit which could be left to default, but it shows the kind of things we want to do. Step by step, this example

1) tells us what we are going to do
2) switches the current directory to LETTERS
3) sets the program path to LETTERS and the root directory together
4) copies WordStar's overlays from the root to LETTERS
5) finally, runs WordStar using the parameter to give the file name
6) afterwards, deletes the overlays
7) changes the directory back to the root
8) and also changes the path back to the root

This is the sort of thing that you should do in setting up our own working batch files.

16.4 Common Problems and Tricks

There are some problems that are common to the use of hard disks and electronic disks. Most of these problems come from shortsighted program developers, who make their programs rather inflexible in the way they use disks. It is appallingly common for programs to be written with the built-in assumption that the only disk drives that will be used are the A-drive and the B-drive.

But your computer system might have other drives. It could have a third and fourth diskette drive, which would be drives C and D. Or if you have either a hard disk or an electronic disk, it is likely to be referred to as the C-drive.

SOME PROGRAMS ARE VERY INFLEXIBLE.

Unfortunately, all too many programs don't allow for this possibility. (By the way, when you encounter programs like this, you should complain loud and long to the programs' authors.)

If your programs are completely flexible about the drives they can use, this is very good. If not, then there are some steps you can take. It may be possible to change the programs either in their source code, or by patching them. In Chapter 20 we'll get into patching a bit. If a program is written in interpretive BASIC, then you are likely to have access to the source code; in other programming languages, you may have the source code as well. Whether we work with a program's source code or try to "patch" the program, our goal will be the same: to change the program's references to *specific* disk drives.

Usually when a program works only with a specific disk drive to access a file, it refers to the filename with a drive prefix, like this:

```
A:FILENAME.EXT
```

The culprit here is the "A:" part, which instructs DOS to look specifically to the A-drive (or some other drive). If we can change items like this in a program, we should change them either to another specific drive that we want to use, or else remove the drive specification entirely so that DOS is being told to use the *current drive* rather than a specific drive.

If it is possible to find and change these elements in a program, then you will be able to get the program to use the disk drives that you want. If you make any changes like this you should be very careful, and you should also test the changes thoroughly before trusting them to work correctly. Yet, generally this is a very simple and safe change to make to a program. Doing it will give you much more flexibility in the use of your programs.

Your version of DOS possibly has a tool which will make this business of using disk drives easier. Some versions of DOS come with a command to reassign disk drives. This ASSIGN command will temporarily reroute a program's requests for one drive to another. If your DOS version has an ASSIGN command, then you can use it to tell DOS to look elsewhere for files that a program needs. For example, if you have a program that expects to work with drives A and B, but you have all of the data on a single hard disk, which is the C-drive, then you could assign all references to A or B to C instead. This will accomplish your goal and save you the trouble of tampering with the program. Naturally the best way to use an ASSIGN command like this is in a batch file, which reassigns the drives before using a program, and then sets them back when you are done.

17

Making Some Software Choices

You almost certainly know by now that you don't just buy a computer. It doesn't work that way. Maybe you can just buy a car—and casually decide on things like the paint color. But for a computer, no. There are lots and lots of tricky choices that you have to make when you set up a small computer and the consequences can be far-reaching.

The choices you have to make fall into two categories: hardware and software. There is little we can give you in the way of general advice about your hardware choices, except to say don't scrimp on memory or disk storage. The hardware choices are so dependent on the particular make and model of computer that general advice is nearly pointless.

But in software, there is some guidance that we can give you, and that is what this chapter is about.

17.1 Choosing Any Program

The best advice I can give you about buying software is to have plenty of money and be prepared to waste some. It's always good advice to have plenty of money, but I'm not being cute here. The most important thing you need to know about buying software is don't expect to pinch pennies.

I'm not saying that the best software is the most expensive. To the contrary, software pricing is a very chaotic part of the marketplace. Software prices don't seem to be set by its cost of production, by its worth to us, or by its quality compared to any competition. So you shouldn't expect to have to pay top dollar to get the best software; nor can you choose the best by looking to the most expensive.

While you're probably already aware that getting all the software you need will probably be expensive, that is not the message we have for you. Our special secret tip to getting the right software is this: be prepared to waste some money.

If you can get all the right software on the first try, good for you. But, more often than you might expect, no matter how carefully you comparison shop and test drive, your first software purchase may not suit your needs once you really begin to use it. What do you do then? Unless your money is in very short supply, and you don't highly value the efficient operation of you and your computer together, you should buy again—this time with a clearer idea of what your true needs are.

Often, you just can't tell what features you really need until you have worked with some program in that subject area. So one of the wisest things that you can do is to buy as carefully as you can, but be prepared to buy again.

I bought four different text editor programs until I found the one with which I wrote this book. Later I bought another one, just because it might be better (it was—but not better enough to be worth retraining myself to use it). My most expensive software buy ever was an accounting program that I came to hate; I gladly bought another. It was cheaper and a little better. Don't be afraid to do this yourself when necessary.

After that advice, what can we tell you about general rules for buying software? Quite a bit. There are more sound, practical principles in selecting programs than you might expect.

The first thing to look for is how well does the program fit into the rest of your system? Are its data files in a standard format, or something weird and wonderful that no other program can touch? Are the data formats well documented so that, if you wish, you can write new programs to use the data? (This is particularly important for accounting data.)

On the subject of programs fitting into the rest of your system is the question of integrated programs. Integrated programs combine several functions that traditionally have been met with separate, isolated programs. Integrated packages are a relatively new item in the software market and a very exciting one. While each part of an integrated package might provide less than all of the features you want, all the parts will work together. And best of all, the "flavor" of the program, its command structure, and the way it presents displays to you, will be consistent.

Then, are the programs hostile to your system? Don't laugh—too many programs are. If a program is copy protected, then it can't be transferred to a hard disk system or an electronic disk, and this means it will not fit into your own work flow as easily as it would otherwise. But the greatest enemies of your system are those few programs which require you to "re-boot" your system to use them. If you have to shut down the operation of your computer and restart it just to use some program, then that is a major disruption of your computer. You may not know it now, but in the future it is likely that you will have your computer doing more than one thing—working with you in the "foreground," while some other tasks are being worked on in the "background." Having to re-boot your system totally disrupts this sort of multiple use of the computer. Even without this multi-tasking, a re-boot of your computer is a stupid waste of time and effort; and you should avoid any programs that call for it.

If your computer system has a hard disk, as more and more of the serious user's systems do, then it is very important to you that your programs not be copy protected. The same applies if you use an electronic disk to speed your work, as I do. Chapter 16 covers the special needs of hard and electronic disks.

I'M SO USER-FRIENDLY, I'M GOING TO ASK YOU A DOZEN QUESTIONS BEFORE I'LL LET YOU GET ANY WORK DONE!

BOLINGER—

Menus, help screens, and the sort of program features that are called user-friendly, are another factor. The standard wisdom is that menus—which are screen displays that list a program's options and features—are always a good thing. You might be surprised to learn that this isn't true. If a program is used only occasionally, or if it is used by relatively non-technical people, then lots of user-friendliness can be very nice. On the other hand, when you use a program a lot, you'll become proficient in using it, and then menus and help-screens get in the way of your work. Example? The text editor used to write this book doesn't have a single help screen or menu screen, and I'm grateful for it. There's another way of approaching menus and help screens. The ideal, really, is for a program to feature menus and such, but keep them out of your way when you don't need them. The fifth text editor that I bought works that way, and it's one of the reasons why its even superior to the one I use (which is flawed but familiar, like one of the family).

Related to the subject of user friendliness is a program's command structure. How do you tell a program what to do? This can greatly affect how easily and efficiently you can use the program. Here again the standard folk wisdom isn't quite true. Use of function keys is slick but may not be the most efficient form of command. The widely popular word processor WordStar uses alphabetic commands rather than function keys, because a skilled typist is disrupted by having to reach for function keys. Heed the lesson of WordStar—for a heavily-used program, different rules apply. What is efficient and friendly for a program that is used casually may be tiresome in a program that you use a lot.

When a program does use function keys, does it use them well for your particular computer? While the alphabetic part of a keyboard is very standard, the rest of it, cursor keys, function keys and all, vary greatly. It is quite possible that a program for your computer has been adapted from another computer. This is particularly true for DOS programs, which are often developed first for the IBM Personal Computer, and then adapted for the general DOS market. Sometimes this can lead to a very inappropriate use of your computer's special keys.

Part of the question of command structure is how menus work. Some menus let you choose from a list with a single key stroke. Others make you move through a list of options with the space bar or cursor keys, and then select your choice with the *enter* key; that looks slick, but is harder to use. Likewise, if you can select from a menu or from a yes-no choice with a single key stroke, do you also have to press the *enter* key? If you do, that's more of a nuisance to use. When a program acts directly on a keystroke (rather than also needing an *enter* key), the program is said to have "live keys" rather than dead keys. Live-key operation is usually better—quicker, easier, more efficient; but for dangerous operations (like anything that could destroy some of your data), a dead-key approach is probably better.

The next thing to consider in selecting programs is customization. Any complex program presents you with a lot of choices. You ought to be able to choose once and be done with it. But many programs demand that you tell them what you want each time you use them. If a program can be customized, then its worth to you may multiply greatly. The best programs in this regard keep a profile data file, which records your customization. The next best possibility is a program that is customized internally through the use of a patcher, which makes the appropriate changes in the program. If you are considering getting a patchable program, find out if the patches are done easily, say through a special-purpose patching program. Some programs can be customized through patching, but the patches have to be done by a skilled technician (usually using DOS's patching tool, the DEBUG program).

Related to customization is whether or not a program comes with its source code. The source code can be very valuable to you, for example, to make customization possible, or to give you guidance in writing programs that use the same data. It isn't always appropriate to get source code, so don't expect it as if you had a natural right to it. Most source code contains proprietary programming techniques, and you can't expect program developers to give away the family jewels. If the source code is in assembly language, you have less reason to want it than if it is in BASIC. And you have more reason to expect the source code for an accounting program than for a word processor. But if the source code is available, that is a factor in selecting one program over another.

Let's summarize the general things you can look for in selecting programs:

- Don't be reluctant to discard a poor program and buy a replacement; finding good programs can be an experimental process.
- Does the program fit into your use of your computer?
- Is the program part of an integrated package?
- Is the program hostile to your work flow?
- Does the program have a good user-interface?
- Is it user-friendly enough?
- Is it too user-friendly to be convenient?
- Are its commands easy to use or a nuisance?
- Is the use of special keys good or poor?
- Can the program be easily customized?
- Is the source code available, if it is appropriate?

After that, let's look at the specific needs in four program areas—word processors, spreadsheets, accounting, and programming languages.

17.2 Choosing Word Processors

What we all call word processing really breaks down into two separate functions, and possibly two separate programs. The two halves of a word processor are a text editor and a print formatter.

The task of a text editor is to work together with you in entering and changing your text material. The job of a print formatter is to take care of page numbering, paragraph justification, headings, footings, underlining, and in general controlling your printing device.

In the best dedicated word processing systems, these two tasks are so well integrated that the person using the system is completely unaware of any separation between the two. This is exactly how it should be. But for small personal computers, word processing programs do not live up to this standard. This means that what we use on our DOS computers is likely to be much clumsier than what it ought to be.

There are two approaches to getting a word processor on a DOS computer. One is to select and buy a text editor and a print formatter separately. The other is to buy a complete word processing program. The first, separate approach appears to be a very unwise one—and it is, usually. However, you may find a text editor so well suited to your working style, that it is better for you to use it separately. Also, for economy you may choose to use the text editor which comes free with your computer—such as DOS's EDLIN editor, which we'll cover in Chapter 19—and buy only an inexpensive print formatter.

Usually the most sensible thing is to buy a complete word processing program, such as the famous WordStar, or one of the many excellent competing word processors. But you should at least consider the alternative.

Selecting a word processor, or a text editor program, is a special area, unlike the purchase of any other software. There are two main reasons for this. One is that there are more text editors and word processors to choose from than there are other types of programs. Programmers seem to love to develop text editors, so the market is flooded with them. This gives you lots of programs to choose from; and frankly you need the variety, for the other thing that sets text editors apart from other programs: their complexity.

Text editors are different from most other programs because they have so many complex commands built into them—commands to insert and delete, commands to copy and move material, commands to set margins, commands to move around in the text, by line, or by word, or by paragraph, and many other commands as well. All these commands have to be dealt with while still making it as easy as possible for you to type in your written text. This is not only very complex in itself, but it also raises a tricky question: how are these commands to be given? With function keys, which vary greatly from computer to computer? With alphabetic command codes, which interfere with the typing of the text? And how is the display going to be formatted? And how is help with the complex commands to be given? With lengthy help menus? With a terse menu area on the screen?

Because of all of that, text editor programs differ widely in their user interface and in the quality of the human engineering that has gone into them. And while we might be able to evaluate different text editors and word processors by some fairly objective standards, different peoples' taste in how they want to work makes a great deal of difference in how happy they will be with one editor or another.

This means that your choice of a word processor may be more difficult than your choice of any other program, if a word processing program is going to be an important tool for you. If word processing is a minor thing for you, then the choice is less critical but still not an easy software choice.

Here are some guidelines to help you make an intelligent decision. First, does the word processor work well with your particular printer? Does it make good use of any special features of your printer? There is little standardization in printer features, and some have a few features that are very valuable—if your word processor can take advantage of them. Next, do you need lots and lots of features, or would a spartan word processor serve you well?

Then, consider the command and menu structure. For a casual, or non-expert user, menus and help screens are necessary to guide you through the complex commands; but for an experienced heavy user, they are a nuisance. And then there are the commands. For an expert typist, alphabetic commands are almost certainly best—this is the approach that WordStar has taken. But for other users, a function-key approach probably will work better. Consider how well the use of function keys matches your computer's keyboard. And also consider customization; do you get to choose what command is assigned to what function key? The two editors I like best on my computer can both be fully customized—that is one of their greatest strengths.

If your word processor will be used a lot, choose very carefully. The difference among word processors is greater than the difference among accounting programs or spreadsheet programs.

17.3 Choosing Spreadsheets

Spreadsheet programs, like the original VisiCalc, are designed to do routine calculations on numbers that are organized in a rectangular grid, or spreadsheet. The most common work for spreadsheet programs is business financial calculations such as budgeting and forecasting, but their use has spread far beyond that.

When we consider spreadsheet programs, we start with the granddaddy of them all, VisiCalc. There are now quite a few competitors for VisiCalc, so you are likely to have a lot of choice. Here are the factors that I think you should consider in looking at spreadsheets.

First, how advanced are its features? The original VisiCalc has been surpassed by many of its later rivals, particularly in terms of the flexible use of cells on the calculation worksheet. SuperCalc, Multiplan, and others may be more advanced than VisiCalc. When Multiplan was introduced by Microsoft, it set a new standard for convenient and advanced features, but by the time you read this there may be a new kid on the block that is even better. On the other hand, consider if you need extra features. If you will be buying template programs to use with your spreadsheet, then all you may need is the lowest common denominator, the features of the original VisiCalc.

Second, who is it from? I would trust VisiCalc's VisiCorp and Multiplan's Microsoft to stay in business, giving us new and better versions. Other spreadsheets might not be supported over time.

Third, is it hostile to your system? SuperCalc can be copied to hard disk systems. VisiCalc and Multiplan can't. Check on the spreadsheets that are available for your computer, and find out if they can be copied to other media, or if they require re-booting the system in order to use them. This is a major factor in how convenient these programs are to use.

Fourth, will it work with standard VisiCalc templates? There are many useful template programs on the market, which can greatly enhance the value of your spreadsheet program. Find out if yours can use them.

Fifth, does it make use of advanced hardware? Many DOS computers can be fitted with fast floating-point processors, like the Intel 8087 arithmetic co-processor. If your use of a spreadsheet is extensive, your calculations can become lengthy. A spreadsheet program that can use the 8087 might be especially valuable to you.

Sixth, does it fit into the other programming tools that you use? If you are using a spreadsheet for some interactive what-if calculations, then you are using the spreadsheet by itself. But many spreadsheet users need to incorporate the results of calculations into reports and proposals. Find out how easily its results can be used by your word processor. This concern, by the way, is one of the strongest arguments for integrated multi-function programs, which we cover in Section 17.5 below.

17.4 Choosing Accounting Programs

Accounting programs are a work horse for many small business computers, and they can be a major source of problems, because a business can become dependent upon them.

Only you and your accountant can judge if a program has the kind of features that you need. Unfortunately, you probably can't find out if a program meets your requirements without not only buying it, but also investing several months effort into using it. This is a nasty fact of life with accounting software. It also tends to be among the most highly priced software and the clumsiest to use. *And* to have the most programming errors in it. In my experience with computer systems both large and small, accounting programs seem to always be a difficult area, and it is rare for a business to be fully happy with its accounting programs.

Keep this in mind when you get a package of accounting programs. Be prepared for more difficulties than you usually encounter with other programs, and take care that you don't expose your business to more danger than you can afford through premature over-dependence upon an accounting package.

Besides your own particular accounting needs, here are some general things that you should look for in accounting programs.

If the program is written in BASIC, as many are, can it be compiled for extra speed? This alone could become extremely important to you.

How well can it be customized? It is with accounting packages that you are most likely to need a program to be adapted to your needs, and to have the program's questions answered once and for all, not over and over again each time the program is used.

One of the ways you might want to customize any program, especially an accounting program, is to change its use of disk drives. It is very common for the authors of application programs like accounting packages to be quite short-sighted about the use of disk drives. Often the programmers either never think that you might want to use their program with a different disk setup than they envisioned, or else they are just too lazy to do what is needed to give you a choice. If you have the source code for the program, as is true for very many accounting programs written in BASIC, you might be able to change the use of disk drives. I've done this myself with the General Ledger program that I use for my own bookkeeping. Even if you can't—or daren't—change the source code for a program, it is often relatively easy and safe to patch a program to change its references to specific disk drives. In Chapter 20 we'll go over the details of how to do this.

Can it be instructed to perform a lengthy series of operations unattended, or does it demand constant human interaction? Some accounting programs will eat up the work time of their users just replying to stupid and unnecessary questions from the programs.

Is the vendor in business to stay? Your general ledger program may not need to be updated next year, but a payroll program probably will, and maybe a fixed assets program as well.

Are all the subjects you need covered included in one package? You don't want a payroll from one software vendor and a general ledger from another. What are all the parts? General ledger, accounts payable, accounts receivable, payroll, fixed assets, and inventory control. Make sure that all the parts you'll need in the future are available with the program you buy now.

Does the accounting package include some kind of general report writer? Large computer users have long ago learned that they need custom reports to supplement their accounting package's standard reports. You shouldn't have to discover that your accounting package is missing a part that you didn't realize you would need.

Converting from manual bookkeeping methods to computerized methods is usually a bloody ordeal. I've personally guided companies large and small through the process, so I know what I'm talking about. The instruction manuals for the accounting package you select may be especially lacking in guidance in this area. Choose carefully. Move slowly. Get experienced help if you can.

We've advised you, in general, to be prepared when necessary to buy more than one piece of software. With computerized accounting there is a parallel to this idea. Be prepared to convert your bookkeeping more than once. You might set out with a chart of accounts that is structured one way, and then later learn that you would be better off with another structure. Or you might want to switch your receivables from "open item" to "balance forward." Be willing to re-convert your accounting if it is called for; the payoff may be tremendous, even though the work involved will probably be a real pain.

17.5 Choosing Multi-function Packages

One of the most exciting and useful developments in program tools has been the appearance of integrated multi-function packages. Typically these packages include several or all of the functions of word processing, spreadsheet calculation, data management, and communications. The advantages of these packages are twofold. First, the functions are integrated so that work and data can flow easily from one function to another. Second, and even more important, only one command language is needed. Without an integrated package, if you need to incorporate spreadsheet calculations into a written report, you will have to use three different command languages—DOS's, the spreadsheet's, and the word processor's—each with its own style and flavor. With an integrated package, there is one style of command that works for all functions.

Since the number one problem of using a computer is learning computer skills, the number one advantage of an integrated package is that it reduces the number of skills that you have to acquire.

Integrated packages are a relative newcomer on the computing scene, so you may not have much choice of packages for your DOS computer. On the other hand, you might even choose your computer on the basis of the integrated programs available for it. (When VisiCalc was the first and only spreadsheet program, quite a few computers were sold just because they would run Visi-

Calc. And at the time that the integrated package 1-2-3 was introduced, some computer pundits were saying that this was another instance where people would buy a computer just to be able to run a particular program.)

What should you look for in an integrated package? The first thing is breadth of features. It defeats the whole purpose of an integrated package if it lacks even one single function that you expect to use a lot. What are the functions that might be in an integrated package?

- text editing (the first half of a word processor);
- report formatting and printing (the other half);
- graph generation;
- spreadsheet calculation;
- data management (storing, organizing, and searching your notes, whether they are mailing addresses, telephone numbers, or paragraphs of written comments);
- small-scale programming (e.g., a program to search your mailing list for some criteria and then place the matched addresses in another file);
- data communications (sending and receiving data with other computers);
- message communications or electronic mail (keeping track of messages sent and received).

When personal computing is fully mature, we will see these services richly implemented on our computers. But for now, the best we can expect is a reasonable number of them, working reasonable well. Consider the functions that you most need and look for them.

Next, consider which functions are fully provided and which are just nominal. One package might have a strong spreadsheet, but a weak text editor. Put your functional needs in priority, and compare your list with various packages' strong and weak points.

The next thing to consider in choosing an integrated package is speed. To make it practical to include many features, the operating speed of a package might be compromised severely. Hopefully not, but it might be. If you will be using an integrated package a lot—and the chances are good that you will—then it must work fast enough to not interfere with the flow of your work.

Finally, consider communications. Communications—sending data and messages between computers—may not be part of your plans now, but as personal computing spreads, communications will become more and more important. So I would advise that you consider communications capability to be part of your list of required features, even if you think that you will never need it.

17.6 Choosing Programming Languages

In Chapter 10 we covered the complex and interesting area of programming languages in more detail, but a little summary here wouldn't hurt.

Don't be shortsighted. Program maintenance usually eats computer centers alive—both in the cost of doing program maintenance, and in the hidden cost of program maintenance that doesn't get done. Choose a program language and programming methodology that makes maintenance practical. This argues heavily in favor of languages such as Pascal and C, and in favor of a fanatical devotion to learning and using structured programming methods.

There are many special advantages to using the language BASIC: it is universally available on personal computers, it is widely known, it is very flexible, and it can be both interpreted and compiled. This argues heavily in favor of using BASIC, but BASIC is dangerously hard to write in a structured way, and it is relatively slow even in compiled form.

There are many advantages to using an extra-high level language, such as a VisiCalc template or a dBase II program. Speed will be sacrificed, but programming brevity and ease of maintenance will be gained.

When you get down to choosing, remember that the quality of the compiler (or interpreter) that you use is as important as the quality of the programming language.

18

Avoiding Shortsighted Mistakes

If you are new to computing, or even if you aren't, you may be worried about making expensive mistakes with your computer. First, expect to make plenty of mistakes, and don't worry too much about it. Computing is a young field, and most of us don't have a lot of experience with it. So making plenty of mistakes comes with the territory; expect it, and be prepared for it. What we'll try to do in this chapter is to help you avoid some mistakes that are especially short-sighted or especially costly.

18.1 Hardware Mistakes

Since computer equipment is so modular and computers are so expandable, it is hard to make a mistake in getting too little equipment. If you end up needing an expansion feature that you didn't need at first, you can always get it later.

This seems to argue in favor of under-buying at first, and adding onto your computer later. But the simple fact is, it usually works the other way—you are usually better off buying more equipment than you think you might need. It is usually better to over-buy than to under-buy when selecting computer equip-ment. Why is this so? Here is the simple reason. It is rare to buy a piece of computer equipment and then later realize that you never needed it at all. And it is a common experience for computer users to waste their time because they don't have a piece of equipment that they need—but are reluctant to add to their system—or waste their money by replacing some part of their system with better (faster, bigger, etc.) components. The market for used parts of personal computers is weak, so if you need to replace your printer or disk drive with a better one, you may not be able to recover much or any of the cost of your first one.

Unless your budget is a severe constraint, it is wiser to over-buy in comput-ing than to under-buy. The history of computing shows that people almost always need more, more, more as time goes by. And if you get plenty to start with, you are usually better off. Obviously you shouldn't buy everything in

IT CAN BE CONFUSING, DECIDING WHETHER TO UNDER-BUY OR OVER-BUY.

sight and spend your money wildly. Yet it is a simple fact of computer life that you are better off, when equipping your computer, to get more rather than less—more speed or more capacity than you might think you will need.

What mistakes are you most likely to make in under-buying? Too little memory, for one. Memory is relatively cheap so you can get plenty. On the other hand, memory is something you can add on but rarely have to replace. Usually, though, there is a large economy in buying memory in big chunks. For example, if you add 128K of memory to your system, and then later add another 128K, it will probably cost much, much more than if you had bought 256K to begin with. Another common under-buy is too little disk capacity. Your data storage needs are likely to grow beyond anything you imagined possible. Adding disk storage is likely to mean discarding your old disk devices, so this can be a real money-waster. If you can add capacity by adding equipment, don't worry about under-buying. But if adding capacity will mean replacing equipment, you would be better off over-buying than under-buying.

The third most likely under-buy is printer quality. Printers that produce a high-quality appearance, especially what's called letter-quality printing, are usually expensive. This is a natural area for computer buyers to economize, but is also one of the most common areas for people to be dissatisfied with their equipment. Since printers can be so expensive, it is harder to blithely recommend that you buy a better printer than you may need. But think carefully. Upgrading to a better printer can be a real waste of money. In my own experience, this is where I have wasted the most money, by buying printers that were less than what I needed.

The biggest thing to consider, of course, is the computer itself. Personal computers today don't come with many limitations on them, particularly DOS computers. It is only in buying game-oriented computers that you are likely to get a computer with too many limitations. But if you are choosing between one model of computer and another, consider deeply the expansion options and the raw computing horsepower. The last thing you want to have to replace, and the most expensive thing to replace, is the computer itself. So if you are choosing between one computer and another, err on the side of more power and more expandability, rather than less.

To recap, the most common and expensive shortsighted mistakes that are made in buying personal computer hardware are buying too little disk storage capacity and too low a quality of printer. An even more common mistake, though a less costly one, is to buy too little memory; this won't waste much money, but it can waste your time. Finally, the most expensive mistake of all is to buy too little in the computer itself—too little expansion capability or too little computing speed ("horsepower").

18.2 Software Mistakes

Making mistakes in buying software can be very expensive, even more wasteful of your time and effort than of your money; and your money can be wasted in basketloads if you make the wrong moves in buying software for your DOS computer. You are more likely to make mistakes in buying software than in buying hardware. It is easy to waste money in this area.

In the last chapter we covered some general rules that can guide you in selecting software. But here, let's take a short look at what are common shortsighted mistakes in buying software.

Probably the most important mistake is to under-estimate how much you will want to tie your use of software together; by that we mean using one piece of software in conjunction with another. Integration is the key here. The more integrated the software, the better. This is again a strong argument in favor of multi-function packages. You may, quite wisely, want to buy the best available word processor and the best spreadsheet program. But you might be even wiser to get an integrated package that did both, even if that means having a second-rate word processor and spreadsheet. The same rule obviously applies to accounting packages. If you are going to need payroll processing in the future, then it would be very shortsighted to buy a general ledger that doesn't have an accompanying payroll module, no matter how superior the general ledger might be.

YOU'RE MORE LIKELY TO WASTE MONEY ON SOFTWARE THAN HARDWARE.

Another common software mistake is to under-estimate how important speed and ease-of-use will become to you. When you start out in computing, speed may not seem extremely important. You may think that it is no big deal that it takes a few key strokes to tell one program to do some operation, while another program could do the same thing automatically through a batch processing command. But as time goes by, it is likely that your use of the computer, and your dependence on it, will grow a lot. Then the speed and ease of use of your computer programs will become major factors in how efficiently you, yourself, can get your work done.

Still another shortsighted mistake in buying programs is to under-estimate how important it is to be able to transfer programs to fast access storage, such as hard disks and electronic disks. As the volume of your programs grows, and as the amount of time you spend working with your computer grows, the worth of hard and electronic disks grows. When that happens, copy protected programs, which cannot be transferred to other disk systems, become real enemies of your system.

18.3 Operational Mistakes

There are three main mistakes that you can make in organizing the operation of your computer. The first one we don't really have to hammer into you, since you will hear it from so many sources: make backup copies of your data. Again and again and again.

Computers are so thoroughly reliable that it is easy to feel that your data is quite secure. But that isn't the case. Your data is in danger in two ways. The lesser danger is from failure of the computer—or its programs—destroying your data. The greater danger is from inadvertent erasure of your data. It is extremely easy to lose your data by a mistaken DEL/ERASE command.

The solution to this operational danger is to frequently make backup copies of your data. Because this can be time consuming, it is tempting to skip doing it. The best and safest way to safeguard your data is to incorporate backup procedures into your working methods, through batch files. Chapter 11 will tell you more about how to do this.

YOUR BEST COMPUTER INVESTMENT IS INVESTING IN THE TIME TO GET ORGANIZED.

The second shortsighted mistake in the operation of your computer is not taking the time to get organized. It is easy to think that you don't need to devote much effort into organizing your use of the system. But the simple fact is, that one of the best investments that you can make of your time is to carefully organize how you use your computer, including placing the right programs together on your disks, and especially working out the most effective batch processing files. And once you've done that, do it again when your work patterns change, or you understand a better way to get organized. The payoff in smooth, easy work is tremendous. I find that it pays off for me to take the time to refine my working procedures roughly once a month. Even after a full year of heavily using the same computer, I still reorganize every month or so; it takes me about a half-hour's effort, and then what I'm working on goes more smoothly.

The third operational mistake is about neglecting to use batch files altogether. There is nothing else in the DOS operating system that can more enhance the smooth and effective operation of your computer system than automating working procedures with batch processing files. Turn to Chapter 11 for more information about batch files.

19

The EDLIN Editor

In this chapter we'll take a look at the text editing program that comes with DOS, the EDLIN program.

19.1 Introducing EDLIN

To begin, we should set the stage to tell you what an editor is for, and how EDLIN fits into the world of editing.

Ordinary written material, such as a letter or report that you or I might write, is dealt with in a special way by computers. Computers have a special format for storing written material: the format known as an ASCII text file. In Chapter 9, where we discuss file formats, you'll find some more details about how ASCII text is recorded in the computer. Here are just a few key things that we need to know about ASCII text files.

The data that is stored in an ASCII text file is the ordinary stuff of written material—alphabetic letters, numbers, and punctuation symbols like the comma and the period. The very words you are reading here are ASCII text, and they are stored in my computer in the form of an ASCII text file. ASCII text files are organized into distinct *lines* of text, which will become very important to us as we learn how to work with ASCII text files. The punctuation that we put into a text file—the commas and the periods—don't mean much to the computer, but the computer adds its own special punctuation to an ASCII file. This special punctuation is used to mark the end of each line, and also the end of the entire ASCII text in a file. This special punctuation—end-of-line and end-of-file—is invisible to us. While we see our own punctuation, the computer keeps its special punctuation hidden from us, so that we don't see the end-of-line markers themselves, but we do see their results, which is the separation of our text into distinct lines.

ASCII text files are widely used in computers, and there are three uses which are particularly interesting to us: ASCII text files are used for word processing data, for the source code of programs (which is what computer programs look like when we write them), and for batch processing files. Most computer users will do word processing on their computers, many will be writing programs, and every one should know how to create and change their DOS batch processing files—so everyone who uses a DOS computer needs to know how to work with ASCII text files.

There is a special kind of program which is designed to help us enter and change ASCII text, and these programs are known as *editors*. A word processing program is basically just an editor with many fancy frills. The frills are important in a word processor, but the heart of word processing is just the entering and revising of written text: in short, editing.

It is hard to use a computer well without an editor program on tap. Not only does much of what we want to do with the computer call for an editor, but also we need an editor to create batch processing files. The key to effective use of our computers lies in using good batch commands, and we need an editor to create the batch processing files, which define what a batch command is to do. So if we want to be proficient in the use of our computers, we must be able to use an editor to create our batch files.

Editor programs are so important that most computer users buy them specially—often getting a complete word processing program which includes an editor. But having an editor is so important that DOS can't rely on your buying a separate one—so DOS includes a simple editing program, called EDLIN. If you don't have another editor, you will need to use EDLIN. But even if you do have a word processing program, you may find that you need to use EDLIN, simply because your word processor may be too powerful to be handy for simple editing tasks. You don't hunt mice with an elephant gun, and you may find that you don't want to use your word processor to create simple batch files. So even if you have another powerful editor, you probably need to learn how to use EDLIN.

There is another very practical reason why you should learn how to use EDLIN. For quick work with batch files, you ought to have a copy of an editor program on each of your program disks. But your main editor, or word processor, may be too large to fit on each disk. So it is good to have a small, compact editing program available, and EDLIN fills that bill.

To use EDLIN effectively you have to understand how it works, and that calls for a little discussion about different ways of editing. EDLIN is a type of editor known as a *line editor* (that's what gave it the name EDLIN) or a command editor. Most good editors, including word processors, are full-screen editors, which means that they show as much as possible of the material being edited on the display screen, and new material is entered right in its proper place on the screen.

While a full-screen editor shows as much of the file as possible, a line editor like EDLIN conceals information, which makes working with it more cumbersome. To display any part of a file, or to do anything else, we must enter *commands*, which tell EDLIN what to do. The commands might be to display part of the file or to make some changes to a file. But whatever we do, it is all done in terms of commands, and the commands operate on the lines of a file.

EDLIN always refers to a file in terms of the numerical order of the lines in the file. If we had a file with three lines in it like this:

```
This is the first line
This is the second line
This is the third line
```

EDLIN IS A CRUDE WRITING TOOL, LIKE A BOX OF CRAYONS.

then EDLIN would refer to these as line numbers 1, 2, and 3. To help us keep track of the line numbers, EDLIN always gives the line number when it displays lines from the file; so if EDLIN were to display the above lines, they would *appear* like this:

```
1: This is the first line
2: This is the second line
3: This is the third line
```

The line numbers that EDLIN shows are *not* part of the data that is in our ASCII text file—it is just shown for reference.

Another thing that you need to know about EDLIN and line numbers is that the lines are renumbered after any change. So if we delete line 2, what was line 3 (which in our example, says "This is the third line") immediately becomes the new line 2. Likewise, if we insert a new line following line 1, the old line 2 gets a new number as line 3.

To make it easier to work with, EDLIN keeps track of its current place among the lines of a file. When EDLIN displays lines, it indicates which is the current place in the file by marking it with an asterisk (*). For example, if the current location in our three-line file was the second line, then it would be displayed like this:

```
1: This is the first line
2:*This is the second line
3: This is the third line
```

When we tell EDLIN to do something for us, we can either tell it to work with some particular line number or to work relative to the current line.

Recall the DOS editing keys which we covered in Chapter 7. These keys are used to help us enter and revise DOS commands, and they work equally well when we are working with EDLIN. For anything we are typing into EDLIN, whether it is a command to EDLIN or data we are entering, we can use the DOS editing keys to revise.

There is one more item we need to cover before we can move onward into the actual use of EDLIN, and that is a safety feature that is built into EDLIN and many other editors. When EDLIN is used to change a file, it does not destroy the old file. Instead, the old file data is kept under a different name—the old data is left in a file with the original filename, and a filename *extension* of BAK, short for backup copy. If we have made some disastrous error in editing a file, the BAK copy will help us recover from the mistake. Because of this backup convention, we can't edit a file which has an extension of BAK—if we need to work with a BAK file, then we must rename it first.

Now we can move on to see EDLIN in action.

19.2 Ordinary EDLIN Commands

We begin using EDLIN entering the EDLIN command name, followed by the name of the file we want to edit. For example:

```
EDLIN B:FILENAME.EXT
```

EDLIN requires that we give it the name of a file to work with (many other editors don't need a file name to start with, but EDLIN does). The file can either be an *existing* file, which we want to change, or a *new* file which we want to create.

When it begins, EDLIN will look for the file we've named, and if it already exists, EDLIN will read it into memory. After EDLIN begins, it will give us one of three messages. If EDLIN doesn't find the file, it will report:

```
New File
```

If we knew that we were creating a new file, that's dandy. If we thought that we were changing an existing file, this means that EDLIN wasn't able to find it—perhaps we misspelled the filename.

If EDLIN finds the file, it will read it into memory if there is enough room for all of the file. It would be a little unusual for us to be using EDLIN with a file which is bigger than will fit into memory, but it could happen. If EDLIN has enough memory space for the file, EDLIN will report:

```
End of input file
```

This message will tell us that EDLIN did find the file, and that there was room for all of it. If there isn't room for the entire file, then EDLIN will give no message at all. This is a little cryptic (which is the sort of thing that makes EDLIN a weak editor), but if we know how to read EDLIN's signs no message means "the file was found, and it's too big to fit into memory."

When a file is too big to fit into memory, EDLIN does not use all the memory available—instead, it keeps a cushion of about 25 percent to give us some working room.

When EDLIN is up and running, it tells us that it is ready for a command by giving its command prompt, which is a simple asterisk (*). To help distinguish when we are working with EDLIN from when we are working with DOS or any other program, EDLIN has this distinct asterisk prompt. So, after EDLIN gives us one if its three messages ("New File", or "End of input file" or no message, meaning "File found and partially read into memory"), EDLIN will give us the asterisk command prompt.

Since we've learned how to start using EDLIN, we might as well make our first order of business learning how to end it. There are two different commands used to end EDLIN's operation. One, E (for end), will write the file from memory to disk, replacing the old file with a new version (and saving the old version as a BAK file). So E-for-end writes the file and then ends operation. To have EDLIN carry out the E command, we type in the single letter, following EDLIN's asterisk prompt, and press the *enter* key, which tells EDLIN to act on the command we have typed.

The other way to end EDLIN's operation is Q (for quit). Q-for-quit is used when we want to stop using EDLIN, but we don't want to write a file back to disk; perhaps we haven't made any changes and don't need to write the file, or perhaps we've make some mistakes in our changes, and we want to discard them. Whatever the reason, if we want to throw away the copy of the file that we have in memory, we use the Q command. As a protection against accidentally losing some work we have done, EDLIN will ask us

```
Abort edit (Y/N)?
```

and unless we answer "Y" for yes EDLIN will continue operation.

Be careful that you keep these two commands straight, or you may write a bad file when you don't want to, or throw away changes that you wanted to keep. E is end *including* writing the changes, and Q is quit *without* writing any changes to the disk copy of the file.

Both of the commands that we have seen so far are given as single letters—E and Q. All of the EDLIN are single letters, which makes it very quick and easy to type them in, as long as we can remember the right letter to use. We always press the *enter* key to tell EDLIN to carry out our commands, just as we do in entering DOS commands.

While the two commands we've seen so far are used by themselves, the other DOS commands take some parameters, which tell them what and where to act. For example, the D-for-delete lines command needs to know which lines to delete. Before we go into the details of each command, let's see how we specify which lines to act on.

When an EDLIN command needs us to tell it what line to act on, we have five different ways we can indicate which line we want to use:

1) We can put in the specific line number, such as 27 or 32500. If we put in a line number that is too big (beyond the end of the lines in memory) then EDLIN acts just as if we had put in the next number after the last line.
2) We can explicitly refer to the line after the last line in memory by typing in a pound sign (#). This has the same effect as entering a line number that is too big.
3) We can indicate that we want to use whichever line is the *current* line by putting in a period (.). A period means, "use the current line number." You'll recall that EDLIN indicates the current line by marking it with an asterisk; after some experience with EDLIN, you'll be able to easily keep mental track of where the current line is, although at first you might be a little confused about it.
4) We can leave the line number blank, and EDLIN will use some default line number which will vary with what makes the most sense for each command.
5) If we're using DOS-2 we can indicate a line number relative to the current line by entering a plus or minus sign and a number, such as "+25" or "−200". This will refer to the line which is that number of lines before (−) or after (+) the current line.

With that background, let's look at some more commands. To add some lines to a file, we use the I-for-insert command. The command is given like this:

*line-number*I

This sets us up to begin inserting lines into the file. The insertion begins *before* the specified line number; and if we leave the line number off, the insertion goes before the current line.

If we are creating a new file, then there is nothing in the file and we have to use the I-insert command to start entering lines into the file. You might expect that with a new file we'd automatically start off inserting information, but EDLIN doesn't work that way—with a new file, the first command that we give EDLIN is the I-insert.

When we give EDLIN the insert command, it sets itself up to let us enter not just one line, but line after line, which is very convenient. At the end of each line, we press the *enter* key to signal the end of that line and the beginning of the next. EDLIN will accept our new lines endlessly. What do we do to stop entering new lines? We give EDLIN the *break* or Control-C command, and EDLIN then knows to stop taking in new lines. When we enter *break*, EDLIN will switch back into command mode, waiting for our next command. To signal this, EDLIN will show its command prompt, the asterisk.One special warning about *break*ing out of insert mode—you should press *break* only after you have pressed *enter* for the last line you inserted. If you press *break* with a line partly entered, it will be thrown away.

The opposite of the I-insert command is the D-delete command. D-delete removes one or more lines from the file we are editing. To delete one line, we enter the command like this, with one line number:

*line-number*D

When we press *enter,* that one line will be deleted; naturally, all the following lines will be renumbered. If we want to delete a group of lines, we give two line numbers, separated by a comma, like this:

*starting-line-number,ending-line-number*D

Both of the lines specified, and any lines in between, will be deleted.

You'll recall that we can always leave a line number specification blank, and a default will be used. If you enter just a D, without a line number, like this:

D

then the current line is deleted. With the range form, if we leave out the first number, like this:

*,ending-line-number*D

then lines are deleted from the current line to the line specified. The reverse *doesn't* work. If you specify

*starting-line-number,*D

it will only delete one line, and not (as we might think) a range of lines from the starting point to the current line.

Naturally we can't do our editing of a file blind. We need to be able to see what we are doing. The L-list command lets us list (that is, display on the screen) lines from the file. Remember that EDLIN doesn't reveal anything about the file we're editing voluntarily. It will only show us exactly what we ask to see, and nothing more. (Full-screen editors show much more information.) The L-list command has a format similar to the D-delete command. We can enter it with no line number, or one line number, or a range of lines:

L
*line-number*L
*starting-line-number,ending-line-number*L

As we mentioned each command has its own defaults, which are tailored to what makes the most sense for it. The defaults are quite different for L-list than they are for D-delete. If we give no numbers, then EDLIN lists 23 lines, centered on the current line—it will show 11 lines before and 11 lines after the current line. This is an easy and convenient way to get a quick snapshot of our current region in the file.

If we enter only the first line number, with or without a comma, EDLIN also shows 23 lines, but starting with the specified line, no matter where the current line is. If you put in just the second line number (with a comma before it, to indicate that it is the second number), then lines are displayed from 11 lines before the current line, up to the specified line.

Do you find this a little confusing? One of the problems with EDLIN is that its rules are too complicated (they are even a little more complicated than what I explained). This is unfortunate, but with a little practice you'll find that the commands like L-list are reasonably easy to use.

The next thing we need to learn about EDLIN is how to make changes to a line that is already in the file. Say we've used the L-list command to find the part of the file we're interested in, so we are ready to make changes. We can delete lines and insert new lines, but how do we just change existing lines? Changes are made with the edit-line command. For this command, we don't have a letter of the alphabet to signal the command; instead, we just enter the number of the line we want to edit. In response, EDLIN displays a copy of the line, as it exists, and then gives us a (seemingly) blank line with the same line number. We can then use the DOS editing keys to make changes to the line, including copying any part of it that we don't need to change. When we have the line the way we want it, we press *enter* and the line is changed. If we decide we don't want to make any changes to the line, we can just press *enter* without typing in any changes and the line will be left as it is.

The edit-line command has a default line number, just like any other command. If we just press *enter*, with no line number, EDLIN will assume that we want to edit the current line. When EDLIN gives us the asterisk command prompt, if we press *enter*, the current line will be displayed and then it is set up for us to change, which we can do with the DOS editing keys.

If we just repeatedly press *enter*, EDLIN will switch back and forth between command mode (with the asterisk prompt) and editing the current line. Each time we switch, the current line location is moved down one. This makes it possible for us to move through the file, line by line, by just repeatedly pressing *enter*. As each line is set up to be edited, we have the option of changing it or moving on to the next line. This is a convenient and quick way to go through a small file, making changes as we need to.

One of the things that an editor needs to be able to do is search through a file to find the location of some text we are interested in. EDLIN has two commands to do this: the S-search command and the R-replace command (which is really a search-and-replace command). We'll start with the S-search command. There are several variations on the S-search. The simplest one is like this:

starting-line-number, ending-line-number S what-to-search-for

The search command searches through the range of lines, looking for the "what to search for." If it is found, then the line with the information is displayed (and made the current line). If EDLIN doesn't find what it is searching for, then it will report with a message "Not found." Each of the three parameters is optional. If the starting line is left off, the search begins with the line following the current line; if the ending line is left off, the search goes on to the end of the file in memory. If the "what to search for" is left off, then EDLIN uses whatever we last gave it as a "what to search for." These three default values make it very easy to continue a search after one instance has been found. After we have had the search command search once, just entering the command

S

with no more parameters, will continue the search from where EDLIN left off. EDLIN will only report exact matches of the information that we asked it to search for. If we are searching for the word "when", like this:

Swhen

then EDLIN would find the word in the middle of a sentence, but it wouldn't find it when the "W" is capitalized at the beginning of a sentence. Some editors can make matches in either upper or lower case, but EDLIN does not—it requires *exact* matches.

There is another variation on the S-search when we put a question mark just before the S; for example

1,35?Swhere

S-search is prepared to search repeatedly when the question mark is used, until we find the instance that we are looking for. Each time EDLIN finds what it is looking for, it displays it, and asks us

O.K.?

If we answer N for no, then EDLIN will go on looking. If we answer Y for yes, then EDLIN will stop looking, so that we can work with the line that was found.

Related to the S-search command is the R-search-and-replace command. This command is entered like the S command, including the optional question mark. But replace is designed to replace what it finds with something else. So we have to enter two sets of characters after the R-command. The two items are separated by a special character, Control-Z. This separator is the same Control-Z character we discussed as the end-of-file marker in Chapter 7. To see what the R-command looks like, here is an example (using just a capital Z to represent the Control-Z key-combination):

1,200Rold informationZnew data

Now the S-search command stops at the first instance that it finds, so that we can do whatever we want with what we found. But the R-replace command has something active to do, so it will automatically repeat its search-and-replace operation all through the range of lines that we give it. In our example, every time that EDLIN finds "old information" anywhere in lines 1 through 200, it will replace it with "new data". Each replacement is displayed so that we can see what is going on.

While the ordinary form of the R-replace command will replace each instance that it finds, the question mark version will stop each time and ask us O.K.? If we answer Y for yes, the replacement is left; if we answer N for no, the line is left as it was, unchanged. *But,* the search-and-replace continues, even if we answer N for no. You will notice that this is an important difference between S-search and R-replace. With S-search, answering yes stops the search while no continues it. With R-replace, answering yes lets the replacement take place while no prevents that one replacement, but the search still continues with *either* a yes or a no answer. So while these two commands are very similar, they respond very differently to the yes-or-no answer.

As you might imagine, it is very easy to make an accidental mess out of using the S and R commands. So you should proceed cautiously until you are comfortable with them.

There are two more commands which are used in that special case when a file is too big to fit into memory. These commands are used to write out some of the file to make room and then to read in more.

The W-for-write command is used to write some lines out of memory. The command is given like this:

*number of lines*W

As many lines as were specified are written from the beginning of the lines in memory. If we don't specify a number of lines, then EDLIN will write just enough lines to get the 25 percent working cushion that it likes to have. After the lines are written, the part of the file that remains in memory is still numbered from line one. So our line numbers don't tell us where the lines are relative to the beginning of the entire file, but only relative to the beginning of what is in memory.

When some space has been made free by writing out part of a file (or by deleting some lines), we can then read in more of the file into memory. This is done with the A-for-append command. A-append is given just like the W-write command:

*number-of-lines*A

If there is enough room, then EDLIN reads as many lines as we have asked it to. If we don't specify the number of lines, then EDLIN will automatically read until memory is 75 percent, leaving a 25 percent cushion of working space.

If EDLIN finds the end of a file, while reading it with the A-append command, it will report it with the message

End of input file

just as it will when it first starts out editing a file.

As you can probably tell from this outline of the ordinary EDLIN commands, EDLIN is not really a convenient and easy editor to use. In practice EDLIN is very clumsy and inconvenient to use, except when you are using it with very tiny files. That, though, is the one thing that I recommend using it for—creating and changing batch files. Little work like batch files are just EDLIN's speed. With anything larger, you should use a more serious editor.

What we have seen so far with EDLIN concerns the commands that are available in all versions of DOS. But DOS-2's EDLIN has four additional commands that are very useful, and we'll cover them in the next section.

19.3 Advanced EDLIN Commands for DOS-2

From the commands that we've seen so far, EDLIN doesn't have any way to move data around, or to duplicate it. If we need to re-arrange our file data, we would be stuck, except for three special commands provided in DOS-2. These commands are C-copy, M-move, and T-transfer.

The C-copy command lets us duplicate some lines, copying them to another part of the file. There are four parameters in this command:

*starting-line,ending-line,where-to,how-many-times*C

Each of the four parameters is optional, expect for the "where to" specification, which must be given. If either the starting or ending lines are left off, then the current line is assumed. If the number of times is left off, then only one copy is made. The copied material is placed before the specified "where to" line, just as it is with the I-insert command.

Usually we would use this command just to duplicate a bunch of material once, but there are times when we might want to use the "how many times" parameter to make several copies. As an example, if we were creating a table or list in a file, we might create a skeleton line (with all the repeated information), copy it as many times as needed, and then fill in the details in each line. Every table and list that you see in this book was created that way (even though I used another editor, not EDLIN).

The M-move command performs a similar function to the C-copy command, but as a move, to take lines out of their current place, and put them somewhere else. With a C-copy, the original copy stays in place; with M-move, it is gone. Duplication makes sense for a C-copy command but not for M-move, so M-move doesn't make multiple copies. There are three parameters for M-move:

*starting-line,ending-line,where-to*M

As with C-copy, the third parameter, "where to", is required and not optional. The starting and ending line numbers will default to the current line if they are not specified.

The third special command that can be used to rearrange data is the T-transfer command. T-transfer is used to read the contents of another file, and to place it into the file being edited. The command is given like this:

*line-number*T*file-name*

The contents of the file are placed in memory, ahead of the specified line number (just as it is with I, C, and M). The file must be specified, naturally enough, but the line number is optional. If it is not specified, then the current line indicates where the new data is to go.

There is one additional command which DOS-2's EDLIN provides, the P-page command. The P-page command is intended for browsing (paging) through a file, and it works just like the L-list command, with one handy exception. L-list leaves the current line unchanged, which might be far from what is being displayed on the screen. The P-page command makes the last line displayed the current line, so that the working location in the file follows what is displayed.

20

The DEBUGer—A Technical Tool

In this chapter we jump into the deep end of the pool and get in way over our heads. Our topic is the DOS programmer's tool command, DEBUG. DEBUG is really quite an advanced tool, and it is not intended for the ordinary user of DOS. But DEBUG may provide capabilities that you need, or you may just want to know what can be done by DEBUG. In this chapter we'll give you a low-level introduction to DEBUG.

20.1 Some DEBUG Background

Freight trucks aren't built like passenger cars, and for good reason. Cars are intended for easy comfortable driving by ordinary people; trucks are built for more rough-and-ready use for professional use by qualified drivers.

Almost everything in DOS is designed for civilian use by the likes of you and me. But there are some special things that need to be done by qualified, technically expert people, and DOS's DEBUG is designed to provide the means to accomplish many important tasks that can't be done except with a sophisticated and complicated tool.

In order for a truck to be able to accomplish its purpose, it can't be made as pretty, or as easy to drive, as an ordinary car. So it is with DEBUG. Much of what DEBUG works with is technical in nature, so the use of DEBUG is equally technical and complicated. This isn't to say that DEBUG is necessarily over your head; you can judge that for yourself. But I can assure you that it is substantially more complicated and technical than any other element in DOS.

The details of using DEBUG are closely tied to the details of the particular microprocessor which is in your computer. Our discussion here will be based on the Intel 86 series of microprocessors, which are used in DOS computers. Most of the features of DEBUG require a rough understanding of the microprocessor, and some of them call for a very thorough understanding.

The first thing you need to know about DEBUG is that it does all of its work in hexadecimal arithmetic; unfortunately, DEBUG doesn't even give us the option of using decimal numbers—everything in DEBUG is done in hexadecimal or hex as it is called.

Hexadecimal arithmetic uses 16 as its base, or radix, instead of 10, which we use. Deep in their hearts, all computers work with binary numbers, so they need to be given, in one way or another, binary numbers. Hexadecimal is simply a shorthand for binary, with each hexadecimal digit standing for four separate binary digits (called "bits"). While our decimal arithmetic uses the ten digits 0 through 9, hexadecimal arithmetic uses sixteen digits, which are represented by 0 through 9, followed by A (with a value of ten) through F (with a value of fifteen).

Here is a table giving a quick outline of the hexadecimal digits:

Hex digit	Decimal equivalent	Binary equivalent
0	0	0000
1	1	0001
2	2	0010
3	3	0011
4	4	0100
5	5	0101
6	6	0110
7	7	0111
8	8	1000
9	9	1001
A	10	1010
B	11	1011
C	12	1100
D	13	1101
E	14	1110
F	15	1111

Hex numbers are interpreted like decimal numbers, but with a base of sixteen rather than ten. If we interpret "12" as a decimal number, it would be, in words:

one times ten plus two equals twelve

but the same "12" interpreted as a hexadecimal number would be:

one times *sixteen* plus two equals *eighteen*

Numbers can be up to four hexadecimal digits long, so they can range from 0 to FFFF, which is equivalent to the decimal number 65,535.

The use of DEBUG involves memory addresses. For Intel-86 computers, complete addresses are five digits long, but they have to be represented by numbers no longer than four digits. This is accomplished by using two numbers to represent an address. The first number, called the segment part, is treated as if it were shifted one place over, the equivalent of multiplying it by "10." The second number, called the relative part, is added to the segment part (shifted over), to get a complete address. It is done like this:

DEBUG IS A POWERFUL PROGRAMMER'S TOOL.

```
1234
5678

179B8
```

When addresses are written out, they are shown with the two parts separated by a colon, like this:

```
1234:5678
```

When DEBUG shows us addresses, it always shows them in that form. When we give DEBUG addresses we can type them in that way, or we can leave off the segment part and the colon and give only the relative part. In that case DEBUG will use a default segment value.

There is one other way that we can specify the segment part of addresses. The microprocessor has *registers*, which are used to hold numbers for addressing memory. Each of the registers has a symbolic name; for example, CS is the name of the *code-segment* register, which customarily provides the segment portion of addresses within a program itself (as opposed to the program's data). Any of the standard symbolic register names can be used, if you know and understand them.

There is much more of a technical summary which we might go into, but rather than lay it all out here we will let it emerge as we discuss the commands that DEBUG can perform.

20.2 The DEBUG Commands

We begin operating DEBUG in one of two ways. We can give the command name, DEBUG, and DEBUG will begin operation by showing us its command prompt, which is a hyphen (-). DEBUG, like EDLIN, has its own command prompt, which is different than the main DOS command prompt. So, when we see a "-" we know that DEBUG is asking us for a command.

The other way to start DEBUG is to give the name of a file after the command, like this:

```
DEBUG A:FILENAME.EXT
```

When we begin DEBUG this way, it will start by reading the file into memory so that we can work with the data in the file.

After we've started DEBUG, we need to know how to stop it. The Q (for quit) command is used to tell DEBUG to end its operation. In response to DEBUG's hyphen command prompt, we type Q, press the *enter* key, and DEBUG ends. As it is for the EDLIN editor, all of DEBUG's commands are single-letter abbreviations.

The first thing we might want to do with DEBUG is to display the information stored in some of memory. Displaying is done with the D-display command. We have to tell DEBUG what we want displayed, which is always a part of our computer's memory; DEBUG needs to know two things about what to display from memory—where to start and how much to show. We must specify where to start as an address (which we saw how to enter in the last section). For how much to display, there are three ways to tell DEBUG how much—we can leave this part of the command blank and DEBUG will show a standard amount, say 80 bytes. Or we can give a second address (relative part only), and DEBUG will display through that address. Or we can indicate the number of characters we want displayed, by keying in L (meaning we're specifying the length we want displayed) followed by the number of bytes (which, unfortunately, must be given in hexadecimal). Here are examples of all three ways of invoking the D-display:

```
D       F000:6000           display from an address, default length
D       F000:6000  6800     display from one address, through another
D       F000:6000  L 100    explicit length, for 100 (hex) bytes
```

These three ways of specifying a section of memory are collectively called a *range*, and several more of the DEBUG commands use ranges; whenever we indicate that DEBUG needs a range, you can give it to DEBUG in any of these three formats.

As a convenience, D-display keeps track of where it has displayed last so that just entering the D command, with no parameters, will display successive parts of memory, which is convenient for browsing.

The information shown by D-display shows the contents of memory in both hexadecimal and character formats, so you can read what is there either way. (The U command, which we are coming to, gives us another way of seeing memory.) Here is a typical D-display:

```
-D 0:0
0000:0000  43 31 E3 00 3F 01 70 00-C3 E2 00 F0 3F 01 70 00  C1c.?.p.Cb.p?.p.
0000:0010  3F 01 70 00 54 FF 00 F0-47 FF 00 F0 47 FF 00 F0  ?.p.T..pG..pG..p
0000:0020  A5 FE 00 F0 87 E9 00 F0-DD E6 00 F0 DD E6 00 F0  %§.p.i.p]f.p]f.p
0000:0030  DD E6 00 F0 60 07 00 C8-57 EF 00 F0 3F 01 70 00  ]f.p°..HWo.p?.p.
0000:0040  65 F0 00 F0 4D F8 00 F0-41 F8 00 F0 56 02 00 C8  ep.pMx.pAx.pV..H
0000:0050  39 E7 00 F0 59 F8 00 F0-2E E8 00 F0 D2 EF 00 F0  9g.pYx.p.h.pRo.p
0000:0060  00 00 00 F6 86 01 00 C8-6E FE 00 F0 F2 00 71 05  ...v...H§§.pr.q.
0000:0070  53 FF 00 F0 A4 F0 00 F0-22 05 00 00 00 00 00 F0  S..p$p.p''......p
```

The information from D-display, and all other DEBUG commands, appears only on your computer's display screen. But you can save a record of it several ways. One is to turn on your computer's echo-to-printer switch, which we discussed in Chapter 7. Another, for DOS-2, is to re-direct the output of DEBUG, say to a file. The display shown above is actual DEBUG output, which was captured in a file using re-directed output and then incorporated into the text of this chapter.

Besides displaying memory, DEBUG also lets us compare two parts of memory with the C-compare command. To work, C-compare needs a *range* to indicate the location and length of the one part of memory, and a second address to indicate the location of the other part of memory. DEBUG will then compare them, byte for byte, and report to us any differences.

Similar to the C-compare command, is the M-move command, which will copy the data in one part of memory to another. Like C-compare, M-move needs a *range* to indicate the move-from locations, and an address to indicate the move-to locations.

Since we have to use hexadecimal numbers with DEBUG, it would be nice to have some aids. Unfortunately, DEBUG gives us no help in converting between decimal and hexadecimal, but it does give us a tool to do addition and subtraction in hexadecimal—the H-hexarithmetic command. To use the H command, we key in H followed by two hex numbers. H will then display their sum and their difference—which gives us easy access to hex addition and subtraction, something that is very useful in working with addresses. But for converting from hex to decimal, we are on our own. To do that, we must turn to a programmer's pocket calculator, or to BASIC (which has easy ways to convert decimal and hex), or to counting on our fingers and toes.

Naturally, we may want to make changes to the information that is stored in memory. DEBUG gives us two ways to do this, with the E and F commands. The E-enter command lets us make direct changes to memory. There are two ways to use the E-enter command, one which lets us just enter data without comment, and the other which lets us see what we are changing first.

The first way of using E-enter is done like this:

E *address list-of-data*

The list of data is stored in memory starting at the address and continuing until everything in the list has been placed in memory. For our convenience, the *list-of-data* can be any mixture of character data and hexadecimal data. If we use characters, then we have to enclose them in quotes to make them distinct from hex numbers. Here is an example:

```
E 0F32:0100 32 "Peter Norton" 32 73 74 69 6E 6B 73 ", doesn't he?"
```

The other way to use E-enter is interactive, with DEBUG showing us the old contents of each byte of memory before we change it. This is very important and useful, because it provides a safeguard against changes being made to the wrong part of memory. Occasionally you may receive patches, which are changes that need to be made to a program. Patches are often given in the form of DEBUG's interactive E-enter commands, so that you can confirm that you are changing what you are supposed to be changing and not something else.

The interactive form of E-enter is invoked by giving E an address, but no list of data to store. E-enter will then display, in hex only, the data at that address and wait for you to key in a new value, also in hex. You either key in a new value, or press the space bar to leave the value unchanged. DEBUG will continue, presenting you with byte after byte to change, until you call the process to a halt by pressing *enter*. You can confirm the changes you made either by later using D-display to show where you made the changes, or by using another feature of E-enter, the hyphen. While you are using the interactive form of E-enter, keying in a hyphen will move you back one byte (just as pressing the space bar will move you forward one). This makes it easy to back-up and confirm what you have done.

The F-fill command can also be used to change the contents of memory. F-fill is used like the automatic form of E-enter, except that we specify a *range* of memory and not just a single starting memory address:

F *range list-of-data*

The reason for the range is that F-fill will duplicate the *list-of-data* as many times as necessary to fill up the range of memory. The list of data can be as long and complicated as you wish, but the most common use for F-fill is to set a block of memory to one byte value, like zero.

We can search through memory for some particular data with the S-search command. S-search needs the same kind of parameters as F-fill: a range (indicate what part of memory to search for) and a list of data, in hex or character formats. S-search will report the address location of each set of data in the range which matches the data list.

Besides the main memory, your computer also has registers which it uses to hold working addresses and temporary results of arithmetic operations. DE-

BUG provides the R-register command so that we can display and change the register values. If we enter the R command by itself, DEBUG will display the contents of all the computer's registers, along with some related information. If we enter R followed by the name of one particular register, then DEBUG will display its contents, and give us an opportunity to enter a new value similar to the way the interactive E-enter command works. To successfully use this command, you must understand quite well how registers are used by your computer, and also how DEBUG uses the registers when it is working.

One of the ways that your computer talks to its various parts and also to the world around it is through an element known as a port. Ports are data paths into and out of your computer's microprocessor. There are many possible ports, and your particular computer will use some of them for special purposes. Generally, you must have a very detailed knowledge of your particular computer's inner workings to be able to understand and use ports. Each port has an *address* which identifies it; these port addresses are similar to, but completely distinct from, memory addresses. Each port can pass data in or out, which is its role in life. DEBUG gives us two commands to move data through ports—I-in reads data from the port and displays it. O-out sends data out the port. The commands are used like this:

I *port-address*
O *port-address data*

While DEBUG gives us the means to display and change data in memory, often our real goal is to display or change data that is on disk. DEBUG provides us with a way to read and write disk data to and from memory. The L-load and W-write commands are used for this. L-load and W-write work in two distinct ways. They can either read and write entire files or specific parts of the disk storage. Let's cover the file part first.

As you'll recall from the beginning of this section, when we start DEBUG we can either start it by itself, or with the name of a file which we want DEBUG to read into memory automatically. If we make changes to the file's data in memory, how do we write it back to the disk? The W-write command, without any parameters, will write the memory copy back to the disk, replacing the original disk copy of the file.

Suppose we want to read another file into memory? How can we do this? It takes a combination of two commands, oddly enough. The first command, N-name, tells DEBUG the name of the file to be read; the second command is L-load, without any parameters (just like writing a file is done with W-write, with no parameters). To read a file we do something like this:

```
N A:FILENAME.EXT
L
```

and then the file is read into memory, just as it would be if we had used that file name when we started DEBUG.

The "naked" form of L-load and W-write is used to read and write complete files, but another form of these commands is used to read specific parts of the disk data. In this case, we specify the memory address we want the data read into, and what part of the disk we want to read from. The command is like this:

L *address drive-number from sector-number sector-count*

The address is the location in memory the data is to be placed to. The drive-number is the equivalent of the letter that DOS uses to identify disk drives, with zero representing the A-drive, one the B-drive, and so forth. This indicates which disk drive the data is to be read from. The from sector-number indicates what part of the disk is to be read; the exact number used depends upon your particular computer, the particular disk format, and also the version of DOS. The sector-count indicates how many disk storage units, called sectors, are to be read into memory.

Writing to specific locations is done with the W-write command, using the same kind of specifications used for an L-load command.

Everything that we have discussed so far has been about and has been working with abstract data. DEBUG also has the ability to work with programs in several interesting ways.

With the D-display command, we saw how to display data in a combined hex and character format. That is just fine if what we are displaying is *data*, but it doesn't tell us much if the information is part of a *program*. To translate raw programs into a more intelligible format, DEBUG gives us the U-unassemble command. U-unassemble translates the hexadecimal of machine language programs into the form of assembly language. Ordinary civilians still won't be able to comprehend it, but anyone who can at least stumble through assembly language programs will be able to decipher some or all of what is being done. Here is an actual example of a U-unassembly done on my computer:

```
F600:0000 E98F7E      JMP      7E92
F600:0003 E8A76B      CALL     6BAD
F600:0006 CB          RETF
```

The display, as you can see, includes the address locations, the data in hex format, and the equivalent assembly language instructions, like "JMP" and "CALL". The assembly language format does not strictly follow what is needed to create an assembly program, but it is closely equivalent.

DOS-2's DEBUG provides the flip side of U-unassemble, the A-assemble command. A-assemble allows us to key in assembly-like instructions, like the "JMP 7E92" that appears above, and have them translated into machine language and stored into memory. While any of us can use the U-unassemble command, and some of us will also be able to understand it as well, only those who are fluent in assembly language can use the A-assemble command successfully. It is more difficult to use DEBUG's A-assemble command than it is to write ordinary assembly programs, since an assembler provides more aid and assistance than DEBUG can. A-assemble is only for proficient experts.

There are two more program-oriented commands which DEBUG gives us. Both of them are quite advanced, and are really only for use by very proficient assembly language programmers. Even then, these two commands are used only in fairly extreme circumstances when programming problems can't be solved by more routine methods. These two commands are T-trace and G-go.

The T-trace command is used to execute a program step by step. With a program ready in memory, T-trace will execute the program's instructions, one at a time, and display the status of the computer, as reflected in its registers. T-trace can be told to stop after each instruction, or to continue for a number of instructions but displaying the results of each one. T-trace is mostly used when a programmer is uncertain about the exact results of some instructions, or of a very small part of a program. T-trace is too laborious to be effective for extensive program testing.

The G-go command also executes a program, but without tracing its results. G-go will execute or carry out a program as quickly as DEBUG is able to. With the G-go command, we can specify locations in the program, called *break-points*, where DEBUG will stop executing it. This is the difference between executing a program by itself, and executing it under the control of DEBUG's G-go command. With break points set, we can run a program and then stop to check the results when an interesting or important part has been reached.

This has been a quick, and only slightly technical overview of what the facilities of DEBUG are. In the next section we'll look at how to use DEBUG to patch or change programs.

20.3 Using DEBUG to Patch

Whatever else we might do with DEBUG, there is one common use that many of us might be using DEBUG for: modifying or patching programs.

There are two different kinds of patching that we might be doing with DEBUG. One is making actual detailed changes, in hexadecimal, to correct a program or to alter it's operating characteristics. For example, some editing and word processing programs are patched with DEBUG in order to customize the way that they operate. When we do this kind of patching, we should be following very careful and detailed instructions that tell us how to make the patches.

The other kind of patching is patching that we might do on our own. This is patching where we don't have to know the exact details of the program that we are changing. Instead, we want to change something more obvious and more easy than a change to the program code. One petty example of this kind of patching is changing a message that a program displays. Another, which we have referred to at several points in this book, is to change a program so that it does *not* tie itself to using specific disk drives.

In order to illustrate how this is done, let's dream up a typical example of how such patching might be done. Suppose we have a program, which we'll call SUPER, and we find that this program really is super in every respect but one: SUPER insists on reading its data from our disk drive B, when we would like it to use whatever default disk drive DOS is currently using. If we can change SUPER so that it doesn't specify a disk drive, then we can move SUPER's data to a hard disk or an electronic disk; in fact, to any disk other than the B-drive that SUPER insists on.

Here is what we would do to try to change SUPER. We don't know in advance if this is going to work—the method is experimental, but there is a very good chance that we will succeed and do no harm in the process.

First we find the SUPER program. It ought to be in a file named SUPER .COM or SUPER.EXE. If SUPER happens to be a BASIC program, it might be stored in a file named SUPER.BAS. Whatever the name, we find it, and copy it to a separate disk (so that we can safely change it without endangering our main copy). In the process, we should note the size of the program file.

Next, we have to consider one picky detail. If the program file has an extension of EXE, then DEBUG will treat it in a special way that makes it possible for DEBUG to use the T-trace and G-go commands. We don't want this for reasons which are rather technical. The main thing is, if we have an EXE file we don't want DEBUG to know about it. So if the file has an extension of EXE, we use the DOS command RENAME to change its extension to anything other than EXE. Let's assume that SUPER is an EXE file, so we will rename it like this:

```
REN SUPER.EXE SUPER.XXX
```

Next, we start DEBUG, and tell it to load the program file. The command is like this:

```
DEBUG SUPER.XXX
```

At this point, DEBUG now has a copy of the SUPER program file in memory. We suspect that inside this program file are specific references to the B-drive, in this form: "B:". So we are going to ask DEBUG to search for them. To use the search command, we have to tell it how much to search, which would be the length of the SUPER.XXX file. If we can translate decimal into hexadecimal, we figure it out. If we can't, we'll tell DEBUG just to search as much as possible. Here is the S-search command that we will use:

```
S 0 L FFFF "B:"
```

Step-by-step, this is what we are asking DEBUG to do: the "S" says we want to search for something. The "0" says to look from the beginning of DEBUG's working memory. The "L" says that we want to search for some length. The "FFFF" says to search for as many bytes as possible; if we knew the exact length of the file (in hexadecimal), we would substitute it here. The last part, in quotes, tells DEBUG that we want to look for the drive specification of "B:".

In response to this command, DEBUG will report where it found "B:". If it doesn't report it anywhere, we are out of luck (sorry) and we have to give up. But instead, DEBUG is likely to report one or even several addresses. If we want to, we can display the data following each address. If DEBUG reported an address like this:

```
04EF:0220
```

then we would use the D-display command to show information from there:

```
D 04EF:0220
```

using exactly the same address that S-search gave us.

When we do this display, we may see only the "B:", but more likely we will see a complete filename, with the "B:" at the front. We're likely to see something like this:

```
04EF:0220 42 3B 46 49 4C 45 4E 41-4D 45 32 32 32 32 32 32
B:FILENAME
```

The combination of the "B:" and the filename is a tip-off that we have found what we want for sure. Our goal is to remove the "B:" part. We can use the E-enter command to replace it with blank spaces, which we do like this:

```
E 04EF:0220 "  "
```

We repeat this process for each memory location that the search command reported that found "B:". When we are done, we write the file back to disk with the W command.

Now we have our modified program file, ready to test. If we renamed it from an EXE file, we need to change its name back:

```
RENAME SUPER.XXX SUPER.EXE
```

Finally, we are ready to test it to see if it works. To play safe, we need to make copies of any current data that SUPER uses just in case the new, modified version gets into any mischief; we'll test the new SUPER with one copy of our data, knowing that if anything goes wrong, we have another, undisturbed copy. Then we try running the SUPER program and see if it now looks for its files not on the B-drive, but wherever we have pointed the DOS default drive. If the test works, then we can start using the modified program with our ordinary data.

The same methods we've described here can be used to locate and change messages that are built into programs. I can think of two plausible reasons why you might want to do this sort of thing. One would be to replace DOS's starting message with your company's own logo; if you want to do that, you'll find the DOS starting message located in the COMMAND.COM file. Another reason would be to translate program messages from English into another language. Whatever your reason, you can use the techniques that we have covered here to make any kind of reasonable changes that you want.

Even if you have no real reason to do this sort of patching work, you might want to give it a try simply to learn the skill of how to do it. It's a skill that might come in handy some day.

Making patches or changes to programs like this is a potentially dangerous process—for we may end up making a program un-usable due to some error on our part or some trick in the program. You need to proceed with caution when you do this kind of work. Under normal circumstances what we have described works just fine, and is surprisingly easy to do.

21

Reference Summary of Commands

In this chapter we'll give you a quick reference summary of the commands which DOS provides, along with some guidance about their use.

21.1 Separate Commands

BREAK

BREAK controls how often DOS will check for the *break*, Control-C key-command which interrupts a program. With BREAK OFF, DOS-2 will check the same as DOS-1—only when output is being written to the display, or when input is being read from the keyboard; with BREAK ON, DOS-2 will check as often as it is able to. This command applies only to DOS-2.

CAT

CAT lists the disk files in an alternative format to the listing given by DIR. CAT is not included in many computer's version of DOS. This command applies only to DOS-2.

CHDIR

CHDIR changes the current directory from one location in the directory tree to another. The current directory can be set independently for each disk drive the computer has. If CHDIR is not given a new directory to switch to, it will simply display the pathname of the current directory, similar to PWD. This command applies only to DOS-2.

CHKDSK

CHKDSK will inspect the status of a disk and report how many files there are, how much space there is, and how much space remains available. CHKDSK will also report on how much memory is available (which has nothing to do with the disk). If CHKDSK discovers any errors in the disks' directory or space allocation table (called the FAT), then it will report them and fix them, either automatically for DOS-1, or under the control of the F-switch for DOS-2.

CLS

CLS will clear the display screen, which is useful for removing extraneous information. This command applies only to DOS-2.

COMP

COMP, also known as FC or FILECOMP, will compare the contents of two files and report any differences. If your computer has the "smart" version of COMP, then COMP will be able to ignore petty differences (such as spaces and upper and lower case differences), and also to search for a matching re-synchronization point when differences are found.

COPY

COPY will copy files with several variations. Individual files can simply be copied from one disk to another; a group of files can be copied, under the control of wild card filenames; one or more files can be copied under new names; and finally, files can be combined, or concatenated, into one file.

CREF

CREF will produce a cross-reference listing of the form that is often used with programming languages. CREF is included with the MASM macro assembler, which may be part of your computer's DOS, or which may be a separately purchased item. CREF is designed so that it can be used quite independently of MASM; but using it with your own programs does require some technical expertise.

CTTY

CTTY is used to re-direct DOS's "console" from the keyboard and display screen to another device—typically a communications line. The main purpose of CTTY is to allow remote control of your computer. This command applies only to DOS-2.

CYPHER

CYPHER is a filter command which can be used to encript or encode data to make it more secure against unauthorized use. Your computer's DOS may not include CYPHER. This command applies only to DOS-2.

DATE

DATE is used to change DOS's record of the current date; it will also display the date, including the day of the week. Normally DATE is used only once when DOS is started up.

DEBUG

DEBUG is a multi-function tool designed to perform technical programming functions relating to the "debugging" of programs. DEBUG can be used to inspect the contents of memory and disks, to change them, and to execute programs under close control. DEBUG is oriented to the technical needs of advanced programmers, and it is not easy to use. DEBUG has a number of sub-commands, which are outlined in Section 22.3.

DEL

DEL, or ERASE, is used to delete one or more files from a disk. When a file has been deleted, it cannot be recovered by ordinary DOS methods.

DIR

DIR is used to display a list of the files in a directory on a disk. DIR will display the entire directory, or a portion selected by filename. The information displayed by DIR includes the file name and extension, the size, and the date and time of the file. Some versions of DOS include an alternate form of DIR named CAT.

DISKCOMP

DISKCOMP is used to compare disks to see if they match *exactly*. DISKCOMP cannot tell if two disks are functionally equivalent (which they would be if they have the same files with the same data); it can only report if they are exact copies of each other, including details that are functionally irrelevant.

DISKCOPY

DISKCOPY is used to make a complete and exact copy of a disk. Although you will often be recommended to use DISKCOPY, the best way to copy data from one disk to another is with the COPY command.

ECHO

ECHO is used to control whether batch file commands will appear on the display screen. ECHO ON, which displays the commands, allows you to see exactly what is happening; ECHO OFF suppresses the command display, which may be irrelevant and confusing. This command applies only to DOS-2.

EDLIN

EDLIN is a simple editor for working with ASCII text files. EDLIN has numerous sub-commands, which are listed in Section 22.2.

ERASE

ERASE is another name for the DEL command, which erases files from disk.

EXE2BIN

EXE2BIN is used to convert programs from the "EXE" format into the "COM" format. This command is intended for use only by program developers—usually only by assembly language programmers.

EXEFIX

EXEFIX is used to convert programs from the "COM" format into the "EXE" format. This command is intended for use only by program developers—usually only by assembly language programmers. Not all computer's versions of DOS include the EXEFIX command.

FC

FC is another name for the COMP command which compares files.

FILECOMP

FILECOMP is another name for the COMP command which compares files.

FIND

FIND is a filter command used to locate those lines in a stream of display data which contain some particular data. This command applies only to DOS-2.

FOR

FOR is an advanced batch file command used to repeat some batch operations for each item on a list of names. This command applies only to DOS-2.

FORMAT

FORMAT is used to prepare disks for use. The disks may be formatted to include a working copy of DOS or not.

GOTO

GOTO is an advanced batch file command used to jump to another part of the file. GOTO can be used to skip over an unwanted portion of the commands, or to skip backwards to repeat commands. GOTO is often used with the IF command. This command applies only to DOS-2.

IF

IF is an advanced batch file command, used to test for some logical condition (such as the existence of a file or an error in a previous program), and then carry out a command based on the test. The command controled by an IF is often a GOTO command. This command applies only to DOS-2.

LIB

LIB is used to control program libraries of the kind that are used by the compilers of languages such as BASIC, Pascal, C, COBOL, and FORTRAN. LIB is intended for use only by advanced programers, and it is not included in some computer's versions of DOS.

LINK

LINK is used in the development of most programs (other than interpretive BASIC programs). LINK is used to combine program parts, including parts taken from a compiler's library. LINK will be used by all programmers, beginning and advanced.

LOCATE

LOCATE is another name for the EXE2BIN command, which converts programs from "EXE" format to "COM" format.

MASM

MASM is a macro assembler used to convert assembly language programs into machine lanuage. MASM, together with CREF, is included in DOS for some computers, and it is a separately sold item for other computers.

MKDIR

MKDIR creates new sub-directories as part of a disk's directory tree. This command applies only to DOS-2.

MORE

MORE is a filter command used to keep display output from rolling off the screen before it can be properly studied. This command applies only to DOS-2.

PATH

PATH is used to instruct DOS about where to look for command program files. PATH can be used to tell DOS to search in several directories and also to search on several disks. This command applies only to DOS-2.

PAUSE

PAUSE is a batch file command used to display a message and wait for a keyboard response.

PRINT

PRINT is used to send disk data files to the computer's printer, while allowing the computer to be used for other purposes. PRINT is a primitive form of print spooler.

PWD

PWD is used to display the current directory (Print Working Directory), similar to the information provided by the CHDIR command. Not all computers include the PWD command. This command applies only to DOS-2.

RECOVER

RECOVER is used to check individual files for damage, and to re-construct the directory of a disk if it has been damaged. RECOVER is a very limited but potentially very useful file recovery command. This command applies only to DOS-2.

REM

REM is a batch file command used to display a message on the display screen.

REN

REN, or RENAME, is used to change the name of one or more files.

RMDIR

RMDIR is used to remove a directory from a disk's directory tree. RMDIR is the opposite of MKDIR, and it is analogous to DEL and ERASE. This command applies only to DOS-2.

SET

SET is used to create or display equations in DOS's environment. SET is an advanced command, which can be used, in conjunction with suitable programming, to control the action of programs. This command applies only to DOS-2.

SHIFT

SHIFT is an advanced batch file command used to shift batch file parameters over one place. SHIFT makes it easier for a batch file to process a list of parameters which can vary in number. This command applies only to DOS-2.

SORT

SORT is a filter command, used to re-arrange lines of display data in alphabetical order. SORT can be used independently of its filter role to simply sort the contents of a file. This command applies only to DOS-2.

SYS

SYS is used to transfer the hidden files (which are part of DOS) to a disk. The main function of SYS is to transfer DOS to a copy-protected disk, or to update the version of DOS on a disk.

TIME

TIME is used to display or change DOS's record of the current time of day. Normally the TIME command is used only once for each time DOS is started.

TREE

TREE is used to display the complete directory tree from a disk. This command applies only to DOS-2.

TYPE

TYPE is used to display the contents of an ASCII text file on the display screen.

VER

VER is used to display the version number of the version of DOS which is being used. This command applies only to DOS-2.

VERIFY

VERIFY is used to instruct DOS to check, or not to check, that any data written to disk was written correctly. For most purposes, it is completely unnecessary to verify the data written to disk. This command applies only to DOS-2.

VOL

VOL is used to display the volume label on a disk. Labels can be placed on disks when they are formatted. This command applies only to DOS-2.

21.2 EDLIN Commands

number—edit a line

Sets up to review and change lines already in the file; use of the DOS editing keys is particularly useful with this command.

A—append

Reads more file data from disk; used only when a file is too big to fit into memory at once; used together with W-write, which will make room by writing out the beginning of the file, from memory to disk.

C—copy

Duplicates lines from one part of the file to another; DOS-2 only.

D—delete

Deletes lines from the file.

E—end

Writes the file to disk and ends the operation of EDLIN.

I—insert

Begins the process of inserting or adding lines to a file; if you are creating a new file, your first command should be I-insert so that you can start entering the data for the new file.

L—list

Displays a group of lines from the file together with their reference line numbers.

M—move

Moves a group of lines from one location in the file to another; DOS-2 only.

P—page

Displays a group of lines similar to the L-list command, but also moves the current location within the file, for convenience; DOS-2 only.

Q—quit

Ends the use of EDLIN, without writing the file back to disk; used if too many mistakes have been made, or when EDLIN is used to browse through a file rather than to change a file.

R—replace

Searches for some data in a file and replaces it with other data.

S—search

Searches for some data in the file and indicates its location.

T—transfer

Inserts the entire contents of another file into the file that is being edited; DOS-2 only.

W—write

Writes part of the file being edited to make room in memory for more lines from the file; this command is mostly used together with A-append for files which are too large to fit into memory.

21.3 DEBUG Commands

A—assemble

Accepts assembly-like commands, and translates them into machine language; for knowledgeable, advanced users only; DOS-2.

C—compare

Compares two areas in memory and reports any differences.

D—display

Displays the contents of an area of memory in both hexadecimal and character formats.

E—enter

Places data into memory; used when patching programs; interactive form displays old data before new data is accepted for greater safety.

F—fill

Places data into memory, duplicating as needed; mostly used to clear memory to zero or some other value.

G—go

Starts executing a program from a particular address; for advanced users only.

H—hex arithmetic

Does addition and subtraction of hexadecimal numbers.

I—in

Reads from the computer's ports and displays the data read.

L—load

Reads from the disk into memory; can load from particular disk locations or load an entire file.

M—move

Moves (copies really) data from one area in memory to another.

N—name

Accepts the name of a file for later use by the L-load command.

O—out

Sends data out of the computer's ports.

Q—quit

Ends the use of DEBUG and returns to DOS for the next command.

R—register

Displays the contents of the registers or makes changes to their values.

S—search

Searches memory and reports the location of some particular data.

T—trace

Executes a program with controlled break points; for knowledgeable, advanced users only.

U—unassemble

Displays the contents of memory in the form of the equivalent assembler instructions; requires knowledge of assembly language to understand.

W—write

Writes data from memory to disk, the reverse of L-load; can write either to particular disk locations or to an entire file.

22

Narrative Glossary

This narrative glossary is intended to provide a very brief rundown of the most common and fundamental terminology used in discussing computers. You can use this narrative glossary in two ways—either by reading it all or by scanning the word list for the terms you are interested in, and then reading the surrounding discussion.

Numbers and Notation

binary

bit

Computers work only with *binary* numbers, that is numbers made up of zeros and ones (0's and 1's). Binary digits are called *bits*, for short. No matter what a computer is doing, it is working with bits. Even if the subject matter is alphabetic characters, or decimal arithmetic, the method is binary numbers.

hexadecimal

Writing many bits, for example 01010100 11101010101, is inconvenient, so several shorthand notations have been developed. The most common is *hexadecimal*, or base-16, notation. Hexadecimal digits have sixteen possible values, from 0 through 15; they are written as 0 through 9, followed by A (representing the value ten), B (meaning eleven), and C through F (with a value of fifteen).

hex

octal

Hexadecimal digits, also called *hex*, represent four binary digits, or bits, at a time. (Another notation, called *octal*, uses the digits 0 through 7 and represents 3 bits·at a time.)

byte

nibble
nybble
characters

The bits that a computer uses are grouped into larger units. A group of eight bits is called a *byte*. Since hex notation represents four bits at a time, it takes two hex digits to represent the value stored in a byte (hex digits are sometimes whimsically called *nibbles*, or *nybbles*). A byte can be used to store 2 to the eighth power of values—256 different values. The values can be interpreted as numbers or as *char-*

acters (such as letters of the alphabet). One byte can hold one character, and therefore the terms bytes and characters are sometimes used interchangeably. The letters of the alphabet and the ten digits, together, are called the *alphanumerics*, although the term is sometimes used loosely to mean any text data.

alphanumeric

When bytes are used to hold characters, some code must be used to determine which numeric value will represent which character. The most common code is the American National Code for Information Interchange *(ASCII)*. In ASCII, the capital letter A has the value 65 (in hex notation, 41), B is 66, and so forth. ASCII includes codes for letters, numbers, punctuation, and special control codes. ASCII proper has only 128 different codes, and needs only 7 bits to represent it; since ASCII characters are almost always stored inside 8-bit bytes, there is room for the 128 ASCII codes and another 128 codes. The other codes are sometimes called *extended ASCII*. ASCII codes are standardized, but extended ASCII will vary from computer to computer. Traditionally, IBM computers have not used ASCII coding to represent characters; instead, they use *EBCDIC* (the Extended Binary Coded Decimal Information Code). *ASCII data*, or an ASCII file, is data which consists of text—that is, letters of the alphabet, punctuation, and so forth—rather than numbers or other data. Sometimes the term ASCII is used loosely to mean *text data*. Properly speaking, an *ASCII file* not only contains the ASCII codes for letters, spaces, punctuation, and so forth, but also contains the standard ASCII codes for formatting, such as carriage return and end-of-file.

ASCII

Extended ASCII

EBCDIC

text data
ASCII file

When a byte is used to represent a number, the 256 different byte values can be interpreted as either all positive numbers ranging from 0 through 255, or as positive and negative numbers, ranging from −128 through 127. These are referred to as *unsigned (0 to 255)* or *signed (−128 to 127) numbers.*

unsigned number
signed number

To handle larger numbers, several bytes are used together as a unit, often called a *word*. For different computers different meanings are given to the term word, but most often it means either two bytes (16-bits) or four bytes (32-bits). For personal computers using MS-DOS a word usually means a two-byte, 16-bit, number.

word

A two-byte word has two to the 16th power different possible values. These can be used as unsigned numbers, with a range of 0 through 65,535, or signed numbers, with a range of −32,768 through 32,767.

Integers, or whole numbers, are not satisfactory for some tasks. When fractional numbers are needed, or a very wide range of numbers is needed, a different form of computer arithmetic is used, called *floating-point*. Floating-point numbers involve a fractional portion and an exponent portion, similar to the "scientific notation" used in engineering. To work with floating-point numbers, computers interpret the bits of a word in a special way. Floating-point numbers generally represent approximate, inexact values. Often more than one format of floating-point numbers are available, offering different degrees of accuracy; common terms for this are *single-precision and double-precision*. Floating-point numbers are also sometimes called *real numbers*.

floating-point

single-precision
double-precision
real numbers

Due to the nature of computer arithmetic and notation, items are often numbered starting from zero for the first element; this is called *zero-origin*. Counting from zero is done especially when figuring a memory location relative to some starting point. The starting point can be called many things, including *base* and *origin*. The relative location is most often called an *offset*. Starting from any base location in memory, the first byte is at offset zero, and the next byte is at offset one.

zero-origin

base
origin
offset

Computer Fundamentals

hardware
software

All of the mechanical and electronic parts of a computer system are called *hardware*. The programs which a computer uses are called *software*.

memory
storage
location
address

The idea of a computer starts with the concept of *memory* or *storage*. A computer's memory consists of many *locations*, each of which has an *address*, and can store a value. For most computers, including MS-DOS computers, each location is a byte; for others, each location is a word.

The addresses of the locations are numbers. The values stored in each location can be either discovered (read) or changed (written). When reading or writing a value, the address of the location must be given.

page

paragraph

segment

displacement

vector

Some computers organize their memory storage into large modular units, often called *pages*. MS-DOS computers do not use pages, but for addressing purposes they divide their memory into units of 16 bytes, called *paragraphs* (a term that was chosen to suggest a smaller division than a page). The memory addressing mechanism for these computers uses two parts—a *segment* value, which points to a paragraph boundary, and a relative value, which points to a byte located at some *displacement*, or offset, from the segment paragraph. The two values, segment and displacement, are needed to specify any complete address; together, they are sometimes called an *address vector*, or just vector.

K

Amounts of computer memory are frequently referred to in units of 1,024, because 1,024 is a round number in binary notation, and almost a round number in decimal notation. The value 1,024 is known as *K*, for kilo; 64K is 64 units of 1,024, or exactly 65,536.

When referring to general capacity, K almost always means 1,024 bytes. However, when referring to semiconductor "chips", K means 1,024 bits. When magazine articles refer to 16K and 64K chips, they mean 16K bits (equivalent to 2K bytes) or 64K bits (equivalent to 8K bytes).

operations

instructions
commands

A computer has the ability to perform *operations* on the values stored in its memory. Examples of these operations are arithmetic (addition, subtraction) and movement from location to location. A request for the computer to perform an operation is called an *instruction* or *command*.

program
code

A series of computer instructions, which together perform some work, is called a *program*. Programs are also called *code*.

processor

microprocessor

The part of the computer which interprets programs and performs the instructions is called the *processor*. A very small processor, particularly one which fits onto a single computer chip, is called a *microprocessor*. The development of microprocessors made personal computers possible. Properly speaking, a computer is a complete working machine which includes a processor and other parts; but the processor part of a computer is sometimes also called a computer.

The memory of a computer is used to store both programs and data. To the memory, there is no difference between programs and data. To the processor, however, only those stored values which represent valid instructions can be a program. The processor reads and writes from its memory both to carry out a program and to access the data that the program uses.

registers

To help it carry out its work, a computer may have a small amount of very specialized memory, which does not have addresses. This specialized memory is referred to as *registers.* Registers are used to make arithmetic more efficient, or to assist in handling addresses.

stack
push
pop
LIFO

Many modern computers, including MS-DOS computers, use a push-down *stack* to hold status information. Data is *push*ed onto and *pop*ped off of the top of a stack, on a *last-in-first-out (or LIFO)* basis.

bus

When a computer uses a common data path to pass data from one part to another, this path is called a *bus.*

peripherals

The memory and processor are the internal parts of a computer. There are many external parts, generally called peripheral equipment, or *peripherals.* Most peripherals must be connected to a computer through some supporting electronic circuitry, called

adapter

an *adapter.* For a complex peripheral, such as a diskette drive, the adapter will include some special logi-

controller

cal circuitry called a *controller.* A controller is often a specialized computer in its own right.

storage

Peripherals may be of many kinds, but they fall into a few simple categories. *Storage* peripherals are used to hold programs and data that can be moved into the computer's internal memory. Examples of

diskettes
hard disks

peripheral storage devices are floppy *diskettes,* cassette tape recorders, and high-capacity *hard disks.*

Other peripheral equipment is used to communicate with people. The equipment used to communicate between people and computers are usually terminals

CRT
display
monitor

composite

RGB

called *terminals*. A terminal most often consists of a typewriter-style keyboard, and a TV-like display screen, called a *CRT* (for cathode ray tube). A printer of some kind may be used instead of a CRT. A *display* screen is called a *monitor*, or simply a display. A color display may accept its color signal information in a combined form, called a *composite*, or separated into its red, green, and blue components, called *RGB*.

Large computers may have many terminals, but small personal computers usually work with only one terminal, which may be built right into the computer system. Having only one terminal is a large part of what makes a *personal computer* personal.

personal computer

modem
asynchronous

communications

RS-232
baud

serial
parallel

Other kinds of peripherals, besides storage and terminals, are printers and telephone connections. Connections between computers and telephones are referred to by the names of some of their parts, such as *modems* and *asynchronous* adapters; all of these terms, in general use, refer to the entire computer-telephone connection, which is generally called *communications*. The most common format for communications connections follows a design standard known as *RS-232*. The speed, or data rate, of a communications line is measured in *baud*, which is bits-per-second. Three hundred baud is a common speed for personal computer communications; 300 baud is about 35 or 40 characters per second. On personal computers, an RS-232 connection is also called *serial*, since it transmits data one bit at a time. A *parallel* connection can transmit more than one bit at a time.

dot-matrix

letter-quality

daisy-wheel
thimble

interface

Computer printers come in many varieties. Many personal computers use an inexpensive *dot-matrix* printer, which creates its printed results by writing a series of dots. *Letter-quality* printers produce results comparable to good typewriters. Most letter-quality printers use a print element that is either a flat disk, called a *daisy-wheel*, or one that is shaped like a large *thimble*.

An *interface* is a connection between any two elements in a computer system. The term interface is used both for connections between hardware parts and software parts, as well as the human interface.

I/O

Much of the equipment that can be connected to a computer is generally referred to as input/output equipment, or *I/O*.

chips

The smallest physical parts that make up a computer may be called *chips*. Chips and other parts are wired together electrically and held mechanically on boards. If there is one principal *board*, it is called the *system board*, or *mother board*. Openings for the addition of more boards are called expansion *slots*, into which are placed memory boards, disk boards, asynch comm boards (telephone connections), and other expansion or peripheral boards.

board
system board
mother board
slot

port

A microprocessor interacts with its world through three means: memory accesses, interrupts, and ports. *Ports* have a port number or port address, and are used for passing data to or from peripheral devices. *Interrupts* are used to get the computer's attention. There are three kinds of interrupts (although all three are handled the same). An *external interrupt* is from the outside world (for example, from a diskette drive). An *internal interrupt* reports some exceptional logical situation (for example, division by zero). A *software interrupt* is a request from a program for some service to be performed; a software interrupt is an alternative to using a call to activate a subroutine. Memory accesses are used to read or write from the computer's memory.

interrupt

external interrupt

internal interrupt

software interrupt

RAM
ROM

The computer's memory can be of several types. Ordinary memory, which can be read or written to, is called *RAM* (random access memory). Memory which contains permanent data is *ROM* (read only memory). Memory can be dedicated to some use; for example, to hold the data that appears on the computer's display screen. If a display screen uses the computer's memory to hold its information, then it is a *memory-mapped* display.

memory-mapped

Programs and Programming Languages

program

Series of computer instructions are called *programs*. Parts of programs which are partially self-contained are called *subroutines*. Subroutines may be procedures if they only do some work, or *functions* if they also result in a value ("open the door" is analogous to a *procedure*; "tell me your name" is analogous to a

subroutine
function

procedure

subprogram routine	function). Subroutines are also called *subprograms,* and *routines.*
	Many subroutines use parameters to specify exactly what work is to be done; for example, a subroutine which computes a square root needs a
parameter	*parameter* to specify what number to use. Many subroutines will indicate how successful their operation was through a *return code.*
return code	
machine language	Computers can only execute programs which appear in the detailed form known as *machine language* However, for the convenience of people, programs may be represented in other forms. If the details of a machine language program are replaced with meaningful symbols (such as the terms ADD or MOVE), then the programming language is known as *assembly language* (also called assembler, symbolic assembler, or *macro assembler*).
assembly language macro assembler	
low-level	Assembler is called a *low-level* language, because assembly programs are written in a form close to machine language. Other forms of programming languages are more abstracted, and produce many machine instructions for each command written by the programmer. These are called *high-level* languages; examples are BASIC, Pascal, FORTRAN, COBOL, PL/I, C, and Forth. Programs which translate high-level language programs into a form usable by the computer, are called *compilers*; for low-level languages, the translators are called *assemblers.* There is no real difference between a compiler and an assembler—they both translate from a human programming language to a form of machine language.
high-level	
compiler assembler	
source code	When a person writes a computer program, the form it takes is called *source code,* or source. When the source code is translated (by an assembler or compiler), the result is often called *object code.* Object code is nearly ready to be used, but it has to undergo a minor transformation, performed by a *link editor,* or linker, to produce a *load module*—which is a finished, ready-to-use program.
object code	
link editor load module	
bug	An error in a program is called a *bug,* and the process of trying to find errors, or trying to fix them, is called *debugging.*
debug	
	There are usually many ways to accomplish an objective with a computer program. The scheme,

algorithm

formula, or method that a program uses is its *algorithm*. For many tasks—even as simple a one as sorting data into alphabetic order—there are dramatic differences in the efficiency of different algorithms, and the search continues for better and better methods.

variable

A program works with symbolic entities call variables. In effect, a *variable* is the name of a place that can hold data of some type. Specific data can be moved into and out of a variable, and the purpose of the variable is to provide a mechanism for manip-

type

ulating data. Variables usually have a fixed *type*, which indicates what sort of data it can accommodate; for example, integer type, single- and double-

string
file

precision, floating-point, and *string* (a collection of text characters). In a program, a *file* is just a special kind of variable, one which can be connected to a diskette file or some device, such as the display screen.

Human Roles

On a personal computer, one person may do everything that is to be done. However, in traditional large computer systems, there is a division of labor, separating human involvement with a computer into various roles. Users of personal computers may wonder about the meaning of various job titles used.

user

The *user*, or end user, is the person for whom computer work is done.

analyst

The systems analyst, or *analyst*, determines the details of the work that the end user needs done, and decides on the general strategy of how a computer will perform the work.

programmer

The *programmer* converts the analyst's general strategy into the detailed tactics and methods to be used. This usually includes writing (and testing) the actual program. However, actually writing and testing the program is sometimes left to a coder.

coder

The *coder* turns the programmer's detailed methods into the program instructions.

operator

The *operator* runs the program on the computer to produce the results needed by the user.

Data Organization

Data is organized and viewed differently, depending upon who or what is looking at it. To the computer itself, data consists of just bits and bytes. To programmers who manipulate data, there are some traditional logical boundaries for data. A complete collection of related data is a *file* (as an example, a mailing list file). One complete unit of the information that is in a file is called a *record;* in a mailing list file, all of the information connected with one address would be a record. Finally, within a record are *fields*, the information of one type; for example, the zip code would be one field in an address record in a mailing list file.

file

record

field

The records that a program reads or writes are *logical records.* Logical records are placed in the storage medium's *physical records*—which are the pieces actually read or written to a diskette. A program sees logical records, while the operating system performs any translating necessary between logical and physical records. On a diskette, a physical record is called a sector.

logical record
physical record

The terms data base and data base manager are used, and abused, so widely that they have no precise meaning. When data is large, complex, and spread across several files, it might be called a *data base.* A *data base manager* is a program—usually large and complex in itself—which can control and organize a data base. Full-scale data base management is far beyond the capabilities of a personal computer.

data base
data base manager

Diskette Vocabulary

sector

Data on a diskette is stored on *sectors*, which can be individually read or written; typically for DOS a sector is 512 bytes. Sectors are the diskette's physical records—the units that are actually read or written. A *track* is the collection of sectors that will fit into one circle on a diskette; a typical disk format has eight sectors in a track. If there is more than one surface on a disk or diskette drive, then a *cylinder* is all of the tracks that are the same distance from the center. Sectors that are in the same cylinder can be read

track

cylinder

seeking

without moving the disk drive's read/write mechanism. Moving the read/write heads from one track/cylinder to another is called *seeking*, and it is relatively slow. Typically there are forty or eighty tracks on each surface of a diskette.

directory
VTOC

FAT (file allocation
    table)

boot record

A diskette needs a table of contents for its files, called a *directory* in MS-DOS. On some other systems, a directory is called a *VTOC (Volume Table Of Contents)*. Some means must be used to keep track of used and unused space on a diskette, and with MS-DOS it is done with the *FAT (File Allocation Table)*. The first sector of each file allocation diskette is dedicated to holding the first part of the operating system's start-up program, called the bootstrap loader, or *boot record*. On each diskette there are four kinds of sectors—boot record, FAT, directory, and data space (where files are stored).

floppy

flippy
hard disk

Winchester

A diskette is flexible, thus it is called a *floppy*. A diskette which can be turned over, to use the other side is a *flippy*. (Double-sided diskettes are not turned over.) A *hard disk* has a rigid platter in place of the flexible plastic of a floppy; the rigid shape allows more precise data recording, and thus higher density and more capacity. The sort of hard disks installed on personal computers today use a collection of methods called Winchester technology so they are also called *Winchester disks*.

Operating Systems

operating system

An *operating system* is a program which supervises and controls the operation of a computer. Operating systems are complex and consist of many parts.

BIOS

One element of an operating system is its *BIOS*, or Basic Input-Output System. The BIOS is responsible for handling the details of input-output operations, including the task of relating a program's logical records to a peripheral device's physical records. At the most detailed level, the BIOS contains routines tailored to the specific requirements of each peripheral device; these routines are called *drivers*, or *device handlers*.

driver
device handler

Usually an operating system is organized into a hierarchy of levels of services. At the lowest level,

logical I/O
physical I/O
services

the device handlers insulate the rest of the operating system from the details of each device. At the next level, relating *logical data* to *physical data* is performed. At a higher level basic *services* are provided—such as accepting output data from a program to be placed into a file.

loader
relocation

error handler

Besides device and data handling, an operating system must supervise programs, including *loading* them, *relocating* them (adjusting their internal addresses to correspond to their exact location in a memory), and recovering from any program errors, through an *error handler.*

command processor

Another element of an operating system is the *command processor,* which accepts and acts on commands given by the computer's user. Commands usually amount to a request for the execution of some service program.

Boundaries are usually drawn in operating systems, isolating the parts which are specific to peripheral devices, and the parts which are specific to a particular computer. Depending upon which level of services is used, for example, a program may work on any computer, any computer which uses the MS-DOS operating system, only on one particular computer using MS-DOS.

INDEX

$$$ extension, 95, 171
% for batch parameters, 132
* wild card, 24, 32, 34, 44, 45, 96, 147
+ switch of SORT, 77
. directory entry, 84
.. directory entry, 84
1-2-3, 206
123 batch file trick, 143
8087, 204
? wild card, 96

A-drive, 23, 27, 149, 162, 193
ABC batch file trick, 142
Ada, 107
Adapter, 253
Address, 251
Algorithm, 257
Aliases for commands, 163
Alphanumeric, 250
Analyst, 257
Appending output, 73, 164
ASCII, 101, 250
ASCII text file, 115, 127, 215, 250
ASM extension, 94
Assembler, 256
Assembler MASM, 56
Assembling, 112
Assembly language, 55, 107, 110, 256
ASSIGN, 195
Asterisk wild card, 24, 32, 34, 44, 45, 96, 147
Asynchronous, 254
AUX device, 79, 94, 151

B-drive, 23, 27, 149, 162, 193
B switch of FILECOMP, 52
BAA batch file, 140, 178
Backup, 171, 190
Bad command message, 30

Bad patches on diskettes, 40
BAK extension, 95
BAS extension, 94
Base, 251
BASIC, 107, 207
BAT extension, 38, 94, 127, 147, 191
Batch file parameters, 132
Batch files, 127
Batch processing, 15
Baud, 254
Binary, 249
BIOS, 259
Bit, 249
Black box, 138
BLD extension, 95
Block device, 148
Board, 255
Boot disk, 157
Boot record, 91, 259
Bootstrap loader, 18
Bottle necks, 184
Brain, electronic, 6
BREAK, 88, 239
Break key, 65, 88, 131, 170
Break points, 235
Bug, 256
Bus, 253
Byte, 249

C-drive, 193
C language, 107, 207
C switch of FILECOMP, 52
CAL extension, 95
CAT, 37, 39, 239
CD, 81, 239
Central processing unit, 6
Chained batch files, 133
Changing default drive, 29
Character, 249
Character device, 148

CHDIR, 81, 153, 239
Chip, 255
CHKDSK, 37, 39, 91, 158, 170, 239
CIPHER, 87
Cleaning diskette drives, 41
Closing a file, 9
CLS, 46, 240
COB extension, 94
COBOL, 107, 125
COD extension, 95
Code, 252
Coder, 257
Colon in TIME, 36
COM extension, 34, 57, 94, 98, 147,
  191
COM1 device, 79, 94, 151
Comma in commands, 32
Command, 252
Command editing, 53
Command processor, 259
Command prompt, 20, 23
COMMAND.COM, 42, 147, 157, 158,
  160, 168
Commands, internal and external, 30
Communications, 254
Communications adapter, 10
COMP, 49, 240
Compiler, 256
Compiling, 112
Composite monitor, 254
CON device, 93, 150
Concatenation with COPY, 44
Console, 148
Console device, 150
Control-C key, 65, 88, 131, 170
Control-Z key, 66, 101, 151
Controller, 253
COPY, 24, 32, 33, 34, 43, 44, 176, 240
Copy protection, 167, 175, 198, 212
CP/M-86, 176
CREF, 56, 240
Cross reference utility, CREF, 56
CRT, 254
CTTY, 79, 240
Current directory, 153
Current disk, 152
Current drive, 195

Cylinder, 258
CYPHER, 240

D-drive, 187, 193
Daisy-wheel, 254
Danger, 42
Data base, 258
Data base manager, 258
Data diskettes, 41
Database programs, 121
DATE, 18, 35, 240
dBase II, 121
Dead key, 200
DEBUG, 54, 241
Debugging, 256
Default drive, 28, 37, 152, 195
Default drive, changing, 29
DEL, 45, 130, 139, 172, 213, 241
Device driver, 259
Device handler, 259
Devices, 148
DIF extension, 95
DIR, 35, 37, 139, 241
Directory, 259
Directory, current, 153
Dirty diskette drives, 41
Disk drives, A and B, 23
Disk file, 9
DISKCOMP, 49, 241
DISKCOPY, 21, 35, 40, 43, 176, 241
Diskette, 8, 253
Diskette labels, 42
Diskette sector, 97
Diskette versus drive, 27
Displacement, 252
Display, 254
DOS, 11
DOS versions, 2
DOS-1 version, 3
DOS-2 version, 3, 15
Dot-matrix, 254
Double precision, 251
Double-sided diskettes, 42
Drive specification, 28
Drive versus diskette, 27
Driver, 259
Dumb and smart, FILECOMP, 51

EBCDIC, 250
ECHO, 133, 138, 241
Echo feature, 65, 74
Editing keys, 59
Editor programs, 52
EDLIN, 52, 101, 127, 202, 215, 241
Electronic brain, 6
Electronic disk, 103, 144, 149, 183
Electronic spreadsheet, 12
End-of-file marker, 101
Environment, 86
ERASE, 45, 130, 139, 172, 213, 241
Error handler, 259
EXE extension, 57, 94, 98, 118, 147, 191
EXE2BIN, 57, 242
EXEFIX, 57, 242
Extended ASCII, 250
Extension to file name, 33, 38
External commands, 30
External interrupt, 255

FAT, 91, 259
FC, 49, 242
Field, 258
File, 257, 258
File allocation table (FAT), 91, 259
File recovery, 45, 155, 172
File size, 89
FILECOMP, 49, 242
Filename, 33, 89
Files, disk, 9
Filter, 71
FIND, 75, 242
Fixed length records, 102
Flippy, 259
Floating point, 251
Floppy, 259
Floppy diskette, 8, 103, 183
FOR, 133, 242
FOR extension, 95
FORMAT, 21, 23, 24, 33, 40, 42, 157, 242
Formatting diskettes, 17
Forth, 107, 125
FORTRAN, 107

Full-screen editing, 53, 221
Function, 255

Generations of files, 190
Generator of data, 70
GOTO, 133, 242
Graphics printer, 10

Hard disk, 8, 81, 103, 183, 253, 259
Hardware, 251
Hex, 249
Hexadecimal, 109, 249
Hidden files, 38, 158, 168
High-level language, 107, 256
Hyphen for switches, 33
Hyphen in DATE, 36

I/O, 9, 255
IBM Personal Computer, 14
IF, 133, 242
Input/output (I/O), 9
Instruction, 252
Interface, 254
Internal commands, 30
Internal interrupt, 255
Interpreter BASIC, 115
Interpreting, 112
Interrupt, 255

Joy stick, 10

K, 7, 252
Keyboard, 148

Labels in batch files, 136
Labels on diskettes, 42
Letter-quality printer, 210, 254
LIB, 56, 118, 243
LIB extension, 95
Libraries, 56
LIFO, 253

Light pen, 10
LINK, 56, 117, 243
Link editing, 56, 117, 256
Live key, 200
Load module, 256
Loader, 259
LOCATE, 57, 243
Location, 251
Logical I/O, 259
Logical record, 258
LOGIN, 87
Loops in batch files, 136
Low-level language, 107, 256
LPT1 device, 94, 152
LST extension, 95

Machine language, 107, 256
Macro assembler, 56, 256
MASM, 56, 243
Master program, 11
MD, 79
Memory, 7, 251
Memory-mapped, 255
Menus, 199
Microprocessor, 252
Microsoft, 11, 14
MKDIR, 79, 243
Modem, 10, 254
Money, plenty of, 197
Monitor, 254
MORE, 75, 243
Mother board, 255
Mouse, 10
Multiplan, 121

Names of files, 33
Nibble, 249
NUL device, 93, 149
Number, signed or unsigned, 250
Nybble, 249

OBJ extension, 116
Object code, 116, 256
Octal, 249

Offset, 251
Opening a file, 9
Operating system, 11, 259
Operation, 252
Operator, 257
Origin, 251

P switch in DIR, 39
p-System, 123, 179
Page, 252
Paragraph, 252
Parallel, 254
Parallel printer connection, 152
Parameter, 256
Parameters for batch files, 132
Parameters of commands, 32
PAS extension, 95
Pascal, 107, 207
Patching, 194, 235
PATH, 81, 85, 191, 243
Paths, 105
PAUSE, 127, 130, 139, 243
Period, directory entry, 84
Period in filename, 34
Peripheral, 253
Personal computer, 254
Physical I/O, 259
Physical record, 258
Pipeline, 69, 139
PL/I, 107
Plenty of money, 197
Plotter, 10
Pop, 253
Port, 255
PRINT, 87, 243
Print formatting, 202
Printer, 10
Printers, letter quality, 210
PRN device, 94, 152
Procedure, 255
Processor, 6, 252
Program, 252, 255
Program diskettes, 41
Program libraries, 56
Programmer, 257
Prompt for commands, 20, 23

PRT device, 94, 152
Push, 253
PWD, 81, 153, 244

Question mark wild card, 96

R switch of SORT, 77
RAM, 255
RAM disk, 149, 183
RAM disk tricks, 144
RAM disks, 103
RD, 79, 244
Real numbers, 251
Record, 258
RECOVER, 87, 155, 244
Recovering files, 45, 155, 172
Redirection, 70
Register, 229, 253
Relocation, 259
REM, 127, 130, 139, 244
REN, 45, 244
RENAME, 45, 244
Return code, 256
RGB monitor, 254
RMDIR, 79, 244
ROM, 255
Root directory, 71, 105, 192
Routine, 256
RS-232, 254
Run-time modules, 119

S switch of FORMAT, 23, 33, 42, 157
SAVE command in BASIC, 115
Sector, 97, 258
Sector size, 97
Seeking, 259
Segment, 252
Semicolon in commands, 32
Serial, 254
Serial printer connection, 152
Services, 259
SET, 86, 244
SHIFT, 133, 244
Signed number, 250

Single-precision, 251
Single-sided diskettes, 42
Size of file, 89
Size of sector, 97
Slash for switches, 33
Slash in DATE, 36
Slot, 255
Smart and dumb FILECOMP, 51
Software, 251
Software interrupt, 255
SORT, 75, 244
Source code, 256
Spreadsheet, 12, 121, 203
Stack, 253
Standard input, 70, 72
Standard output, 70, 72
Starting message of DOS, 19
Storage, 251, 253
String, 257
Structured programming, 108
Sub-directories, 71, 105, 189
Subprogram, 256
Subroutine, 255
Suspend feature, 66
Switch identifier, 33
Switches of commands, 33
SYS, 40, 42, 169, 244
System board, 255
System disk, 23, 42, 91, 157

Templates, VisiCalc, 204
Terminal, 254
Terrible idea, 80
Text data, 250
Text editors, 199, 202
Text file, 115, 127
Text files, 215
Text formatting, 202
Thimble, 254
TIME, 18, 20, 35, 245
Time stamp of file, 89
TMP extension, 95, 171
Tokenized BASIC, 115
Track, 258
TREE, 81, 245
Tree-structured directories, 71, 79, 189

TXT extension, 95
TYPE, 46, 245, 257

UCSD p-System, 123, 179
Unassembly, 55
Unerasing files, 45, 155, 172
Unsigned number, 250
User, 257
USER device, 93
User friendliness, 199

V switch of COPY, 33
V switch of FORMAT, 42, 158
Variable, 257
VC extension, 95
Vector, 252
VER, 46, 245

VERIFY, 88, 245
Versions of DOS, 2
Vertical bar character, 75
VisiCalc templates, 204
VOL, 46, 245
VTOC, 259

W switch of DIR, 139
W switch of FILECOMP, 52
Wild cards, 96
Winchester disk, 8, 103, 183, 259
Word, 250
Word processing, 13, 52, 202
WordStar, 200

Zero origin, 251